The Political Economy of Asian Regionalism

Giovanni Capannelli • Masahiro Kawai
Editors

The Political Economy of Asian Regionalism

Springer

Editors
Giovanni Capannelli
Asian Development Bank Institute
Chiyoda-ku
Tokyo, Japan

Masahiro Kawai
Asian Development Bank Institute
Chiyoda-ku
Tokyo, Japan

ISBN 978-4-431-54567-5 ISBN 978-4-431-54568-2 (eBook)
DOI 10.1007/978-4-431-54568-2
Springer Tokyo Heidelberg New York Dordrecht London

Library of Congress Control Number: 2013957366

Printed on acid-free paper

Springer is part of Springer Science+Business Media (www.springer.com)

Preface

One of Asia's distinct characteristics lies in the diversity of its economies, their endowment of natural resources and human capital, the level of development, and institutional effectiveness. Despite such diversity, Asia has succeeded to become one of the most dynamic regions in the word today. Alongside economic success, since the early1980s, Asian economies have also started to become more interdependent with each other.

While the path towards economic integration was initially led by market forces through the creation of regional production networks, the Asian financial crisis of 1997–1998 triggered the beginning of significant initiatives for regional cooperation and integration. This development has led to the idea that Asia could think of forming a region-wide economic community in the years to come.

This book contributes to the theoretical and empirical literature on Asian regionalism, or the combination of market integration and cooperation initiatives, with a focus on the innovations needed to reform Asia's institutional architecture for regional cooperation and integration.

After reviewing the key issues and challenges related to the political economy of Asia's economic cooperation and integration, the book discusses different aspects of regionalism from political and economic perspectives. Distinguished scholars, experts, and practitioners contribute with their ideas to discussing the rationale for regional collective action and the perspectives for creating an Asia-wide economic community.

The eight chapters review the trend of Asian economic integration with a focus on the implications of the global financial crisis. In addition to analyzing issues such as trade and finance, the study deals with the implications of Asian regionalism on the introduction of domestic reforms in individual countries and reviews the key issues related to the development of regional institutions for integration.

A key message from the book is that regional and global cooperation has become the trend for Asia's future. As Asia is expected to become the largest economic region in the world by 2015, Asian countries have to strengthen regionalism while increasing their voice in international forums and providing more global public goods.

The initial drafts of the papers included in the book were presented at the Asian Development Bank Institute (ADBI) annual conference held in Tokyo, Japan, on 3 December 2010. These drafts have been substantially revised to address comments by peer reviewers. The final chapters have also been updated to reflect key developments that occurred after their initial drafts.

I take this opportunity to thank the chapter authors for their contributions to this publication, and to my co-editor, Giovanni Capannelli and the ADBI team, for their effort in organizing the conference and collecting the papers for this book. I would like to thank in particular Zhihai Xie for providing assistance on the book project and Ainslie Smith for editing the manuscript.

Tokyo, Japan Masahiro Kawai

Contents

Contributors

Amitav Acharya

Amitav Acharya is professor at the School of International Service and chair of the ASEAN Studies Center, American University, Washington, DC. He previously held academic appointments with Bristol, Nanyang Technological, York, and Harvard Universities. His research focuses on Asian international relations, regional institutions, and comparative politics. *Whose Ideas Matter: Agency and Power in Asian Regionalism* (Cornell 2009) is one of his latest books. A Canadian citizen, he was born in India and educated in India and Australia.

Giovanni Capannelli

Giovanni Capannelli is special adviser to the Dean, ADBI. His research interest covers Asian economic development and regional integration issues. With ADBI since 2010, he has led the ASEAN 2030 study and several other research projects. Prior to joining ADBI he was with ADB in Manila for eight years, working as principal economist for the Office of Regional Economic Integration and the Pacific Department. Giovanni Capannelli also served as faculty member of the Asia–Europe Institute, University of Malaya, and as economist at the Tokyo delegation of the Bank of Italy. He is an economics graduate of Bocconi University, Milan, and holds a master's degree and PhD in economics from Hitotsubashi University, Tokyo.

Gregory Chin

Gregory Chin is associate professor of political science at York University, Toronto and a fellow of the Center for International Political Economy at Peking University. He was the inaugural China Research Chair of The Centre for International Governance Innovation (CIGI) from 2010 to 2013, and from 2012 to 2012 was the founding director of CIGI's Global Development Program. From 2003 to 2006 he was first secretary in the Canadian Embassy, Beijing, and he worked previously for Canada's foreign affairs and trade ministry and the Canadian International Development Agency. His research focuses on monetary affairs of the People's Republic of China, Asian regionalism, the BRICS, and global governance reform.

Philippa Dee
Philippa Dee is adjunct associate professor at the Crawford School of Public Policy at the Australian National University. She was previously assistant commissioner at the Australian Productivity Commission. Her main research area is the economics and political economy of services trade reform, identifying where it can contribute to better domestic regulation more generally. She was educated at Victoria and Canterbury Universities in New Zealand and at Simon Fraser University in Canada.

Masahiro Kawai
Masahiro Kawai is ADBI's dean and CEO. He was previously head of ADB's Office of Regional Economic Integration and concurrently special advisor to the ADB president in charge of regional economic cooperation and integration. Before that he was in academia, first as an associate professor of economics at Johns Hopkins University and later as a professor of economics at the University of Tokyo. He also served as chief economist for the World Bank's East Asia and Pacific Region and as deputy vice minister for international affairs of Japan's Ministry of Finance. His recent publications focus on economic regionalism. He holds a BA in economics from the University of Tokyo and a PhD in economics from Stanford University.

Soyoung Kim
Soyoung Kim is professor of economics, Seoul National University. He previously held positions at the University of Illinois and Korea University. He also works as a consultant for several international and regional financial institutions and an advisor for various institutions and government. His main research interests are international, macro, monetary, and financial economics. His research articles have been published in numerous journals. Soyoung Kim received his PhD in economics from Yale University.

Nagesh Kumar
Nagesh Kumar is chief economist of UNESCAP and director of ESCAP South and South West Asia Office, New Delhi. He earlier served as director of Macroeconomic Policy and Development Division, at ESCAP headquarters, Bangkok. Previously, he was director-general of Research and Information System for Developing Countries, Delhi. He has served on the boards of the Exim Bank of India and the International Centre for Trade and Sustainable Development, Geneva. He has published over 15 books and 90 research papers. He holds a PhD in economics from the Delhi School of Economics.

Anne McNaughton
Anne McNaughton is a senior lecturer at the College of Law, Australia National University. Prior to joining the Australia National University in 2001, she taught at the University of New South Wales. Her research interests include comparative contract and commercial law, regulation and transnational governance with a particular focus on the EU legal system and systems of private regulation. Anne McNaughton graduated with a bachelor of arts from the University of Newcastle and a bachelor of law from the University of New South Wales. She holds master of law degrees from Eberhard-Karls-Universität, Tübingen, Germany and the University of Technology, Sydney.

See Seng Tan
See Seng Tan is associate professor, deputy director of the Institute of Defence and Strategic Studies, and head of the Centre for Multilateralism Studies at the S. Rajaratnam School of International Studies, Nanyang Technological University, Singapore. A student of Asian security, he is the author and/or editor of 9 books and has published over 40 refereed academic papers. His latest book is *The Making of the Asia Pacific: Knowledge Brokers and the Politics of Representation* (Amsterdam University Press 2013). He was educated at the University of Manitoba and Arizona State University.

Shujiro Urata
Shujiro Urata is professor of economics at the Graduate School Asia–Pacific Studies, Waseda University, Tokyo. He is also affiliated with the Research Institute of Economy, Trade and Industry, the Japanese Centre for Economic Research, and the Economic Research Institute for ASEAN and East Asia. He specializes in international economics and has published a number of books and articles on international economic issues. He received his PhD in economics from Stanford University.

Doo Yong Yang
Doo Yong Yang is associate professor of international studies at Kyung Hee University, Gyeonggi-do global campus, Republic of Korea. From January 2008 until September 2009 he was a senior research fellow at ADBI. Previously he worked for the Korea Institute for International Economic Policy and the Bank for International Settlements. His field of research is international finance, focusing on monetary policy and exchange rates and managing capital flows. He holds a PhD in economics from the University of Colorado at Boulder.

Panel Discussion Speakers[1]

Iwan J. Azis
Iwan J. Azis is head of ADB's Office of Regional Economic Integration. Before joining ADB, he was professor at Cornell University. His expertise is on macrofinancial economics and regional institutions. He has published numerous books and articles on current development issues. An Indonesian national, he obtained his PhD and master's degree from Cornell University, and his bachelor's degree in economics from the University of Indonesia.

Haruhiko Kuroda
Haruhiko Kuroda was appointed governor, Bank of Japan, in March 2013. He was previously president and chairperson of the Board of Directors of the Asian Development Bank, a position he assumed in 2005. Before joining ADB, he was

[1] These experts presented their views and ideas at the ADBI annual conference panel discussion without presenting a formal paper.

special advisor to Japanese Prime Minister Koizumi, and professor at Hitotsubashi University. In a career spanning nearly four decades, he has represented Japan's Ministry of Finance at a number of international monetary conferences as vice minister of finance for international affairs. Haruhiko Kuroda holds a BA in law from the University of Tokyo and an MPhil in economics from the University of Oxford.

Keng Yong Ong
Keng Yong Ong is the high commissioner of Singapore to Malaysia. Before being appointed to this position in July 2011, he served as director of the Institute of Policy Studies in the Lee Kuan Yew School of Public Policy at the National University of Singapore. He was concurrently ambassador-at-large in the Singapore Ministry of Foreign Affairs and Singapore's non-resident ambassador to Iran. He was ASEAN secretary-general from January 2003 to January 2008 and Singapore's ambassador to India and Nepal from 1996 to 1998. He is a graduate from the University of Singapore and Georgetown University.

Pushpanathan Sundram
Pushpanathan Sundram is the managing director of EAS Strategic Advice Asia in Singapore. He is also a senior fellow at the Singapore Institute of International Affairs. From December 2008 to April 2012 he served as ASEAN deputy secretary-general for the ASEAN Economic Community and was previously principal director of the Bureau for Economic Integration and Finance at the ASEAN Secretariat. He received his bachelor's degree in economics and political science from the National University of Singapore and master's degree in public policy from the Lee Kuan Yew School of Public Policy, National University of Singapore.

Jianmin Wu
Jianmin Wu is chairman of the Shanghai International Studies Center and vice chairman of the China Institute for Innovation and Development Strategy. From 2003 to 2008 he served as president of the China Foreign Affairs University. From 1999 to 2003 he was the PRC's ambassador to France, and from 1996 to 1998, to the United Nations Office in Geneva and to other international organizations in Switzerland, as well as ambassador to the Netherlands. From 1965 to 1971 he acted on many occasions as interpreter for Chairman Mao Zedong and Premier Zhou Enlai.

Abbreviations[2]

ABF	Asian Bond Fund
ABMI	Asian Bond Markets Initiative
ACFTA	ASEAN–PRC Free Trade Agreement
ACIA	ASEAN Comprehensive Investment Area
ACU	Asian Currency Unit
ADB	Asian Development Bank
ADBI	Asian Development Bank Institute
ADMM	ASEAN Defence Ministers' Meeting
AEC	ASEAN Economic Community
AFAS	ASEAN Framework Agreement on Services
AfDB	African Development Bank
AFDM	ASEAN Finance and Central Bank Deputies' Meeting
AFTA	ASEAN Free Trade Area
AIA	ASEAN Investment Area
AMF	Asian Monetary Fund
AMRO	ASEAN+3 Macroeconomic Research Office
APEC	Asia–Pacific Economic Cooperation
APSC	ASEAN Political-Security Community
APTA	Asia–Pacific Trade Agreement
ARF	ASEAN Regional Forum
ASA	ASEAN Swap Arrangement
ASC	ASEAN Security Community
ASCC	ASEAN Socio-Cultural Community
ASEAN	Association of Southeast Asian Nations
ASEAN+3	ASEAN, the People's Republic of China, Japan, and the Republic of Korea
ASEAN+6	ASEAN, the People's Republic of China, Japan, the Republic of Korea, India, Australia, and New Zealand

[2] In this report, "$" refers to US dollars, unless otherwise stated.

ASEC	ASEAN Secretariat
ASEM	Asia–Europe Meeting
ASPAC	Asia and Pacific Council
ATIGA	ASEAN Trade in Goods Agreement
AUSFTA	Australia and United States Free Trade Agreement
BIMP–EAGA	Brunei Darussalam–Indonesia–Malaysia–Philippines East ASEAN Growth Area
BIMSTEC	Bay of Bengal Initiative for Multi-Sectoral Technical and Economic Cooperation
BIS	Bank for International Settlements
BSA	Bilateral swap arrangement
CAFTA	PRC–ASEAN Free Trade Agreement
CAREC	Central Asia Regional Economic Cooperation
CARIFORUM	Caribbean Forum of African, Caribbean, and Pacific states
CCIEE	China Center for International Economic Exchanges
CEPEA	Comprehensive Economic Partnership in East Asia
CEPT	Common External Preferential Treatment
CER	Closer Economic Relations (Australia and New Zealand)
CGIF	Credit Guarantee and Investment Facility
CJK	PRC, Japan, and Republic of Korea
CLMV	Cambodia, Lao People's Democratic Republic, Myanmar, and Viet Nam
CMI	Chiang Mai Initiative
CMIM	CMI Mutilateralization
CUSTA	Canada–US Trade Agreement
EAEC	East Asian Economic Caucus
EAEG	East Asia Economic Grouping
EAFTA	East Asia Free Trade Agreement
EAS	East Asia Summit
ECO	Economic Cooperation Organization
EEC	European Economic Community
EFTA	European Free Trade Association
EMEAP	Executive Meetings of East Asia and Pacific Central Banks
EMI	European Monetary Institute
EPA	Economic Partnership Agreement
EPRD	Economic Policy Review and Dialogue
EPU	European Payments Union
ESCAP	Economic and Social Commission for Asia and the Pacific
EU	European Union
FCL	Flexible credit line
FDI	Foreign direct investment
FLAR	Fondo Latinoamericano de Reservas
FoBF	Fund of Bond Funds
FTA	Free trade agreement
FTAAP	Free Trade Area of the Asia–Pacific

G7	Group of Seven
G10	Group of Ten
G20	Group of Twenty
GATS	General Agreement on Trade in Services
GATT	General Agreement on Tariffs and Trade
GCC	Gulf Cooperation Council
GDP	Gross domestic product
GMS	Greater Mekong Subregion
GTAP	Global Trade Analysis Project
GTI	Greater Tumen Initiative
ICT	Information and communication technology
IDB	Inter-American Development Bank
IMF	International Monetary Fund
IMT–GT	Indonesia–Malaysia–Thailand Growth Triangle
IORARC	India Ocean Rim Association for Regional Cooperation
JACIK	Japan, ASEAN, the PRC, India, and the Republic of Korea
Lao PDR	Lao People's Democratic Republic
MAPHILINDO	Malaysia, Philippines, and Indonesia
MCSDSEA	Ministerial Conference on Economic Development in Southeast Asia
MFN	Most favored nation
MNC	Multinational corporation
NAFTA	North American Free Trade Agreement
NATO	North Atlantic Treaty Organization
OECD	Organisation for Economic Co-operation and Development
OPEC	Organization of Petroleum Exporting Countries
OREI	Office of Regional Economic Integration (ADB)
PAFTAD	Pacific Trade and Development Conference
PAIF	Pan-Asian Bond Index Fund
PBEC	Pacific Basin Economic Council
PCL	Precautionary credit line
PECC	Pacific Economic Cooperation Council
PIF	Pacific Islands Forum
PRC	People's Republic of China
PTA	Preferential trade agreement
R&D	Research and development
RCEP	Regional Comprehensive Economic Partnership
RIETI	Research Institute of Economy, Trade and Industry
ROOs	Rules of origin
RTA	Regional trade agreement
SAARC	South Asian Association for Regional Cooperation
SAFTA	South Asia Free Trade Area
SARS	Severe acute respiratory syndrome
SASEC	South Asia Subregional Economic Cooperation
SEADA	Southeast Asia Development Association

SEATO	South East Asia Treaty Organization
SMEs	Small and medium-sized enterprises
SPECA	Special Programme for the Economies of Central Asia (UN)
SWOT	Strengths–Weaknesses–Opportunities–Threats
TAC	Treaty of Amity and Cooperation
TNC	Trade Negotiating Committee
TPP	Trans-Pacific Partnership
TRIPS	Trade-related intellectual property rights
TS	Trilateral summit
UK	United Kingdom
UN	United Nations
US	United States
WTO	World Trade Organization

Chapter 1
The Political Economy of Asian Regionalism: Issues and Challenges

Giovanni Capannelli and Masahiro Kawai

Abstract This chapter provides an overview of the political economy of Asian regionalism, where the term "regionalism" refers to cooperation initiatives and market integration trends. It discusses the aim and objectives of regional collective action, highlights some of the key regional economic cooperation efforts, identifies the major issues and challenges, and analyzes the perspectives for creating a region-wide economic community in Asia in the long run. Contributions by various experts to understanding the political economy of regionalism are presented in a sequential manner focusing on topics covering the implications of the global financial crisis on the trend of regionalism in Asia, opportunities emerging in the areas of trade and finance, the implications of regional cooperation on the introduction of domestic reforms in individual Asian economies, and the development of regional institutions for integration. The chapter suggests the Asian model for regionalism has several distinct characteristics related to historical circumstances and marked diversity across economies, which makes it very distinct from the European model.

Keywords Asian economic community • Domestic structural reforms • Economic integration • Regional cooperation • Regionalism

1.1 Introduction

The path of Asian economic development and regional integration has changed in the aftermath of the global financial crisis of 2008–2009. Led by the People's Republic of China (PRC) and India, emerging Asian economies are now playing a more prominent role in the global economy. Asia as a whole has become the engine

G. Capannelli (✉) • M. Kawai
Asian Development Bank Institute, Tokyo, Japan
e-mail: gcapannelli@adbi.org; mkawai@adbi.org

G. Capannelli and M. Kawai (eds.), *The Political Economy of Asian Regionalism*,
DOI 10.1007/978-4-431-54568-2_1, © Asian Development Bank Institute 2014

of global economic growth and strengthened economic regionalism. Individual countries have experienced sustained growth since 2010 and the region is expected to maintain momentum for some time despite the many challenges and risks it faces.

With the center of global economic gravity rapidly shifting toward Asia, scholars and policymakers around the world have shown increasing interest on the trends and prospects of Asian regionalism. A number of studies analyzing the region's long-term economic development path have recognized the important role played by intensifying economic interdependence among countries in shaping the future of Asia (Kohli et al. 2011; World Bank 2012; Asian Development Bank (ADB) and Asian Development Bank Institute (ADBI) 2014). Understanding the political economy of Asian regionalism, with reference in particular to regional market integration and cooperation initiatives, has become a central issue for the analysis of international relations and the definition of business strategies across the world.

Since the end of World War II, members of the European Union (EU) have made remarkable progress in economic, political, and social integration, showing unprecedented results for independent states deciding to share part of their sovereignty in defined areas with regional neighbors. No other region in the world can claim levels of achievement for common institutions and the creation of mechanisms to jointly manage a wide range of functions and activities like those adopted by the EU. The process underlying the evolution of the EU has been used as a reference—and a benchmark—for regional integration and cooperation around the world.[1]

But the circumstances that led to the creation of the EU are rarely observed elsewhere. In Asia, the Association of Southeast Asian Nations (ASEAN), considered by many scholars as one of the most successful regional groups, has followed a different path. Created in 1967, it gathers today ten member countries with remarkably diversified levels of economic development, and with very different political and social systems, as well as different cultural and religious values. Despite its diversity, ASEAN has made considerable progress over the years and it has been able to introduce a plan to create an ASEAN Community by the year 2015, structured on three "communities" in the political-security, economic, and socio-cultural areas.[2] Beyond Southeast Asia, the wider East Asian region—embracing the PRC, Japan, the Republic of Korea, Taipei,China, and Hong Kong, China—is where even in the absence of common institutions and specific mechanisms to promote regionalism, market forces have induced closer economic integration through the establishment of production networks in industries such as electronics, home appliances, and automobiles.

Increased regional economic interdependence has both positive and negative effects. On the one hand, countries become more vulnerable to the risk of contagion

---

[1] Although the sovereign debt and banking crisis that hit Europe in 2010 has shaken the EU, particularly the eurozone, in one of its major achievements—the common currency—Europe is responding through closer integration among the eurozone members.

[2] The original timeline was set for 2020, but prompted by the positive trends in economic dynamism, regional leaders, at the Cebu Summit in 2007, decided to accelerate the creation of the ASEAN Community to 2015.

from negative shocks originating in regional neighbors and have to sacrifice some national interests and priorities in favor of regional ones. On the other hand, closer integration offers greater opportunities for benefitting from economies of scale, lower business costs, greater competitiveness, and higher productivity with a potential to foster economic growth. Economic cooperation in infrastructure connectivity, trade and investment, finance, and regional public goods' provision can internalize spillover effects and strengthen economic integration. Recent findings suggest that Asian opinion leaders believe the benefits of economic regionalism largely outweigh the costs (ADB 2008, 2010).

However, the extent of economic integration and cooperation varies across Asia's subregions. The economies of Northeast Asia and Southeast Asia are highly integrated within and between the subregions. The economies of South Asia, Central Asia, and the Pacific countries are still poorly integrated within their respective subregions and so are the links across these and other subregions (ADB 2012). Although data show a marginal improvement in indicators of regional integration over the last 10 years, there is still room to intensify regional economic interdependence.

Given the pronounced diversity across Asian economies, societies, and political systems, regional cooperation initiatives are not expected to proceed at the same speed and depth experienced in Europe. During the last 10 years, however, Asian countries have shown great interest in forging regional partnerships in a wide range of areas, leading eventually to a distinct brand of regionalism that can work even under conditions of different levels of economic development, different political systems, and distinct national interests. Asia has developed a unique and multidimensional approach to regionalism, based on flexibility and consensus, which is an essential element in understanding its institution-building process.

The Asian Development Bank Institute (ADBI) organized a conference focused on the "Political Economy of Asian Regionalism" with a view to deepen understanding of the underlying processes leading up to the idea of forming an Asian economic community in the long run.[3] This volume gathers the papers presented at that conference, properly updated to account for recent developments. It also embraces the key ideas discussed by a panel of experts including Jianmin Wu, former President of the China Foreign Affairs University, Iwan J. Azis, Head of the Office of Regional Economic Integration of the Asian Development Bank (ADB), Ong Keng Yong, former ASEAN Secretary-General and currently High Commissioner of Singapore in Malaysia, and Haruhiko Kuroda, former President, ADB and currently Governor, Bank of Japan.

[3]A study by the Asian Development Bank (ADB 2010) discussed the idea of an Asian economic community being a region-wide overarching institution, gathering all Asia's subregions (Central Asia, Northeast Asia, Southeast Asia, South Asia, and the Pacific), covering areas such as infrastructure, trade and investment, money and finance, as well as the provision of regional public goods in health, education, environment, disaster risk-management, and human and drug trafficking. The study suggested the possibility for such an Asian economic community to be established in the next decades, but it also clarified that given Asia's pronounced diversity, the region's institutional architecture will maintain a much greater degree of flexibility than Europe's, without the implementation of a grand plan for Asian regionalism.

1.2 Perspectives on the Political Economy of Asian Regionalism

ASEAN Centrality in Asian Regionalism

Successful regional collective action requires leadership that in turns builds upon strong capabilities in terms of political legitimacy and financial resources. In Chap. 2, Amitav Acharya argues that one of the key factors why Asian regionalism was unable to emerge as a driving force in the post-war period is that none of its aspiring leaders possessed both capability and legitimacy. Although the United States (US) and Japan could have been "materially" capable of providing leadership and direction, they lacked political legitimacy. At the same time, large and diverse countries such as India, the PRC, and Indonesia could have had enough legitimacy in leading a pan-Asian regional movement, but they lacked the needed resources.

ASEAN as a group could also have possessed political legitimacy to lead regionalism in Asia, but it never had enough human and financial resources. As a result, while ASEAN has made significant normative contributions to the regional order, its institutional mechanisms have proven ineffective in solving regional problems, attracting criticism as being merely "talk shops". Acharya argues, however, that ASEAN institutions have played a fundamental role in preventing Asia from degenerating into a hegemonic order and foresees an increasing importance of ASEAN as a group to move Asia's overall regional agenda. He suggests that as the Indian and the PRC economies continue to grow at a sustained pace, they could eventually possess both the resource capability needed to lead the regional process together with legitimacy. But the old-time rivalry between the PRC and India—and their enormous social and political challenges domestically—could prevent their emergence as regional leaders for the provision of collective goods, suggesting, in turn, that ASEAN remains the most suitable candidate to lead Asia's integration.

The challenges and opportunities facing ASEAN countries were presented in the panel discussion by Ong Keng Yong, who stressed the importance of the decision to create an ASEAN Community, based on political-security, socio-cultural, and economic pillars. ASEAN is characterized by the diversity of its members, the widespread use of decisions based on consensus, and the practice of moving step-by-step at a pace comfortable to all. Thus, creating an ASEAN Community represents both a challenge—which may eventually push for a structural revision of some of the group's basic principles—and an opportunity for strengthening the group's identity by working closely together in dealing with common challenges.

ASEAN benefits from its strategic location between the PRC, India, and Australia, and from the existence of close production, trade, and transport networks that have enabled it to play a prominent economic role in the region. ASEAN's customized institutional processes and mechanisms have helped it to formalize a habit of consultation and cooperation among stakeholders from within and outside the region. As the ASEAN Community gradually becomes a reality, regional initiatives are expected to bring more sustainable, inclusive, and rapid growth to ASEAN member countries, as well as contributing to manage global concerns such as environmental protection, climate change, and energy and food security.

ASEAN's role in the regional and global institutional architecture is predicated on the notion of centrality. The group has been playing an increasingly important role in Asia's regionalism not only because of the political rivalry between the PRC and Japan and the resource capability and legitimacy shortage from the PRC and India, but also—and more importantly—because it has been able to develop mechanisms and processes that deliver a strong sense of ownership from a large number of stakeholders around a core group of countries that are not perceived as threats by others. With ASEAN following an approach of "open regionalism"—where the discriminatory component against non-members is kept at a minimum—non-ASEAN members, including countries outside Asia, have found merit in tightening ties with the group, implicitly supporting the idea of its centrality.

Since early 2013, this approach has been strengthened by the starting of negotiations to form the Regional Comprehensive Economic Partnership (RCEP), an ASEAN-born plan aiming to build a wide free trade and investment area by pooling together the five existing ASEAN+1 agreements signed with the PRC, the Republic of Korea, Japan, India, and Australia and New Zealand, and to possibly expanding membership beyond these countries. ASEAN's centrality in the wider Asian architecture is therefore compelling. Its process requires time as it builds from the bottom up. Although some member countries aiming to achieve quick dividends from regional collective action may not be completely satisfied with its performance, over time ASEAN has been able to gradually institutionalize regional processes from informal gatherings into strategic forums.

ASEAN's approach is to develop consultation and cooperation by networking. Such regional camaraderie has become a distinctive feature of ASEAN's diplomacy that has allowed it to play a central role in bringing major world powers together. Today, a number of important regional and global meetings revolve around the ASEAN Summit. A key process started with the creation of the ASEAN Regional Forum (ARF) in 1994. This was followed by the establishment of the ASEAN+1 summits with the PRC, Japan, the Republic of Korea, India, Australia, and New Zealand, the ASEAN+3 Summit (which puts the PRC, Japan, and the Republic of Korea together), and the East Asia Summit (including also Australia, India, New Zealand, the Russian Federation and the US). By means of these gatherings, ASEAN has positioned itself as playing an "honest broker" role, while providing the venue, synergies, and continuity of processes for stakeholders to effectively cooperate.

ASEAN's centrality is also an important feature in ensuring regional peace and security, which is a prerequisite for economic growth and constructive external relations with non-regional powers. Past conflicts in continental Southeast Asia, ongoing territorial disputes among Asian countries and insurgencies within member countries reinforced the resolve of ASEAN leaders to strengthen the group's role in promoting peace and security. Accordingly, ASEAN has engaged major world powers with strategic interests in Southeast Asia in multiple and overlapping structures, thereby obtaining more stability than it would have had otherwise by using a single arrangement.

Multilayered Asian Regionalism and Economic Globalization

The importance of maintaining a multilayered regional cooperation agenda is stressed in Chap. 3 where Gregory Chin finds that given the emergence of an increasingly multipolar world economy, Asia's future standing as a major global center for growth and development relies on its effectiveness to promote a system based on multiple, variable geometries. In other words, while the European model, based on rigid and central institutional structures, is proving unrealistic for other regions of the world, Asia's multispeed, multitrack approach can accommodate the greater diversity that characterizes the global economy and it can more effectively be emulated as a model for regional cooperation. Moreover, the nesting of regional initiatives into wider global frameworks is a striking feature of the cooperation approach followed by Asian countries, which stresses the importance of complementary relations between regional and global structures.

Chin's analysis shows how Asian regionalism and economic globalization have evolved in the aftermath of the global financial crisis. He finds that while the first order response from Asian countries was to join global efforts, the crisis did trigger advances in Asia's policy cooperation, especially through the enhancement of monetary and financial initiatives, such as the multilateralization of the Chiang Mai Initiative and the deepening and widening of bond markets promoted by the ASEAN+3 countries—originally established to respond to the Asian financial crisis of 1997–1998. The chapter confirms therefore the theoretical proposition in historical institutionalism that crises have a catalytic effect in stimulating regional innovation.

Before the Asian financial crisis, regional economic integration was mainly driven by market forces. The crisis triggered the creation of the ASEAN+3 group as well as other functional initiatives, and the establishment of their institutional processes. Intergovernmental cooperation assisted Asian economies to emerge out of the global financial crisis of 2008–2009: today it is playing an even more important role in bringing the region together.

One dimension useful to understand how Asian regionalism is thriving with accelerating regional dynamics, is the increasing shift from global to regional players in the provision of public goods that transcend national boundaries. Typically, international public goods used to be provided by global institutions or global powers outside the region such as the US. Today, however, Asian countries are taking collective action to provide an increasing number of regional public goods. Asian groups and institutions are becoming important providers of regional public goods in the region. For example, ADB and the United Nations Economic and Social Commission for Asia and the Pacific provide policy, knowledge, and financial support for economic regionalism. In the financial area, institutions such as the Chiang Mai Initiative and its multilateralization (CMIM) and the ASEAN+3 Macroeconomic Research Office (AMRO) are actively promoting regional cooperation. Other major initiatives were put together to promote Asian bond markets and credit guarantee and investment. In the trade and investment area, the RCEP led by the ASEAN+6 countries has the potential for not only liberalizing trade and investment

Table 1.1 Institutional families in global and Asian economic governance

Function	Global institutions	Asian examples
Macroeconomic stability	International Monetary Fund *Surveillance, crisis lending, systemic stability*	Asian Monetary Fund (to evolve from CMIM/AMRO) *Regional surveillance, crisis lending, stability*
Development finance	World Bank *Global public goods: poverty, environment, food and energy*	Asian Development Bank *Regional development priorities, regional infrastructure lending*
Trade liberalization	World Trade Organization *Global disciplines, dispute resolution, Article XXIV*	Regional Comprehensive Economic Partnership (under negotiation) *Asia-wide deeper agreements*
Financial system stability	Financial Stability Board *Global standards, colleges of regulators*	Asian Financial Stability Dialogue (to be designed and created) *Asia's regulatory initiatives*

AMRO ASEAN+3 Macroeconomic Research Office, *CMIM* Chiang Mai Initiative Multilateralization
Source: Revised version of Table 2 in Kawai et al. (2010)

among the member economies, but also for harmonizing trade and investment rules in the region. These regional institutions provide a large number of regional public goods being used by their member countries. Asian economies can use these regional public goods to complement those provided by global institutions such as the World Bank, the International Monetary Fund (IMF), and the World Trade Organization (WTO). Table 1.1 shows how regional and global institutions work on the provision of international public goods.

On trade and investment there is an ongoing debate how Asian countries should remain open to the rest of the world at a time when the WTO Doha Round negotiations are stalled. One way of achieving it would be for Asian countries to forge free trade agreements (FTAs) with major non-Asian economies. In this context, a discussion is ongoing over the path toward the creation of a Trans-Pacific Partnership (TPP) agreement—a high quality FTA led by the US for a subgroup of Asia-Pacific Economic Cooperation (APEC) economies—and its relationship with the RCEP concept, and whether the two will be competing or complementary arrangements. Indeed the merits of shaping these agreements as complementary rather than competing ones are many. In particular, a TPP can be useful even for Asian regional integration because the participating countries need to go through structural domestic reform, which will make it easier for them to connect with other Asian countries.

Another example of increasing importance of regional initiatives is the area of political and military security. The United Nations Security Council has played an important role in dealing with security issues in Asia. However, the ARF and the six-party talks process are regional arrangements that are now having more leverage in addressing security issues among Asian countries. One of the major achievements in Asia's security arrangements is the enlargement of ASEAN's Treaty of Amity and Cooperation (TAC) bilaterally with the PRC, India, Japan, the Republic of Korea, and other regional stakeholders, including Australia, the Russian Federation and the US. Moving forward, it may be possible to further multilateralize the TAC among Asian countries, so that major powers including the PRC, Japan, India, and the Republic of Korea would be able to sign a treaty committing themselves internationally not to use force to resolve regional disputes.

As Asian countries are becoming more economically interdependent, Asia as a region requires higher degrees of integration. Under such circumstances, Asian leaders' attitudes toward regional cooperation have changed. While in the past Asian leaders were skeptical about the possibility of establishing a regional economic community, in recent years many leaders of key Asian countries have not only declared their support to the idea of regionalism and deeper Asian integration, but also have made concrete proposals for creating various communities that could push for the creation of an Asia-wide community in the future.

Examples of these proposals include Australia's former Prime Minister Kevin Rudd's idea on the creation of an "Asia-Pacific Community", Japan's former Prime Minister Yukio Hatoyama's suggestion to establish an "East Asian Community", the PRC's former President Hu Jintao's suggestion to promote a "Harmonious Asia", the Republic of Korea's former President Lee Muyng-Bak's proposal of a "New Asia Initiative", and India's Prime Minister Manmohan Singh's commitment to build an "Asian Economic Community". Although it is unclear whether any of these proposals will eventually take shape, remarkably they all point towards the same direction of an Asia-wide community. We have not yet seen the new leaders of the PRC, Japan, and the Republic of Korea—President Xi Jinping, Prime Minister Shinzo Abe, and President Park Geun Hye, respectively—declare their willingness to continue to support the idea of creating an Asian community, but the economic reality towards regional economic integration is undeniable.

1.3 Driving Forces: Regional Cooperation in Trade and Finance

The financial crisis that hit Asian economies in 1997–1998 and the global financial crisis of 2008–2009 provided a tremendous stimulus to regionalism and offered a unique opportunity to introduce structural reforms in Asian countries aimed at strengthening domestic resilience and promote economic development. As a result, Asia's economic interdependence has increased both in trade and finance.

Market forces related to the expansion of regional production networks and the rise of the PRC and India have prompted progress in trade and investment integration. Cooperation initiatives also largely contributed to regional trade and investment integration through an exponentially rising number of regional FTAs, trade facilitation schemes, and the development of economic corridors under subregional cooperation programs such as the Greater Mekong Subregion (GMS), the Central Asia Regional Economic Cooperation (CAREC), the South Asia Subregional Economic Integration (SASEC), and others.

Trade and Investment Agreements

Shujiro Urata in Chap. 4 analyzes Asia's FTAs. While since 2000, Asia has witnessed a proliferation of free trade and investment agreements, no region-wide FTA has been established—unlike in Europe. Several initiatives, however, were started aiming to broaden the regional coverage of existing FTAs. These initiatives include the East Asia Free Trade Area (EAFTA) among the ASEAN+3 countries and the Comprehensive Economic Partnership in East Asia (CEPEA) among the ASEAN+6 countries (ASEAN+3 plus Australia, India, and New Zealand), which has de facto been renamed the RCEP. Urata explains how these initiatives aim at reducing the cost of bilateral and plurilateral FTAs, especially the so-called "spaghetti bowl" effect, due to different issues covered by various FTAs and diverse rules of origin and other provisions affecting the complex web of overlapping agreements.

Urata concludes that wider groups in terms of membership, such as CEPEA, lead to larger trade benefits with greater trade creation effects and smaller trade diversion. However, his analysis also suggests that a smaller FTA such as an EAFTA is easier to manage because of its smaller membership. His recommendation for Asian governments is to continue conducting negotiations on different FTAs in tandem until authorities can negotiate a framework agreement in favor of one group or the other. Given ASEAN's centrality in the process leading to the formation of an Asia-wide FTA, the initiative recently undertaken to establish the RCEP by pulling together existing ASEAN+1 FTAs is a reasonable process that leads to de facto CEPEA negotiations.

The rationale for strengthening regional trade and investment integration was explained by Iwan Azis in the panel discussion when he stressed that intra-Asian trade is destined to grow and regional cooperation to strengthen due to reasons such as the failure of the global approach to trade and investment negotiations under the WTO, and the rapid economic growth inducing an expansion in domestic incomes and a related push to increase regional demand for final products. The increasing trend in regional trade interdependence has been determined mainly by stronger intra-Asian trade in intermediate goods such as parts and components of electronics, home appliances, and automobiles. Final goods have been produced mostly for export to markets outside Asia, mainly the US and Europe. However, sluggish growth in the US and Europe and buoyant domestic economic dynamism in Asian countries is expected to push for an expanding role of regional demand for final goods, creating therefore even closer trade interdependence.

Monetary and Financial Cooperation

Maintaining stable exchange rates is an important condition to ensure growth in intraregional trade flows. Before the global financial crisis started in 2008, exchange rates among key Asia currencies were relatively stable, except for the won–yen exchange rate. Owing to that stability, intraregional trade grew steadily for about a decade. But as the crisis hit, the Asian exchange rates started to fluctuate widely, often in opposite directions, breaking their stability and disrupting trade flows. The immediate effect of the global financial crisis on the Asian economies was observed in the trade channel (Kawai and Zhai 2010). Policymakers need to be reminded of such implications and promote exchange rate stability to ensure growth in regional trade interdependence.

The issue of exchange rate coordination provides an important link between trade and financial cooperation. More broadly, progress in real sector issues such as production networks, trade and investment, and infrastructure development require sound financial systems and regional financial stability. In turn, sound financial systems and regional financial stability nurture further trade and investment activities in the region. Here is where a clear connection is made between trade and investment cooperation on the one hand, and monetary and financial cooperation on the other.

Soyoung Kim and Doo Yong Yang discuss the prospects for closer monetary and financial integration in Asia in Chap. 5. As Asia faces not only the impact of the global financial crisis, but also increasing challenges related to the management of volatile capital flows and the need to resolve global imbalances, its financial architecture needs to move beyond the region and establish close and effective global connections.

Kim and Yang argue that rigorously, consistently applied regional financial surveillance—associated with peer pressure—is important for strengthening domestic financial architecture and ultimately mitigating risks emerging from sustained volatility of capital flows and instability of macroeconomic conditions. They make the case for the creation of a regional financial institution aiming to serve as a venue for building consensus among key policymakers and other stakeholders (central banks, ministries of finance, and financial supervisory agencies) about regional and global financial standards. Such a new institution—an Asian Financial Stability Dialogue—was proposed earlier by ADB (2008).

The concept of this new regional financial institution gravitates around the ASEAN+3 Finance Ministers' Meeting process—established in the aftermath of the Asian financial crisis—which plays a major role in promoting monetary and financial cooperation in the region. Its major contributions include the Chiang Mai Initiative (CMI) to provide liquidity support for economies facing short term needs for foreign exchange reserves, the Asian Bond Markets Initiative (ABMI) to promote development of domestic capital markets, and the more recently established Credit Guarantee and Investment Facility (CGIF) to help deepen local-currency corporate bond markets.

While the CMI has evolved and has now been multilateralized by replacing bilateral contracts for currency swaps among central banks with a regionally pooled reserve fund, the overall situation faced by ASEAN+3 countries has changed. At the time of the CMI creation the issue was to deal with the exchange rate depreciation against the US dollar. Today, however, Asian countries are facing appreciation problems fuelled by, among other things, massive capital inflows to the region. Overall, the risks and challenges for Asian countries today are somewhat opposite to those of a decade ago. This new situation needs to be reflected in the mandate and functions delegated to regional financial institutions.

For example, the AMRO was established in 2011 with a mandate to conduct regional macroeconomic and financial monitoring. The ASEAN+3 countries need to consider revising and expanding the AMRO's mandate to include wider issues of macroeconomic management and exchange rate coordination. There is also merit to include a peer review process to the region's financial surveillance mechanism. At the same time, as Kim and Yang—as well as Chin—explain in greater detail, the size of the multilateralized CMI may still need to be expanded and its link with IMF programs eliminated.

1.4 Promoting Domestic Reforms: The Case of ASEAN

When countries consider the opportunity to join regional institutions and other schemes for regional cooperation, they usually conduct an—often implicit—cost-benefit analysis. Such analysis typically includes on the positive side various effects such as economies of scale related to faster economic growth and poverty reduction, benefits from regional public goods offered, the internalization of regional spill-overs and other externalities, and the collective increase in the regional countries' voices in global forums. On the other hand, the negative side of the equation usually includes effects such as diversion of trade and financial flows due to discrimination against non-members of the group, loss of national economic policies' independence, greater transmission of shocks and turbulence among members, and problems related to preserving local identity, culture, and traditions.

In Chap. 6, Philippa Dee and Anne McNaughton contribute to the analysis of the costs and benefits of regionalism by discussing how closer integration and cooperation among neighbors may also promote, as a positive effect, the introduction of domestic structural reforms in member countries. They examine both the theoretical arguments and empirical evidence concerning the link between domestic reforms and regionalism and argue that in Asia the case for reciprocity in domestic reforms is weak and difficult to be drawn directly by regional cooperation initiatives. For example, they find that while in the EU the enforcement mechanism used by the European Court of Justice played an important role in explaining the introduction of domestic reforms by member countries, the same has not been the case in Asia. At least, it is difficult to prove the existence of a direct and unequivocal link between the adoption of domestic reforms and the need to fulfill requirements of regional cooperation schemes.

The positive effects of regional cooperation on domestic efficiency can be important, but they tend to be of a more indirect nature, as in Europe. Dee and McNaughton argue that the success of the EU case was mainly due to the empowerment of domestic constituents that took action against uncompetitive regulations. In particular, their analysis suggests the EU was able to promote economic reforms in sensitive, behind-the border areas because it was able to overcome sovereignty losses by internalizing the political battle to domestic interests. Asia could learn important lessons from such experience as it moves toward a gradual deepening of its regional institutional settings.

ASEAN countries, for example, are required to fulfill a variety of commitments for the realization of the ASEAN Economic Community (AEC) by the end of 2015, demanding the introduction of domestic reforms to comply with regional requirements.[4] However, progress in some areas is slow because of the time required to align domestic laws, rules, and regulations with AEC requirements. Overall, although ASEAN's tariff liberalization is now largely completed the free flow of goods and services remains hampered by non-tariff and behind-the-border barriers especially those related to technical regulations and product standards which require indeed the introduction of domestic structural reforms.[5]

Once commitments are reflected in domestic systems through new regulations and laws, ASEAN countries proceed through signing mutual recognition agreements and other similar obligations allowing them to fulfill their AEC pledges that not only apply to the liberalization of trade and investment but also to trade and investment facilitation measures through the simplification and harmonization of conformity assessments, customs procedures, and other provisions.[6] It remains, however, difficult for ASEAN countries to transpose regional commitments directly into domestic laws and regulations, even if they have already signed and ratified the agreements. Problems, especially for ASEAN's least developed member countries, are not only due to lack of political will or commitment but also to the actual capacity of individual countries to implement the adopted measures. In other words, regional

[4] All economic sectors are targeting 2015 for the completion of the AEC, except the financial sector where the timeline is set for 2020.

[5] In the area of trade in goods, the ASEAN Free Trade Area (AFTA), based on Common External Preferential Treatment (CEPT) was realized on 1 January 2010, as Brunei Darussalam, Indonesia, Malaysia, Philippines, Singapore, and Thailand eliminated tariffs for products originating from other ASEAN members on 99.7 % of total tariff lines. Riding on the momentum of AFTA realization, the ASEAN Trade in Goods Agreement (ATIGA) entered into force on 17 May 2010. ATIGA requires the introduction of domestic structural reforms as it included provisions on enhanced rules of origin; disciplines the application of non-tariff measures and the elimination of non-tariff barriers; and adopts standards, technical regulations, and conformity assessment procedures, as well as sanitary and phyto-sanitary measures.

[6] The area of services liberalization remains one of the most difficult due to a plethora of different domestic regulations and contrasting business interests and pressure groups from ASEAN member countries. Progress has been made with the entry into force of the ASEAN Multilateral Agreement on the Full Liberalization of Air Freight Services in 2009 and the ASEAN Multilateral Agreement on the Full Liberalization of Passenger Air Services in 2010 as part of the wider effort to introduce an ASEAN open skies' policy in line with the AEC objectives.

integration tends to have a more direct, positive effect on the introduction of domestic structural reforms on more developed countries that possess enough capacity to plan and properly implement the necessary measures related to such reforms.

1.5 Regional Institutional Architecture

Following the considerable progress Asian countries has made in recent years to strengthen economic links among themselves and with the rest of the world, economic integration is helping Asia expand its markets, connect peripheries with centers of growth, and reduce poverty. Asia's prolonged economic momentum has significantly driven the idea of establishing a region-wide community, as countries gradually realize that regionalism is a powerful force that can help build peace and prosperity. Creating a proper governance framework for Asia's integration is essential to sustain development and increase the region's contribution to the global economy.

As discussed above, Asian leaders have been showing increasing interest in the idea of forming a regional community. ASEAN is working to create its own community by the end of 2015, covering not only economic, but also political-security and socio-cultural areas. The ASEAN+3 group has been promoting financial cooperation through the ABMI, the CMIM, and the AMRO. The ASEAN+6 countries are looking into ways to establish a region-wide FTA, while the South Asian Association for Regional Cooperation is making efforts to promote closer economic integration among its member countries. CAREC is another case of successful subregional infrastructure and transit cooperation. The Pacific Island Forum has been working to create a community among Pacific island economies. These initiatives, and many others, represent steps countries in Asia and the Pacific have been taking toward creating a more integrated regional community. As a consequence, new and articulated institutional architecture for cooperation is taking shape in Asia.

One principle underlying the formation of such new institutional architecture is based on the notion of regional "principal subsidiaries" that is, Asian versions of global institutions—either new or existing institutions.

Looking at the functional areas of institutions such as the IMF and WTO, the idea of creating an Asian Monetary Fund has been on the table for several years, and more recently the proposal of establishing an Asian Trade Organization has been put on the table by some regional economists. Moving forward, the international community should consider forming a global energy agency and regionally, an Asian energy agency. Creating a world environmental organization and its regional version of an Asian environmental organization would also be useful as the region needs to ensure its energy and environmental security. By extension of this concept, global and regional institutions could be formed in emerging areas, where countries would find it useful to provide global and regional public goods and agree to delegate some powers to these institutions and replace part of their national sovereignty with shared sovereignty at global and regional levels.

Institutions for Asian Regionalism

Giovanni Capannelli and See Seng Tan in Chap. 7 analyze Asia's institutions for regionalism. After reviewing the main intergovernmental institutions for regionalism currently present in Asia, they argue that the institutional architecture needs reform and innovation aimed at improving governance structures, ensuring stakeholders' closer participation in decision making, and promoting greater delegation of powers from national to regional agencies. Capannelli and Tan also propose the creation of new regional institutions to face emerging Asia's and global challenges. Although the region is not short of institutions promoting integration, the majority of such institutions remain a functional nature, with only very few overarching organizations operating under a broad mandate to promote cooperation and integration with regional members. In particular, they also argue that, given its roots in the regional order, institutional efficacy is a function of the ability and willingness by member countries—especially the more influential stakeholders—to collaborate regionally.

Capannelli and Tan explain that the formation of regional production networks in East Asia has occurred mainly through market forces in the absence of regional cooperation initiatives and that besides the role played by the ASEAN Secretariat in supporting the formation of a single market and production base under the AEC Blueprint, an Asia-wide market has emerged without much support from regional institutions. Although this approach has served well the region in the past, the changes experienced since the onset of the global financial crisis in 2008 have rendered more urgent the need for closer intergovernmental cooperation at global and regional levels. The emerging challenges Asian countries are facing include rising income inequalities, strengthening global competitive pressures, increasing environmental threats, and worsening territorial disputes.

Deeper institutionalization inevitably invites the idea of forming an Asia-wide community. One key issue being debated is whether the process should follow a bottom-up or a top-down approach. While Asia has been reluctant to adopt a "grand-plan" for regional integration in the style of the EU, the majority of views agree that moving from the top down is the only way to ensure that institutions for Asian integration receive enough powers delegated by national agencies and to ensure that regional issues and priorities are reflected in domestic strategies. At the same time, a top-down approach needs to nurture a bottom-up process to provide enough space for including different constituencies and ensuring ownership and participation from a wide group of stakeholders.

During the panel discussion, Wu Jianmin elaborated on two key principles that Asian authorities on regional cooperation should be following. One principle is to recognize that there are important lessons to be learnt from the past and to use the historical experience of cooperation as a guide to help move Asian regionalism in the future. In this respect, it is clear that Asian economic cooperation was not born out of a grand design for regionalism, but of the pragmatic approach followed by Asian authorities to respond to crises. When the Asian financial crisis started in 1997, countries realized they could effectively count only on their own efforts.

Although the IMF and the Group of Seven (G7) offered many recipes to individual economies, proposed solutions only exacerbated underlying problems instead of solving them. What really worked was the kind of close cooperation Asian countries were able to establish among themselves. The Asian experience also shows that focusing on areas where member countries can directly benefit from cooperation initiatives is a key factor to the success of regionalism.

A second key principle is the sense of urgency to build a region-wide Asian community. Asian countries have not seen such opportunities emerging in the last four to five decades and they will regret their inability to seize the moment. Moreover, the global financial crisis of 2008–2009 urged a drastic revision of the export-oriented growth model East Asian countries have adopted over the last few decades as demand from Europe and the US has slowed down. Asia has realized that it is time to revisit this model and create new demand generated from within the region, to spur and sustain economic growth.

An Asian Economic Community?

Based on these principles for cooperation, the process leading to the possible formation of an Asia-wide economic community is described in Chap. 8 by Nagesh Kumar, who explains how the Asia and Pacific region has emerged as the growth pole of the world economy since the early 2000s, and how the Asian economies require rebalancing in favor of greater domestic consumption and exploiting the potential of regional economic integration, especially in the aftermath of the global financial crisis of 2008–2009.

Kumar makes an argument similar to the one put forward by Urata in Chap. 4, that by unleashing the synergies for broader trade creation, a proposed FTA such as the RCEP among the ASEAN+6 countries could be a growth engine not only for the region but also for the rest of the world. Kumar argues that monetary and financial cooperation among Asian countries can generate additional aggregate demand for sustaining economic dynamism by efficiently intermediating between the region's excess savings and unmet investment needs. He concludes that by forming credible schemes for regional integration, Asia will be able to find its place in the global framework for economic governance and contribute to building a more democratic and multipolar world economy. In turn, given the countries' increasing economic interdependence, Asian integration is seen as a key factor to ensure global peace and stability.

Haruhiko Kuroda, during the panel discussion, offered his insights on four priorities policymakers should consider as they make conscious efforts to form an Asian economic community. The first priority is to adopt appropriate economic policies that should be seen primarily as a national effort to achieve inclusive and sustainable development. Countries can learn from each other and share development experiences with regional neighbors. As Asian economies develop stronger ties among themselves, inclusive growth should become a region-wide aim. In the absence of a proper redistributive mechanism, some economies or some economic groups may end up losing, while others will gain, making the process unsustainable over time. It is therefore important to promote inclusive regionalism by creating an incentive system that does not distort the market but promotes innovation and economic growth.

The second priority is to strengthen the regional institutional architecture for economic cooperation. The study *Institutions for Regional Integration: Toward an Asian Economic Community* (ADB 2010) reviewed the strengths and weaknesses of Asia's existing regional organizations and observed that Asia already has a large number of institutions and forums aiming to promote economic integration. The study highlighted that existing institutions are usually established to deal with functional issues. Asia still lacks overarching institutions that are important pillars of a regional community of any sort. Given its historical and economic background, it may well take several decades before Asia can establish such region-wide institutions. The EU, for example, operates through the Commission, the Council, the Parliament, the Court of Justice, and many other institutions that cover a wide-spectrum of functional areas. In Asia today, only ASEAN can be seen as an institution aiming at building the idea of a region from its broad economic, political-security, and sociocultural pillars. Eventually, Asia will need some sort of overarching institution and political leaders should acknowledge, earlier more than later, the necessity for such an institution.

A third priority is to fulfill Asia's responsibility in supporting the global commons to ensure that the region grows in harmony with the rest of the world. The key issue is to properly nest Asian regionalism in global discussions and frameworks. For instance, Asia needs to promote green growth and ensure environmental sustainability in harmony with global developments. Asian countries must also be able to maintain regional financial stability—an essential element of global stability—and to share their experiences of rapid economic development with other regions in order to promote a robust growth process worldwide. Asia, being an emerging center of political and economic interest, has to shoulder more responsibility to support the international community.

Finally, the fourth priority is to generate more tangible benefits from regional initiatives so that local constituencies would be inclined to understand and support plans and processes for economic integration. Strengthening physical connectivity and regional infrastructure is one clear example where benefits are evident to everybody. Other areas of cooperation where advantages are visible are in managing negative externalities, such as communicable diseases and cross-border pollution. On the other hand, positive spillovers can be generated in areas such as education. For example, introducing a student mobility program—similar to the Erasmus Programme of the EU—would open up education opportunities across national boundaries and have a tremendous impact on improving the social dimension of Asian regionalism. Given that integration in Asia is still an elitist idea, student exchange programs could greatly contribute to increasing the degree of understanding at the grassroots level of the benefits generated by regional cooperation initiatives and involving local communities more directly in the regional integration process through a bottom-up approach.

What kind of region-wide community will Asian countries be able to establish? Kuroda further shared his views on this question. He stressed the fact that Asia is too broad and diverse to follow the European model and, due to its diversity, it will likely continue to be organized through a multiplicity of functional institutions and various forums dealing with specific issues. While in the long run Asia will need to experience the growth of more overarching institutions in the style of Europe, a significant degree of flexibility will remain necessary to face emerging challenges. Given its distinct characteristics, Asia's integration process is not expected to follow the European model.

Even if more overarching institutions are created, it is unlikely that Asian countries will be willing to form a strong regional bureaucracy or provide the adequate human and financial resources needed to create strong secretariats. In order to establish effective regional institutions, national governments must be ready to delegate a sufficient amount of powers to them and share part of their sovereignty. National priorities receive, however, much higher attention than regional ones in the agendas of Asian politicians. At the same time, the perception of benefits accruing from regionalism remains limited to a few social groups. More grassroots-level support is needed to promote cooperation and the formation of a region-wide community. The progress of regionalism in Asia is to be understood in a pragmatic way: it is only in the long run that Asia will eventually be ready to create strong regional institutions. The journey, however, has already started and, step-by-step, Asia's collective efforts can transform a shared vision into action and reality.

Asia is expected to become the largest economic region in the world by 2015 (ADB and ADBI 2014). While Asia needs an increased voice in international forums, Asian countries have to provide not only more regional public goods but also increase their contribution to the provision of global public goods. As Asia's role becomes more prominent in global discussions, the world is also demanding Asia to be more responsible. Eventually, the question is not whether regional cooperation will strengthen or not, but rather what kind of regional cooperation will take shape. Cooperation has become the trend for Asia's future.

References

Asian Development Bank (ADB). (2008). *Emerging Asian regionalism: A partnership for shared prosperity*. Manila: Asian Development Bank.

Asian Development Bank (ADB). (2010). *Institutions for regional integration. Toward an Asian economic community*. Manila: Asian Development Bank.

Asian Development Bank (ADB). (2012). *Asian Economic Integration Monitor*. July. http://aric.adb.org/pdf/aeim/AEIM_2012July_FullReport.pdf.

Asian Development Bank and Asian Development Bank Institute (ADB and ADBI). (2014). *ASEAN, the PRC, and India: The great transformation?* Tokyo: Asian Development Bank and Asian Development Bank Institute.

Asian Development Bank Institute (ADBI). (2014). *ASEAN 2030: Toward a borderless economic community*. Tokyo: Asian Development Bank Institute.

Cheong, I., Kim, H., & Cho, J. (2010). Business use of FTAs in Korea. RIETI Discussion Paper Series 10-E-038. Tokyo: Research Institute of Economy, Trade and Industry.

Kawai, M., Petri, P., & Sisli-Ciamarra, E. (2010). Asia in global economic governance: A case for decentralized institutions. In M. Kawai, J.-W. Lee, & P. A. Petri (Eds.), *Asian regionalism in the world economy: Engine for dynamism and stability* (pp. 3–32). Cheltenham: Edward Elgar.

Kawai, M., & Zhai, F. (2010). Asia's post-global financial crisis adjustment: A model-based dynamic. *Asian Development Review, 27*(2, December), 122–151.

Kohli, H. S., Sharma, A., & Sood, A. (Eds.). (2011). *Asia 2050: Realizing the Asian century*. New Delhi: Sage Publications for the Asian Development Bank.

Kohpaiboon, A. (2010). Exporters' response to FTA tariff preferences: Evidence from Thailand. RIETI Discussion Paper Series 10-E-039. Tokyo: Research Institute of Economy, Trade and Industry.

Pomfret, R., Kaufmann, U., & Findlay, C. (2010). Use of FTAs in Australia. RIETI Discussion Paper Series 10-E-042. Tokyo: Research Institute of Economy, Trade and Industry.

Takahashi, K., & Urata S. (2010). On the use of free trade agreements by Japanese firms: Further evidence. *Business and Politics*, *12*(1), Article 2.

World Bank. (2012). *Building a modern, harmonious, and creative high-income society*. Washington, DC: World Bank.

Chapter 2
Foundations of Collective Action in Asia: Theory and Practice of Regional Cooperation

Amitav Acharya

Abstract This chapter argues that the collective action in Asia by its regional organizations has historically suffered from a "capability–legitimacy gap": a disjuncture between the capability (in terms of material resources) of major Asian powers to lead regional cooperation on the one hand and their political legitimacy and will as regional leaders on the other. Successful collective action requires leadership with both capability (as suggested by rationalist theories) and legitimacy (as suggested by constructivist approaches). A central point of the chapter is that the putative or aspiring leaders of Asian regionalism throughout the post-war period never had both. Actors who were materially capable of providing leadership and direction (the United States [US] and Japan) lacked the necessary legitimacy, while those who possessed legitimacy (India and the People's Republic of China [PRC]) in the 1940s and 1950s, the Association of Southeast Asian Nations (ASEAN) since 1967, and Indonesia (in the context of Asia as a whole) have lacked the necessary resources. (Although the US is not an Asian country, it can be regarded as a resident Asian power and a player in Asian regionalism. The PRC was known as China before 1949). The result has been that while the ASEAN-led Asian institutions have made a significant normative contribution to regional order, they have not proved to be effective instruments of regional problem solving. But the capability–legitimacy gap has both costs and benefits. While Asian regional institutions remain weakly institutionalized and attract criticism as "talk-shops," they have helped to ensure that Asia does not degenerate into a hegemonic order or a concert of power. It remains to be seen whether regionalism in an era of a rising PRC and India could bridge this gap. It is theoretically possible that the PRC and India could develop and possess both the resources and political will and standing to provide collective goods and lead Asian regionalism, but their mutual rivalry might prevent this.

A. Acharya (✉)
American University, Washington, DC, USA
e-mail: aacharya@american.edu

G. Capannelli and M. Kawai (eds.), *The Political Economy of Asian Regionalism*, DOI 10.1007/978-4-431-54568-2_2, © Asian Development Bank Institute 2014

Keywords Asian cooperation • Asian foreign relations • Asian regional institutions • Regionalism

2.1 Two Concepts of Collective Action

In its conventional understanding, collective action is defined as the "ability to refrain from individually profitable actions for the sake of the common good" (Bandiera et al. 2005). This understanding of collective action is rationalist, focusing on material incentives, strategic interaction, cost-benefit calculations, logic of consequences, relative gains, and individualist rationality, in the provision of public goods. The foundation work on this notion is Mancur Olson's book *The Logic of Collective Action: Public Goods and the Theory of Groups* (Olson 1965). The notion of collective action permeates the neo-liberal institutional (or contractual) approach to international institutions. A key element of Olson's theory is the problem of exploitation of the strong by the weak, or free riding. The problem of collective action can only be resolved by a hegemon, because only a hegemon can provide all states with public goods while accepting sacrifices, thereby willingly nurturing free riders. Yet, since the hegemon can do this informally or bilaterally, there is little scope for multilateralism. From this perspective, collective action by large groups led by weak states can be ruled out.

A different and newer understanding of collective action may be derived from the constructivist school of international relations. Here, collective action assumes that actors may be guided by the "logic of appropriateness", rather than simply by the "logic of consequences". It is rooted in a communitarian, rather than individualist rationality. While the first concept of collective action stresses capability, the second stresses legitimacy. Unlike the first, the second concept does not assume that hegemony is essential to the realization of collective action or cooperation. Cooperation and collective action can take place even through institutions not dominated by one (unipolarity) or more great powers (concert). Non-hegemonic institutions, or institutions in which weak powers attempt to provide leadership and direction, can also lead to outcomes serving common interests and to the realization of common security and economic benefits by relying on socialization and normative pressure. Moreover, while the rationalist position holds that only a hegemon can address the problem of free riding, from the constructivist position, free riding is not necessarily an obstacle to collective action. Instead, free riding can be part of a normative bargain where the strong power/s can satisfy their legitimacy needs by offering public goods and accepting the norms that are championed by the weaker states.

The rationalist approach leads us to expect that only small groups will be successful in providing collective action. As Olson puts it, "In general, social pressure and social incentives operate only in groups of smaller size, in the groups so small that the members can have face-to-face contact with one another" (Olson 1965: 62). Moreover, "In a smaller group, one person makes up a larger percentage of the resources of that group, so the addition or subtraction of a single member to that organization can determine the success of the group. There are also social pressures that work much better on the 'small' than on the 'large'" (Moffatt).

The constructivist view, which focuses on socialization, and its micro-processes such as persuasion, teaching, mimicking, social influence, and argumentation, are not stymied by group size. Indeed it may be argued that some of these processes work better in larger groups. The greater the number of actors within a group, the stronger would be the pressure on each member (including new, skeptical, and non-cooperating members) to conform to the norms of the group. The costs and benefits of multilateralism are seen not in terms of free riding or efficiency (although this may be present), but group identity, the quality of regional existence, and the appeal of a certain normative purpose.[1] Moreover, this concept of collective action takes note of the possibility that actors, including great powers, would be guided by consideration of whether the benefits of socialization exceeds its costs, or whether the risks of not being socialized (isolation, loss of leadership, material gains like market access and opportunity to increase their domestic welfare from foreign investment and transnational production, and allocation of more welfare-diverting resources to the defense sector) would outweigh the costs of being socialized (free riding by weaker states). The problem of free riding does not disappear, but is offset by the fact that incentive for a leading power or powers to provide public goods, (or lead in the collective provision of such goods) is based on communitarian rather than individualist thinking. Accepting a certain amount of free riding becomes key to legitimacy, and hence to justifying the inequities of power distribution. Thus, the stronger and more resource-rich actors voluntarily accept, or even encourage free riding.

In short, the possibility of collective action is contingent upon capability as well as legitimacy. Neither is sufficient by itself. Capability rests on material forces, legitimacy on normative considerations. As this chapter is concerned with Asian regional institutions, I argue that the type of collective action that has been foundational to Asian regional institutions today (as well as historically) is based largely on the second concept. But the usefulness of this second concept lies in its highlighting what I call the "capability–legitimacy gap" in institution building, or the mismatch between capability and legitimacy, of putative leaders of Asian regional institutions. The Asia–Pacific's strongest powers, the United States (US) in both economic and military terms, and Japan in economic terms, could not build viable regional institutions, even if they have the capabilities—economic and military—to do so. And those powers that might have had legitimacy, at least initially, to lead regional institutions, lacked the capability to provide collective good. In this category we might include the People's Republic of China (PRC) and India, the early leaders of Asian regionalism in the post-World War II period. But subsequently, they also lost their legitimacy as regional leaders.

This might explain a major historical puzzle of Asian international relations. Asia has no shortage of great powers. But the PRC, Japan, India, as well as the US have not been able, either singly or jointly (for example, Japan–US), to create and shape a

---

[1] Olson considers normative or "moral incentives" behind collective action, but dismisses them as "selective incentives." Olson (1965), p. 61 (footnote 17).

lasting regional organization. As a result, Asian regionalism continues to be led by its weaker states, especially the Association of Southeast Asian Nations (ASEAN).

Why so? The concept of collective action may be useful here in explaining why Asia's regional institutions have continued to be led by weak states and why the contribution of such a regional order is not to be dismissed. As a consequence, the task of shaping and leading Asian regional institutions have been left in an anomalous way to a coalition of Asia's weaker states, a coalition which has greater legitimacy, but little capability. Instead, this group has relied on normative suasion. The problem of free riding, while pervasive, and which rationalists may regard as a major obstacle to cooperation, has been managed because the legitimacy deficit and needs of the stronger powers. They have been willing to trade capability for legitimacy.

I illustrate this argument with the help of a brief analysis of three different phases of Asian regionalism. I show that in each phase, the region's principal powers suffered from a legitimacy deficit that prevented them from organizing regional cooperation in a sustainable manner, despite having the material capabilities to do so. This included not only the two powers who were obviously capable of providing collective goods while accepting sacrifices, namely the US and Japan, but also countries such as the PRC and India who were politically quite influential at least during the early post-war period. One outcome of the mismatch between capability and legitimacy—or what I would call the capability–legitimacy gap, is that Asian regionalism today remains "led" by a coalition of the region's weaker states. While many scholars and analysts ponder whether the rise of the PRC and India can change this equation, I argue that this is unlikely until and unless these two Asian powers acquire both legitimacy and capability. Neither is sufficient to ensure their ability to create and lead viable regional groupings.

2.2 The Development of Asian Regionalism[2]

A simple approach to historicizing Asian regionalism would be to divide it into three broad phases, with each having sub-phases or moments that capture important initiatives and developments. This schema starts from the end of the Second World War, although it might be argued that regional concepts and regionalist movements did exist before the war (Acharya 2010). The evolution of Asian regionalism is summarized in Table 2.1.

Phase I: The First Asian Relations Conference (1947) to the Creation of ASEAN (1967)

This period saw a contest between two concepts of regionalism. The first was represented in the very first Asian (broadly defined to include West and Central Asia,

[2] This section draws heavily from Acharya (2009).

Table 2.1 Evolution of Asian regionalism

Features	1947–1955	1956–1989	1990–2009
Geographic scope	Pan–Asia, Afro–Asia (both inclusive of West Asia, but not Central Asia)	Microregional political cooperation Macroregional economic cooperation (Pacific Community Concept)	Mainly Asia–Pacific, East Asia
Key drivers	Nationalism Decolonization Superpower rivalry	Economic development, regime security, conflict mitigation, free trade	Economic interdependence, superpower retrenchment, rise of the PRC and India, transnational threats
Leadership	India, Indonesia, Myanmar	Indonesia (post-Sukarno); Japan; ASEAN as a group; Australia, Japanese scholars, think tanks, and leaders	ASEAN as a group, PRC (?)
Intergovernmental institutions	Asian Relations Organization, Southeast Asia Treaty Organization	ASA, MAPHILINDO, ASPAC, ASEAN, SAARC	APEC, ARF, APT, EAS, ASEM, SCO
Institutional design	Inclusive, deliberative, consensus, organizational avoidance	Exclusive, deliberative, ASEAN Way (consensus, non-legalistic, organizational minimalism); open deliberative as well as integrative regionalism	Inclusive, deliberative, ASEAN Way Plus (flexible engagement), incremental institutionalization
Military cooperation	Intra-mural: None Extra-mural: Bilateral (US treaties) and multilateral (SEATO)	Intra-mural: Bilateral (ASEAN) Extra-mural: Bilateral (US treaties) multilateral (FPDA, SEATO till 1970s)	Intra-mural: Bilateral (ASEAN) Extra-mural: Bilateral (US treaties) multilateral (FPDA, SEATO till 1970s)
Economic purpose and form	Bandung Economic Committee: collective self-reliance, commodity price increase, raw material cartel, increased shipping rates	Developmental regionalism (ASEAN PTA), market-led, transnational production networks	Trade liberalization (ASEAN FTA, AEC, ASEAN–PRC FTA) Financial cooperation (after 1997: APT, Chiang Mai Initiative)
Conflict management role	Intra-mural: None Extra-mural: Indochina (Colombo Powers); Taipei,China (Bandung Conference)	Intra-mural: Sabah dispute (ASEAN) Extra-mural: Cambodia (ASEAN)	Intra-mural: None Extra-mural: Spratly Islands (PRC)

(continued)

Table 2.1 (continued)

Features	1947–1955	1956–1989	1990–2009
Civil society participation and forums	Epistemic communities: Institute of Pacific Studies Nonofficial forums: Calcutta Conference; New Delhi Socialist Conference (1955)	Epistemic communities: ASEAN–ISIS, PBEC, PECC Nonofficial forums: Forum Asia	Epistemic communities: CSCAP, NEAT Nonofficial forums: ALTSEAN, APA, Focus on Global South, SAPA
Cultural flows	Chinese and Indian cultural diffusion in Southeast Asia	Japanese cultural products American culture	Movies from India and Hong Kong, China; songs from Taipei,China; Chinese cuisine; TV dramas from the Republic of Korea; cultural products from Japan; new tourism

AEC ASEAN Economic Community, *ALTSEAN* Alternative ASEAN Network on Burma, *APA* ASEAN People's Assembly, *APEC* Asia-Pacific Economic Cooperation, *APT* ASEAN Plus Three, *ARF* ASEAN Regional Forum, *ASA* Association of Southeast Asia, *ASEAN* Association of Southeast Asian Nations, *ASEM* Asia-Europe Meeting, *ASPAC* Asia and Pacific Council, *CSCAP* Council for Security Cooperation in the Asia Pacific, *EAS* East Asia Summit, *FPDA* Five Power Defence Arrangements, *FTA* free trade agreement, *ISIS* Institute for Strategic and International Studies, *MAPHILINDO* Malaysia, Philippines, Indonesia, *NEAT* Network of East Asian Think Tanks, *OPTAD* Organization for Pacific Trade and Development, *PAFTAD* Pacific Trade and Development, *PBEC* Pacific Basin Economic Council, *PECC* Pacific Economic Cooperation Council, *PRC* People's Republic of China, *PTA* Preferential Trading Arrangements, *SAARC* South Asian Association for Regional Cooperation, *SCO* Shanghai Cooperation Organization, *SEATO* South East Asia Treaty Organization, *SAPA* Solidarity for Asian People's Advocacy, *US* United States
Note: This table incorporates four dimensions of Asian regionalism: Regionalization, Regional Institutions, Regional Identity, Semiofficial (Second Track Dialogues), and Nonofficial Regionalism (Regional Civil Society Networks)
Source: Author's compilation

with Australia invited as well) conferences, convened by India in 1947 and 1949. Called the Asian Relations Conferences, their primary goal was to create political pressure for decolonization (although none took on a militant anti-colonial character), and to give a collective voice or identity to the nationalist aspirations and newly independent countries of Asia. The high point of this phase was the Asia–Africa conference in Bandung, Indonesia in 1995, which, despite its name, was conceived and dominated by Asian actors. Here, the purpose shifted beyond decolonization to developing rules of conduct in international affairs and exploring ideas and avenues for economic (including energy) cooperation. While the Asian Relations gatherings were convened by India, with the PRC (under Nationalist rule) showing a strong interest in hosting and offering leadership as well, the Bandung Conference, was led by a coalition of five states: India, Indonesia, Pakistan, Ceylon, and Burma.[3]

[3] Ceylon was renamed Sri Lanka in 1972. Burma became known as Myanmar in 1989.

The PRC, by now under communist rule, was offered a major platform to break out of its isolation by reassuring its suspicious neighbors. Both the first Asian Relations Conference and the Bandung Conference discussed political security as well as economic matters, but the sentiment of the day was economic nationalism, rather than economic liberalism as understood in developed countries in terms of advancing free trade.

A parallel approach to regionalism during this period, which became prominent in the 1950s, might be called regionalism within "great power orbit". This was represented at first in the efforts of the US, backed by the United Kingdom (UK), to create a regional collective defense organization. Established in 1954, the South East Asia Treaty Organization (SEATO) was geared to meet the perceived threat of subversion from the PRC. It also envisaged economic assistance to vulnerable countries.

But neither of these two frameworks of regionalism could take roots in Asia. Simply put, neither succeeded in creating viable regional bodies. This outcome can be explained in terms of the aforementioned capability–legitimacy gap. The leaders of the New Delhi and Bandung conferences had more legitimacy than capabilities (although they too suffered from some legitimacy deficit), while the powers behind SEATO had more capabilities than legitimacy.

To elaborate, while India, as the leader of the Asian Relations Conferences was able to provide some material assistance to nationalist forces fighting the Dutch in Indonesia, the same assistance was not provided to Ho Chi Minh. Part of the reason was political; India's then Prime Minister Nehru, mindful of resentment against the role of Indian troops in supporting British colonial era wars throughout Asia and other continents, and not wanting to want to complicate the political situation in Indochina with foreign (Indian) intervention, was very cautious in offering material help to nationalists in Asia. But his reluctance also stemmed on limited Indian resources that was still reeling from the effects of partition and struggling to find its economic feet after centuries of colonial rule. A further constraint on the prospects for pan-Asian regionalism had to do with suspicions of both India and the PRC in the minds of the region's lesser powers. One statement by a Burmese participant returning from the 1947 Asian Relations Conference in New Delhi is revealing: "It was terrible to be ruled by a Western power, but it was even more so to be ruled by an Asian power" (Henderson 1955).

At the Bandung conference, Nehru's role in championing the cause of communist the PRC (represented by then Premier Zhou En-Lai), along with the alleged arrogant manner in which Nehru treated hosts Indonesia and other delegates, created misgivings on the part of the other countries about Indian leadership. The economic outcome of the Bandung conference included "an increased readiness to undertake development, by self-help and mutual aid, in the economic field" (Cable 1955). There were calls for collective action to stabilize "prices of, and demand for, primary commodities," and for concerted action "to induce the shipping companies to adopt a more reasonable attitude", "for more raw materials to be processed before export", "for the encouragement of the establishment of national and regional banks and insurance companies," "for the exchange of information on matters relating to oil," and "for consultations between the Bandoeng countries before the international meetings" (Gilchrist 1955). These proposals, especially for exchange of information on oil prices, might have foreshadowed the Organization of Petroleum Exporting Countries (OPEC) cartel, and the demand for collective bargaining to raise commodity prices, was something ASEAN would pursue later. Moreover, neither India nor the PRC were able to offer the kind of resources to start a regional economic arrangement comparable to the British Commonwealth-sponsored Colombo Plan, and Japan, despite taking an active interest on economic issues at Bandung, was not in a political position to provide any leadership at this stage.

In contrast to the New Delhi and Bandung meetings, the problems facing SEATO had much more to do with legitimacy than resources. Although SEATO was neither the North Atlantic Treaty Organization (NATO) nor the Marshal Plan for Southeast Asia, the amount of US economic aid that went with it was not insubstantial. In 1957, for example, the SEATO area received over US$600 million in US economic aid (Time 1958), a level of aid that would continue into the 1960s, as will be discussed shortly. Neither was SEATO without military power.[4] There is evidence that the US took the prospect of intervention by the PRC in Indochina very seriously and developed contingency plans for collective action; plans that included the possible use of nuclear weapons[5] (Buszynski 1983; Gravel 1971; Herring and Immerman 1984). SEATO's difficulties in ensuring its credibility and eventually survival had more to do with legitimacy (especially lack of Asian representation) than military power. SEATO ran into a headlong contest with the regionalist sentiments found in the Asian Relations Conferences and at the Bandung Conference. Its legitimacy as a group representing the interests of Southeast Asia was questioned because only two Southeast Asian countries—Thailand and the Philippines—were represented in the alliance. And several influential newly independent countries, including India, Indonesia, Burma, and Ceylon, questioned the very legitimacy of a Cold War defense pact because it was created and dominated by a foreign superpower. Some Asian leaders like Nehru saw such collective defense pacts as a new form of foreign dominance. For Nehru, "the majority of Asian countries [and the] overwhelming majority of Asian peoples will not be participants in the organization. Some it may be anticipated would even be strongly opposed to it, thus rendering South East Asia a potentially explosive theater of the Cold War" (UK Foreign Office 1954a). Myanmar turned down the invitation to attend the Manila conference that saw the creation of SEATO on the ground that "an alliance with a big power immediately means domination by that power. It means the loss of independence" (Nu 1955). The Indonesian government argued that SEATO would undermine its "independent foreign policy" (UK Foreign Office 1954b). The fate of SEATO seemed to have been sealed by its

[4] I have discussed this extensively in Acharya (2009), Chap. 3.

[5] According to the *Pentagon Papers*, "In the event of a massive Chinese troop intervention…it is quite possible that the US would have retaliated with strategic nuclear weapons against targets in China" (Buszynski 1983).

failure to attract any new Asian members beyond the original three—Pakistan, the Philippines, and Thailand.

The weakness of SEATO is not the only example of US failure to organize a regional association in Southeast Asia and Asia more generally. One might also look at the Johnson administration's blueprint from the mid-1960s for a Southeast Asia Development Association (SEADA). The "major political purposes" behind this initiative included the US desire "to dramatize the seriousness of our long-term commitment to Asian development in forms which enlarge the role of Asian leadership and which strengthen Asian unity" (US Department of State 2000a). As such the grouping was intended to "bring together the peoples and governments of Southeast Asia in a constructive association for economic development action, in cooperation with each other and with the advanced nations; to build regional political unit and reduce tensions; to commit the advanced countries and the United Nations to a deeper interest in the development and, indirectly, the security of this vulnerable region..." (US Department of State 2000b).

Membership of SEADA was to include both developed country donors and a broadest number of regional countries, with the possible exception of North Viet Nam. US officials even contemplated the direct or indirect involvement of the Democratic People's Republic of Korea and the Soviet Union. In creating this grouping, the US was prepared to organize an aid program that would have amounted to "at least US$1 billion per year in all forms of foreign economic assistance for development, plus at least US$200 million annually in foreign private investment." The US was ready to provide half of the amount. At this stage, US economic aid to the potential membership of the Southeast Asia Development Association was running "at about US$385 million per year", while its military assistance programs in the prospective member countries totaled US$330 million (US Department of State 2000b). A different official estimate put the combined total of US economic and military aid to Southeast Asia at a higher level: with economic aid "of the rough order of magnitude of US$530 million", and military aid expenditures at US$310 million for financial year 1964 (US Department of State 2000a).

Overall, US officials estimated that supporting such a regional grouping would require "a figure of US$6.4 billion for a 10 year period would represent a 20 % increase over present levels". If military aid was included, the figure would have been US$8 billion over 10 years (US Department of State 2000a).

But the SEADA idea failed to take off, despite the US willingness to commit substantial resources. Part of the reason had to do with the distraction and difficulties caused by the ongoing war in Viet Nam, which proved enormously costly for the Johnson administration both in economic and domestic political terms, and made it difficult to mobilize support and resources. But there is also little evidence that Southeast Asian countries endorsed the idea with any degree of enthusiasm. Instead, by this time, there had emerged indigenous interest and approaches to regionalism in Southeast Asia, represented by the Association of Southeast Asia (ASA) in 1960 and MAPHILINDO (Malaysia, Philippines, and Indonesia) in 1963. Although both were short-lived (ASA because it did not include Indonesia, and MAPHILINDO because of Indonesian President Sukarno's aggressive policy of *konfrontasi*—literally confrontation against Malaysia), these tentative efforts were subsumed by the creation of the Association of Southeast Asian Nations (ASEAN) in 1967—a formal intergovernmental organization.[6] ASEAN gave Indonesia the legitimacy, based on an implicit normative bargain whereby Indonesia (under the new regime of Suharto) undertook a policy of restraint (nonintervention and nonaggression) towards its smaller neighbors (such as Malaysia and Singapore—targets of its earlier *konfrontasi*), while its neighbors accepted Indonesia's legitimacy as a regional elder, if not leader per se. In effect, this put Indonesia within a "golden cage,"[7] a normative formula that neither India in relation to South Asia nor the PRC in relation to Southeast Asia, was able to enjoy. ASEAN reflected a shared concern with regime security against communist insurgencies in all its member states, as well as a rejection of outside influence and meddling in Southeast Asian affairs, a limited attempt to prevent Southeast Asia being dominated by outside powers and insulate it from the effects of the Cold War. As such, ASEAN repudiated the SEATO approach to hegemonic regionalism, and focused on conflict resolution among its members, as well as creating a regional space where great power intervention might be discouraged, if not entirely avoided. Economic cooperation was not seriously considered at the beginning, but the first tentative steps would be taken in the 1970s.

The fate of SEATO and SEADA illustrates that hegemons cannot resolve the collective action problem through provision of collective goods through multilateral institutions unless they enjoy a degree of legitimacy before the weaker actors in the collectivity. Overall, the evolution of regionalism in Asia during this period was hardly a fit with the rationalist theory of collective action. It shows overwhelmingly that regionalism was used by newly independent states to bolster their legitimacy as actors and agents of international relations. There was little emphasis on developing free trade areas or collective defense arrangements. The idea of hegemonic leadership was resisted, not just in the case of the US and UK sponsorship of SEATO, but also possible dominance by the PRC and India of an Asian regional grouping. Hence, the Asian Relations Organization set up by India in 1947 did not find much support and withered away. Before its communist takeover, the PRC's bid to host a second Asian Relations Conference was viewed with similar suspicion. And at Bandung while there was "acceptance of the principle of multilateral trade," and demand for "collective action stabilizing prices of, and demand for, primary commodities", but this was "not intended to form a regional bloc" (Gilchrist 1955).

---

[6]In a way, these two short-lived experiments in Southeast Asian regionalism—ASA and MAPHILINDO—showed the importance of regional legitimacy on the part of Indonesia, the main regional actor.

[7]"Golden cage" is a metaphor to describe Indonesia's predicament in being recognized as the de facto leader of ASEAN in exchange for not accepting a commitment to exercise restraint toward its smaller neighbors and not to threaten or coerce them.

Phase II: ASEAN's Formation to the Pacific Community Idea

While the most powerful actor that sought to shape and create regionalism in Asia during the first phase was the US, during the second phase, the role could be said to belong to Japan. Unlike the US that sought to create both security and economic regionalism, Japan's interest was mainly economic, with security being an indirect goal, a by-product of economic cooperation.

In 1966, a new regional organization in Asia emerged: the Asia and Pacific Council (ASPAC). ASPAC suggested a more activist role by the region's middle powers—Japan and Australia—in encouraging regionalism, but it never took off, thanks to lukewarm response from the ASEAN members, some of which, like Indonesia saw ASPAC (in which Australia and Japan were active members) as a Western enterprise geared to their Cold War agenda. Neither Australia nor Japan enjoyed the legitimacy within ASPAC that Indonesia enjoyed with ASEAN. To quote a secret British memo on ASPAC, "excessive Australian zeal" and Japan's disproportionate economic power within ASPAC were two important reasons that might produce the "collapse" of the grouping. It characterized the atmosphere surrounding ASPAC as "unreal" due to "the presence of these two countries which, though professing Asian sympathies and loyalties, are in fact much closer to the US or to Western Europe in their way of looking at the area's problems" (British Embassy 1968). This assessment of Japan's role is important, since according to some observers, Tokyo was so "preoccupied" with ASPAC and the Ministerial Conference on Economic Development in Southeast Asia (MCSDSEA)—also started in 1966—that it "did not take ASEAN seriously," when the grouping came into being in 1967 (Yamakage 1997). Another British assessment in 1972 noted that, "ASPAC's effective development as an instrument of regional collaboration has suffered from the hostility of some of its South East Asian members to anything implying Japanese leadership" (ASPAC 1972). Yet another British memo blamed Japan's "half-baked statements about new groupings" on the awareness of the Japanese government "of the continuing resentment in South East Asia against them arising from the war, and also from current Japanese economic domination" (British Embassy 1973). It is noteworthy that while ASPAC (1966) and ASEAN (1967) were set up within a year of each other, they reflected very different normative settings, and ASEAN was to outlive ASPAC that folded in 1975. Japan's subsequent emphasis on network-style regionalism might have been the result of its realization that an intergovernmental regional organization led by Japan would not be acceptable to most Asians.

A more promising development with a longer-lasting impact during this period was the emergence of the Pacific Community idea. This coincided with Japan's reemergence as an economic powerhouse. Much of it was the result of proposals by individual leaders (Japanese prime ministers) and scholars (such as Kiyoshi Kojima) in the 1960s and 1970s. In the beginning these proposals were confined to the advanced industrial countries of the Pacific—Japan, Australia, the US, and Canada—but concerns about legitimacy and viability saw the gradual extension to include the ASEAN countries, which came to feature more centrally in these frameworks. This Pacific Community movement progressed almost exclusively without formal institution building, through discussions and elaborations within epistemic communities—such as the Pacific Economic Cooperation Council (PECC)—and other Track-II forums[8] (Table 2.2). They attracted a great deal of academic debate over the merits of open and consultative regionalism, versus closed and integrative type, before settling decisively in favor of the former. As economic linkages in Asia and the Pacific grew, there was growing momentum toward the establishment of a formal regional organization, which occurred with the Asia–Pacific Economic Cooperation (APEC) forum in 1989.

Japan's role in Asian regionalism at this stage came to the fore and deserves special notice. Although initially uninterested in ASEAN (it focused more on ASPAC and MCSDSEA) Japan came to value ASEAN as a vehicle initially for regional stability and subsequently for its economic objectives. Not only were ASEAN members a source of raw materials for Japan's industrialization, but also a market for Japanese products and more importantly, as a final link in the Japan-centered regional production network that rapidly emerged following the 1985 revaluation of the yen. Initially, Japan's economic role in support of ASEAN took the form of official development assistance. Between 1975 and 1987, 65 % of Japan's foreign aid went to Asia, with ASEAN's share ranging from 32 to 44.7 % (Akrasanee and Prasert 2003). Later, Japan's economic role in support of ASEAN also involved massive foreign direct investment (FDI). As capital-rich Japanese companies headed southwards in the post Plaza Accord period, Japan's FDI in ASEAN from 1988 to 1993 amounted to $22 billion. (The Plaza Accord of 1985 resulted in an upward valuation of the yen). According to some estimates, from 1990 to 2000, Japan had invested 20 % of all net foreign direct investment in Southeast Asia, a figure that was as much as $52 billion from 1990 to 1998 (Akrasanee and Prasert 2003).

Yet, at no stage was Japan considered as a sponsor or leader of ASEAN. This had much to do with continuing misgivings about Japan's wartime role in Southeast Asia, compounded by perceptions of economic exploitation by Japanese corporations of Southeast Asian countries. Anti-Japanese actions in Southeast Asia included Thailand's boycott of Japanese goods in 1972, Malaysia's complaint against Japanese synthetic rubber, anti-Japanese demonstrations at universities, and riots in Indonesia during the visit by Japanese Prime Minister Kakuei Tanaka in January 1973 (Akrasanee and Prasert 2003).

Japanese leadership understood these sentiments, as underscored by the Fukuda Doctrine of 1977, where Prime Minister Takeo Fukuda reaffirmed Japan's commitment to anti-militarism, and pledged to strengthen Japan's economic and political relationship with Southeast Asian countries on the basis of mutual trust and equality. Japan's role in Asian regionalism continued to focus on the economic domain and exercised though epistemic communities and Track II forums rather than formal intergovernmental organizations with a political-security focus.

[8] Nonofficial meetings in which government officials may participate in their private capacity.

Table 2.2 Epistemic communities and the Pacific community idea: 1960–1980

Idea	Source of idea	Impact/outcome
Asian Marshall Plan (1960)	Morinosuke Kajima, Japanese businessman and MP	Influenced by growing pan-European cooperation idea
Economic Cooperation in the Pacific Area (1963)	Japan Economic Research Centre (JERC)	JERC emerged as key Japanese institution for research and dissemination on Pacific cooperation concept
Economic Cooperation for Development and Trade in the Pacific (1964)	Conference organized by the East-West Center, Honolulu, US	Stirred Japanese academic Kiyoshi Kojima's interest in Pacific free trade
Pacific Economic Community (PEC) (1965)	Kiyoshi Kojima's landmark paper to a JERC Conference proposed a Pacific Free Trade Area	Attracted the interest of Japanese foreign minister Takeo Miki, who sent Kojima to travel through the Pacific in early 1967 to ascertain interest in the PEC idea
Pacific Basin Economic Council (1967)	Australia-Japan Business Cooperation Committee	Separate group but supportive of Pacific Community concept
Pacific Trade and Development Conference (PAFTAD) (1968)	Convened by Kojima with support from Japanese foreign minister Takeo Miki under the auspices of JERC	PAFTAD became a major platform for promoting the Pacific Community concept and precursor to the OPTAD idea
Pacific Basin Cooperation Study Group (March 1979)	Proposed by Japanese prime minister Masayoshi Ohira and chaired by Saburo Okita who became foreign minister in November 1979	First mention of "open regional cooperation" concept that became "open regionalism": the mantra of Pacific economic cooperation
Organization for Pacific Trade and Development (OPTAD) (July 1979)	Study for the US Senate Foreign Relations Committee by Peter Drysdale (Australia) and Hugh Patrick (US)	Abandoned the idea of a free trade area of the advanced Pacific nations only in favor of an OECD-type informal and consultative and information providing association
Pacific Community Seminar, Canberra (15–17 September 1980)	Mooted by prime ministers Ohira of Japan and Malcolm Fraser of Australia, this government sponsored meeting had tripartite (official, business, and academic) representation	Established a standing committee, which later came to be known as the Pacific Economic Cooperation Council (PECC) to undertake information exchanges and research on regional economic cooperation; stimulated national committees of Pacific Economic Cooperation in Japan, US, Republic of Korea, Thailand, and Canada, as well as ASEAN Pacific Cooperation Committee. Played pivotal role in the formation of Asia–Pacific Economic Cooperation (APEC), the intergovernmental economic cooperation grouping of the Asia-Pacific

APEC Asia–Pacific Economic Cooperation, *JERC* Japan Economic Research Centre, *OPTAD* Organization for Pacific Trade and Development, *PAFTAD* Pacific Trade and Development Conference, *PEC* Pacific Economic Community, *PECC* Pacific Economic Cooperation Council, *US* United States

Source: Acharya (2009)

In the meantime, ASEAN not only survived initial crises challenging its survival, especially the dispute between Malaysia and Philippines over Sabah, and tensions in Singapore-Indonesia relations, but also went from strength to strength as a political organization. A new stage in ASEAN's evolution would start with the US withdrawal from Viet Nam in 1975. Thereafter, ASEAN would seek to develop more overt political-security cooperation, but no multilateral military ties. Following Viet Nam's invasion and occupation of Cambodia that began in December 1979, ASEAN developed a more formal diplomatic and political role—its highpoint as a diplomatic community—with respect to the Cambodia conflict. ASEAN strictly disavowed European Economic Community (EEC) style economic integration, and gave birth to the type of informal, consensus-oriented regional interactions with an avoidance of legalization and bureaucratic centralism that came to be known as the ASEAN Way.

During this period, ASEAN countries, along with, the Republic of Korea, Japan, and Taipei,China, continued to enjoy close economic and security relations with the US. The US continued to provide two crucial public goods: (i) an extended security umbrella that would be credited by some (for example, former Prime Minister Lee Kuan Yew of Singapore) for providing the non-communist governments of Asia a cushion to focus on their economic development; and (ii) access to US markets, even at the cost of incurring significant trade deficits. The US implicitly backed ASEAN, but was careful not to openly advertise it. ASEAN members—then consisting of only Indonesia, Malaysia, Singapore, the Philippines, Thailand, and from 1994, Brunei Darussalam—maintained an officially non-aligned or "autonomous" posture, partly to avoid provoking the Soviet Union, the PRC, and Viet Nam. The fact was that despite providing public goods, the US had lost SEATO and had little to do with the origins and functions of ASEAN. This suggests the importance of legitimacy over capability in building regional institutions and illustrates my earlier claim that the problem of free riding need not obstruct efforts at collective action through regional groups if it is part of a normative bargain whereby the actor providing the collective good sees free riding as a way to satisfy its legitimacy deficit.

Among other Asian powers, the PRC and India were pretty much out of the picture when it came to the development of Asian regionalism in this phase. Defeat in the 1962 border war with the PRC had led to a considerable erosion of Indian influence in Southeast Asia. India, with a growing domestic instability and after the 1965 and 1971 wars with Pakistan, became more preoccupied with domestic and South Asian affairs. While New Delhi showed some interest in joining ASEAN in the 1970s, ASEAN was reluctant to let India in, partly out of concerns of Indian dominance, and for getting embroiled in the India–Pakistan and India–PRC rivalries. The PRC, despite Zhou En-Lai's impressive show at the Bandung Conference, failed to gain much legitimacy in the region as a result of its policy of supporting communist movements in Southeast Asia. And with the Cultural Revolution, the PRC too became more internally preoccupied. This left the space for ASEAN to develop Asian regionalism in its own way.

Overall, the development of Asian regionalism during this phase marked the beginnings of interest in trade liberalization. The chief reason for this interest was the need to manage the growing economic interdependence in the Asia and Pacific region, fuelled by trans Pacific trade and Japanese investment in East Asia. The search for a Pacific Community or a Pacific trade institution was aimed at reducing transaction costs, prevent unilateralism, and manage conflicts over issues such as trade deficits and protectionism. Outwardly, this conformed to the rationalist concept of collective action. But the pursuit of a free trade agenda through a regional organization of the Asia-Pacific was secondary to the reality of trans Pacific economic relations prevailing at this time, which was driven by a non-institutionalized, market-driven or "open regionalism" in which a number of Asian economies, including the newly industrializing economies (Hong Kong, China; Republic of Korea; Taipei,China; and Singapore) relied heavily on access to the US market and protection from its security umbrella to boost their economic prospects and regime survival. To the extent that this dependence on the US was largely through bilateral understandings and alliances, we cannot accurately include it under the purview of collective action under multilateral institutions. The impetus for a Pacific Community came from Track-II or epistemic communities, such as the Pacific Trade and Development (PAFTAD), the Pacific Basin Economic Council (PBEC), and the Pacific Economic Cooperation Council (PECC). These were led mainly by protagonists from the middle powers such as Japan and Australia. The US remained indifferent to the prospect for a Pacific trade organization and hostile to a Pacific security organization. While the original plan for a Pacific regional trade organization resembling the Organisation for Economic Co-operation and Development (OECD) (mooted in Japan and Australia) encompassed only the developed economies of the Pacific, it was not long before the need for including the ASEAN countries was recognized as critical to the legitimacy and viability of any such grouping. Hence, it was not the model of a regional institution under hegemonic leadership with a small number of countries that came to dominate the thinking and approach of Asian and Pacific regionalists during this period, but rather the alternative model focusing on the issue of group identity, inclusive regional socialization and the normative elements of open regionalism and cooperative security.

Phase III: The Post-Cold War Period

The foregoing discussion shows that neither the US nor Japan, despite their strong support for regional collective action in Asia (US in the military and economic arena, Japan mainly in the economic arena), could create and shape a regional institution on their own. ASEAN remained the main platform for Asian regionalism. Asian regionalism went through some major changes in the post-Cold War period. Aside from APEC's beginning in Canberra in 1989, ASEAN at its first post-Cold War summit in Singapore adopted a new vision and direction, which would mean increasing security cooperation, an ASEAN Free Trade Area, and greater participation in Asia-Pacific multilateral security cooperation. The major breakthrough for the latter was the establishment of the ASEAN Regional Forum (ARF) in 1994 in

Bangkok. ARF became Asia's first multilateral security organization, albeit security defined not in military or collective defense (alliance) terms, but as cooperative security measures aimed at building confidence and avoiding conflict.

The ARF marked the beginning of the extension of the ASEAN model of regionalism to the wider Asia and Pacific region. The ARF itself was ASEAN-led, and anchored on ASEAN's normative framework, which meant it was not a fundamental break from the mold of Asian regionalism that had developed during the Cold War period. Sovereignty, non-interference and the avoidance of leadership by great powers (or a concert of power model) were affirmed. ASEAN itself made little shift from the principle of non-interference in dealing with human rights questions and resisted US and European sanctions against its new member, Myanmar.

A parallel development at this stage was the proposal in 1990 by the then Malaysian Prime Minister Mahathir's idea of an East Asia Economic Grouping (EAEG, later modified to East Asian Economic Caucus, or EAEC). Mahathir's proposal came as a result of the breakdown of the General Agreement on Tariffs and Trade (GATT) Uruguay Round Talks and the growing fear of the break of the multilateral trading system into regional blocs, a fear fuelled by the creation of the North American Free Trade Agreement (NAFTA) and the advent of the European Single Market. Mahathir clearly sought Japanese leadership of his proposed East Asian bloc. But Japan was reluctant, partly due to fierce US opposition to it, and partly due to its own nervousness about taking on a leadership role in Asia while there were unresolved concerns about Japan's wartime past. Even Singapore's then Prime Minister, Lee Kuan Yew, who greatly adored Japan's economic achievements, would say that allowing Japan to send peacekeeping troops abroad would be "like giving chocolate liqueur to an alcoholic" (Japan and the World 2009; Kaufman 2008).

The Asian financial crisis of 1997–1998 was a turning point in Asian regionalism. In response to the crisis, and criticism of the failure of existing Asian regional institutions, including APEC, ARF, and ASEAN to come up with an effective response, pressures grew for redefining the ASEAN way, diluting the principle of non-interference, engaging in new forms of cooperation that had been neglected or avoided in the past (including financial cooperation). As a result, the idea of an East Asian community drew support, as broader Asia Pacific groupings such as APEC and ARF looked ineffectual. The ASEAN+3 mechanism and eventually the East Asia Summit (EAS) were the outcome of this process of regional redefinition, carried out ostensibly because an East Asia identity seemed more natural and attainable than an Asia-Pacific identity.

By the late 1990s, the PRC's spectacular rise has created the possibility of Beijing assuming a leadership role in regional institutions, although few expected it to supplant Japan. During the Asian financial crisis, in December 1997, Japan announced a special yen loan facility of ¥600 billion to help Asian countries affected by the crisis. And less than a year later, under the New Miyazawa Initiative announced in October 1998, Japan offered $430 billion in aid to assist the recovery of ASEAN countries (Akrasanee and Prasert 2003). But after Japan's crisis-induced proposal for an Asian Monetary Fund (AMF) in 1997, backed by its own substantial financial resources (which it used to bail out countries like Malaysia) fell through (again due to US pressure), the PRC could be seen as an alternative to Japanese and ASEAN leadership of Asian regionalism. But the PRC was not acceptable as a leader of pan-Asian regional institutions (the Shanghai Cooperation Organization, a smaller subregional body is different), as subsequent events have shown. The PRC's desire to keep the membership of the East Asia Summit to the ASEAN+3 countries has been frustrated with the inclusion—at the insistence of ASEAN members such as Indonesia and Singapore—first of Australia, New Zealand, and India when the EAS first convened in 2005, and with the admission of the US and the Russian Federation in 2010. In the end East Asia would itself be given a functional as opposed to geographic meaning, as the rise of the PRC created concerns of a PRC takeover of strictly East Asian regional groupings. What is clear is that while Asian regionalism would be meaningless without participation from the PRC, they would not be politically acceptable with PRC dominance. While the participation of these countries gives the EAS more weight in dealing with regional security issues—the presumed focus of the EAS—the dream of an East Asian Community, mimicking the European Union (EU), once proposed by Japan's Hatoyama government as a counter to the idea of a more comprehensive Asia Pacific Community proposed by Australia in 2008 (by then Prime Minister Kevin Rudd) has been displaced. The failure of the Hatoyama and Rudd initiatives also underscores the problems of legitimacy that Japan and Australia face, in regional institution building.

The evolution of the EAS also attests to the importance of the capability–legitimacy gap in shaping Asian regionalism. Japan–PRC competition ensures that the two Asian powers, despite the immense resources each can bring to regionalist endeavors, will not come together to jointly set the terms of the fledgling regional grouping. Each will contest the legitimacy of the other as regional leader, while ASEAN will not take comfortably to a PRC–Japan condominium because of its misgivings about either of them as great powers (more so towards the PRC than a relatively stagnant Japan these days) This is in sharp contrast to the deep-rooted Franco-German rapprochement after World War II, which paved the way for the emergence and consolidation of regionalism that is the European Union today.

Asian regional institutions have performed unevenly since the 1997 crisis. A growing concern with transnational dangers, exemplified by the 2002 and 2005 Bali terrorist bombings, the 2003 severe acute respiratory syndrome (SARS) outbreak, and the 2004 Indian Ocean tsunami saw concerted action, featuring those countries most directly involved and those who were in a position to provide support. These were generally positive developments attesting to the importance and relevance of regional collective action. They also helped to redefine the role of ARF, reorienting it more towards humanitarian and transnational issues. But collective action in the economic arena fared less well. The progress of the Chiang Mai Initiative (CMI) of establishing bilateral currency swaps and eventually a multilateral arrangement was noteworthy, but thanks to its small size, its efficacy remains to be tested. The CMI has also been criticized for lacking autonomy from global regulatory authorities like the International Monetary Fund (IMF), but this need not be a serious obstacle, as the concerted approach by the IMF and the EU in bailing out Greece attests. On a more disappointing note, APEC continued to decline as bilateral trade arrangements took center stage, its once paradigmatic vision of creating a multilateral free trade zone for the Pacific all but abandoned in favor of the US-led Trans-Pacific Partnership (TPP).

A key issue facing Asian regionalism today is the question of leadership. Through the above crises, and now with the flaring up of the South China Sea disputes, the role of ASEAN as occupying the "driver's seat" in Asian regional institutions, such as ARF and EAS, has come under increasing scrutiny. But despite this, no major change seems likely to the principle of "ASEAN centrality", which has now been recognized by all other players, including the US.

2.3 Conclusion

In understanding the problem of collective action in Asian regionalism, it is not enough to apply the pathway outlined by rationalist theories like Olson's. Such a task requires taking stock of the normative, social, and functional determinants of Asian regionalism that have shaped its historical trajectory and continue to influence its direction despite the recent shocks of crisis.

A major obstacle to collective action in Asian regionalism is not the problem of free riding in a large group of actors, as specified by rationalist theory, but the capability–legitimacy gap that a constructivist approach, as employed in this chapter, would identify. In other words, through history in Asian regionalist efforts, we have seen too often that those who were materially capable of providing leadership and direction have lacked the necessary legitimacy, while those who have possessed legitimacy have lacked the necessary resources. In the former category we include the US and Japan, while in the latter category belong India and the PRC in the 1940s and 1950s, and ASEAN since its formation. Never have the two attributes really coincided. As a result, while the ASEAN-led Asian institutions have made a significant normative contribution to regional order, they have not proved to be effective instruments of problem solving or collective action.

Yet, the persistence of a capability–legitimacy gap in Asian regionalism is not without benefits. While this means Asian regional institutions will not become like the EU, this does not mean they do not make other kinds of contributions. Among other things, it has ensured that Asia does not degenerate into a hegemonic order or a concert of power. It ensures that the PRC does not become a regional hegemon. Can a rising Asia overcome this capability–legitimacy gap? Might we expect the PRC and India to one day acquire both the resources needed for organizing regional collective action and the legitimacy required for making it effective and lasting? But even in the case of the PRC, while it increasingly acquires the material resources for regional leadership, it is still a long way from possessing the ideational and the soft power required for organizing the region. A key mechanism of collective action tolerance or encouragement of free riding in return for the legitimacy is yet to be found in the case of the PRC. Until now, the PRC has been seen as the target to be socialized and co-opted into regional institutions. This is in keeping with the PRC's own policy "not to lead". But this has to change and may be already changing. The question of a more proactive PRC providing both leadership and resources to regional institutions has not been addressed yet. The key policy challenge for the region is to encourage the emergence of the PRC as a genuine provider of regional public goods while discouraging it from succumbing to the temptations of unilateralism and bilateralism. Part of the process of fostering this development would depend upon the PRC's own domestic developments, including the emergence of a more transparent and open domestic political system, and learning by the PRC's policymakers of the benefits of constructive regional leadership. The other part requires collective social bargaining by others in the region with the PRC over the terms of its leadership. The PRC's role as a substantial provider of regional public goods will be vital to the success of Asia's regional institutions and the security and prosperity of the region. Some of the key questions facing the future of collective action in Asian regionalism are what the PRC leadership might mean in institutional terms, the full economic and strategic implications of a new type of Asian regionalism with the PRC as its leader, and the role of other Asian powers such as the US, Japan, India, and the Russian Federation in such an order.

References

Acharya, A. (2009). *Whose ideas matter: Agency and power in Asian regionalism*. Ithaca, NY: Cornell University Press.

Acharya, A. (2010). Asia is not one. *The Journal of Asian Studies, 69*(4), 1001–1013.

Akrasanee, N., & Prasert, A. (2003). The evolution of ASEAN-Japan economic cooperation. In *ASEAN Japan cooperation: A foundation for East Asian Community*. Tokyo: Japan Center for International Exchange. http://www.jcie.org/researchpdfs/ASEAN/asean_narongchai.pdf.

Asian and Pacific Council (ASPAC). (1972). March. FCO 24/1269, TNA.

Bandiera, O., Barankay, I., & Rasul, I. (2005). Cooperation in collective action. April: http://econ.lse.ac.uk/staff/bandiera/collective.pdf.

British Embassy in Tokyo to Foreign and Commonwealth Office. (1973). Japan and Asian Regional Cooperation. London. 26 April. FCO 15/1727, TNA.

Buszynski, L. (1983). *SEATO: The failure of an alliance strategy*. Singapore: Singapore University Press.

Cable, J. E. (1955). Chancery Singapore, to South East Asia Department, Foreign Office, London. *Asian-African Conference*. 7 May. D2231/345, FO 371/116984, TNA, PRO (Set 5).

British Embassy in Jakarta to Foreign and Commonwealth Office, London. (1968). A.S.E.A.N. Membership and A.S.E.A.N. A.S.P.A.C. Relations. 26 August. FCO 15/23, TNA.

Gilchrist, A. G. (1955). Office of the Commissioner-General for the UK Singapore, to F. S. Tomlinson. Foreign Office, London. *The Economic Recommendations of the Bandung Conference*. 7 June. D2231/370D, FO 371/116986, TNA, PRO.

Gravel, M. (Ed.). (1971). *The Pentagon papers: The defense department history of United States decision making on Vietnam*. Boston, MA: Beacon.

Henderson, W. (1955). The development of regionalism in Southeast Asia. *International Organization, 9*(4), 462–476.

Herring, G. H., & Immerman, R. (1984). Eisenhower, Dulles, and Dien Bien Phu: 'The day we didn't go to war' revisited. *Journal of American History, 71*(2), 343–363. September.

Japan and the World. (2009). Facts and details. http://factsanddetails.com/japan.php?itemid=827&catid=22&subcatid=149.

Kaufman, Z. D. (2008). No right to fight: The modern implications of Japan's Pacifist Postwar constitution. *Yale Journal of International Law, 33*(1), 266–273.

Moffatt, M. The logic of collective action: special interests and economic policy. http://economics.about.com/cs/macroeconomics/a/logic_of_action.htm.

Nu, U. (1955). Speech to the National Press Club, Washington, DC in July 1955. Cited in J. Barrington. The concept of neutralism: What lies behind Burma's Foreign Policy? *Perspective of Burma. An Atlantic monthly supplement.* February 1958. http://www.theatlantic.com/magazine/archive/1958/02/the-concept-of-neutralism/6834/.

Olson, M. (1965). *The logic of collective action: Public goods and the theory of groups*. Cambridge, MA: Harvard University Press.

Time. (1958). SEATO: Mature four-year-old. 24 March. http://www.time.com/time/magazine/article/0,9171,868316,00.html#ixzz1QuVc5YfB.

UK Foreign Office. (1954a). Inward telegram to commonwealth relations office. 2 August 1954. FO 371–11875. TNA-UK.

UK Foreign Office. (1954b). Foreign office to Djakarta Embassy. 13 August 1954. D 1074/295. FO 371/111875. TNA-UK.

US Department of State. (2000a). Memorandum from the Counselor of the Department of State and Chairman of the Policy Planning Staff (Rostow) to the President's Special Assistant for National Security Affairs (Bundy). Washington, March 30, 1965. In *Foreign Relations of the United States, 1964–1968, Volume XXVII, Mainland Southeast Asia; Regional Affairs*, Document 56. http://history.state.gov/historicaldocuments/frus1964-68v27/d56.

US Department of State. (2000b). Memorandum from the Administrator of the Agency for International Development (Bell) and the Under Secretary of State for Economic Affairs (Mann) to President Johnson. Washington, undated. In *Foreign Relations of the United States, 1964–1968, Volume XXVII, Mainland Southeast Asia; Regional Affairs,* Document 61. http://history.state.gov/historicaldocuments/frus1964-68v27/d61.

Yamakage, S. (1997). Japan's national security and Asia-Pacific's regional institutions in the Post-Cold War era. In P. J. Katzenstein & T. Shiraishi (Eds.), *Network power: Japan and Asia.* Ithaca, NY: Cornell University Press.

Chapter 3
Asian Regionalism After the Global Financial Crisis

Gregory Chin

Abstract This chapter examines the evolving dynamics between economic globalization and Asian regional interdependence, and asks whether and how the global financial crisis impacted Asian regionalism. The analysis suggests that the global crisis did trigger advances in regional policy cooperation from 2008 onwards, especially in the area of financial and monetary cooperation. Although the first order response of Asian countries was to join the broader global effort to contain financial freefall at the world level, there emerged a second order response at the level of regional institutional building, specifically to "multilateralize" the Chiang Mai Initiative, and to develop a regional trust fund to help strengthen Asian bond markets. This finding reconfirms the theoretical proposition in historical institutionalism that financial crises have a catalytic effect in stimulating regional innovation. At the same time, we see evolution in the pattern of Asian regionalism in two respects: first, the recent advances in Asian regionalism are being driven primarily, at this stage, by the rise of the PRC and India—although each in their own way, and to varying degrees. The current advance in regionalism also builds on momentum provided by pre-existing programs of regional financial cooperation, namely the Chiang Mai Initiative, and "regional connectivity" programs that have also been championed by Japan and ASEAN countries, such as the GMS, CAREC, and BIMSTEC initiatives. Second, Asian economies appear to be pursuing inclusive regionalism, which attempts to strike a balance between helping themselves and helping the global economy. Asia is striving for modes of regional cooperation that are, on balance, complementary with the current global macroeconomic rebalancing agenda of the G20, and supportive of global integration and openness. The main policy findings are that Asia's future standing in an increasingly multicentered world economy will be determined by its effectiveness in advancing a multilayered international cooperation agenda. Yet achieving such international gains will depend on Asia's willingness to make

G. Chin (✉)
York University, Toronto, Canada
e-mail: gtchin@yorku.ca

G. Capannelli and M. Kawai (eds.), *The Political Economy of Asian Regionalism*,
DOI 10.1007/978-4-431-54568-2_3,

serious advances in regional collective action and global leadership, especially in areas of financial and monetary cooperation.

Keywords Asian regionalism • Chiang Mai Initiative • Globalization • Regional connectivity • Regional financial cooperation

3.1 Introduction

How did the 2008–2009 global financial crisis affect Asian regionalism, how did Asian economies respond, and in what ways could their responses reshape economic globalization more broadly? The chapter offers two main empirical findings. First, Asian economies were generally better positioned to weather the crisis, compared to other parts of the world, and Asian governments responded initially by taking insulating measures at the national and bilateral levels to protect their economies from external shocks, and by joining the global effort—through the Group of Twenty (G20) process—to contain the global financial freefall (Chin 2010a). Second, Asian governments have been keenly aware of the potential contagion effects of the recessions in the United States and the European economies, and they have maintained their self-insurance measures, while at the same time, they have moved ahead gradually with regional cooperation measures that promote sustainable and equitable growth, and integration, within the Asian region, and that share the benefits of East Asian growth more broadly across the world economy.

The central argument is that the global financial crisis did trigger advances in regional integration in Asia from 2008 onwards, especially in the realm of financial and monetary cooperation, and also with the rising regional activism of the People's Republic of China (PRC), and integration outreach between East Asia and India. As a first order response, Asian states responded initially to the crisis at national, bilateral, and global levels. However their second order response was to give increased attention to regional institution-building, in three ways: firstly, to "multilateralize" the Chiang Mai Initiative, and to develop a regional trust fund to help strengthen Asian bond markets; secondly, the PRC becoming a key driver of intra-Asian regional cooperation initiatives; and thirdly, the simultaneous rise of, and growing cooperation between the PRC and India, which gives further momentum to Asian regionalism. It should be noted, however, these post-crisis advances in regionalism build on pre-existing programs of regional financial cooperation: the Chiang Mai Initiative and pan-Asian connectivity programs, in which Japan and the Association of Southeast Asian Nations (ASEAN) have played key roles in championing, such as the Greater Mekong Subregion (GMS), the Central Asian Economic Cooperation (CAREC) forum, and the Bay of Bengal Initiative for Multi-Sectoral Technical and Economic Cooperation (BIMSTEC).

The above observations do not ignore the reality of inter-state rivalry within the region (see Chap. 2). However, from a longer-term perspective, we also see the counter-trend of gradual and incremental gains in regional cooperation.

This chapter focuses on the dynamics of international cooperation. The analysis builds on established studies in the political economy of regionalism to highlight the role of crises in preconditioning advances in regionalism, as critical junctures, wherein state and corporate actors respond to evolving policy preferences and capabilities by promoting regional options (Kuroda and Kawai 2002; Calder and Ye 2004; Chin and Stubbs 2011). The chapter concludes with a discussion of the theoretical-conceptual and policy implications of the analyses.

3.2 Global Financial Crisis as Catalyst: First and Second Order Responses

It is understandable that during the height of the global financial freefall in the third quarter of 2008, economies in the Asian region sought direct bilateral and unilateral tools to immediately stem the damage from the crisis by enacting bilateral currency swap agreements (Chin 2010a). They also quickly joined the globally coordinated response of the G20 leaders' summits in Washington DC in November 2008 and in London in April 2009—to try to contain the potential spread of contagion. The Asian members of the G20—the PRC, Japan, the Republic of Korea, Indonesia, Australia, Turkey, and arguably the Russian Federation—made important contributions to the G20 leaders' process at the Washington and London meetings (Chin 2010b).

In hindsight, the combination of unilateral, bilateral, and global responses to the crisis were the first order responses of economies in Asia and elsewhere. However, after some lag effect, Asian governments responded at the regional level: a second order response. Even within the G20 process, a new regional dimension emerged. To prevent the spread of financial crisis, G20 leaders gave their support to new lines of rapid financing, to be organized and disbursed by regional development banks, to support developing and low-income countries to enact countercyclical policy.

At the London G20 in April 2009, the leaders instructed the International Monetary Fund (IMF) to greatly increase its emergency lending capacity to support the emerging economies and developing countries in preventing financial contagion. The "20" agreed to triple the resources of the IMF to $750 billion. G20 leaders also told the IMF to undertake a major overhaul of how it lends money by offering larger amounts and tailoring loans to countries' varying strengths and circumstances. This included introducing more flexible and rapid funding facilities, especially to meet the needs of developing countries, which were facing a global liquidity freeze. At the London meeting, the G20 also set a target of more than doubling the concessional lending to the world's poorest countries.

Strong lobbying from the emerging countries also resulted in consensus support for the recommendations of the G20 Working Group 4—for multilateral development banks to provide support to countercyclical efforts to offset capital flight and maintain demand by providing financing for fiscal expansion, support to social safety nets, trade financing, bank recapitalization, and infrastructure investment in emerging markets and low-income countries (G20 Working Group 4 2009).

Most importantly, the G20 leaders agreed (in London) to support an Indonesian proposal to devolve a portion of the new commitments for the IMF to the Asian Development Bank (ADB), to finance flexible, fast-disbursing, and front-loaded instruments that provided rapid assistance to ("well-governed") developing countries in the region that were facing financing gaps because of the global crisis. With the G20 backing, ADB rapidly introduced a new countercyclical instrument—the Countercyclical Support Facility—to provide budget support of up to $3 billion to crisis-affected developing countries in Asia (ADB 2009). Regional development banks in other parts of the developing world quickly followed the ADB example, and also drew on a portion of the new funds committed to the IMF to establish new regional-level lending facilities to promote rapid countercyclical financing support within their regions.[1]

Prior to the global financial crisis, ADB was already lending more than the World Bank inside the region, similar to the Inter-American Development Bank (IDB) and Fondo Latinoamericano de Reservas (FLAR) that were providing more crisis-related financing in South America than the IMF. However, the new temporary, rapid, countercyclical funding facilities that were created at the regional level during the crisis represent an expansion of the role of regional development banks beyond medium-term development assistance and poverty reduction programs in Asia, Africa, and Latin America.

The global financial crisis also triggered advances in already existing regional initiatives in Asia; supplemental or alternative modes of international cooperation at the regional level. The warnings from the Obama administration, in statements by Lawrence Summers, the White House economics director and Treasury Secretary Timothy Geithner that the "US is going to be less the consumer importer of last resort", and that "other countries are going to need to be in a different position as well" (Summers 2009), weighed heavily on Asian exporters. US President Obama reinforced the warning, and the anxiety of Asian governments, when he followed up at the APEC Summit in Yokohama in November 2010 by emphasizing that the economic crisis had shown the limits of depending on US consumers and Asian exporters to drive growth: "Going forward, no nation should assume that their path to prosperity is simply paved with exports to America" (Obama 2010). At the same time, the actual recovery of the developed economies from the financial turmoil of 2008–2009 has been fragile. With US unemployment still above 9 % in late 2010, Europe facing massive debt problems, and the possibility of a decade of high unemployment and potential social unrest looming in developed economies, Asian authorities recognized that they needed to rely less on the US and European consumer for final demand, and to put more attention on domestic and regional demand.

As the world economy started to teeter in 2008, due to the worsening US subprime mortgage crisis, economies in Asia prepared to further strengthen the Chiang Mai Initiative (CMI) by "multilateralizing" the emergency fund, and increasing the total pool of emergency funds from $90 billion to $120 billion. Although the total

[1] The author thanks an Indonesian participant at the G20 summits in Washington and London for sharing this information.

amount of funds of the multilateralized CMI or CMIM ($120 billion) is a small percentage of Asia's accumulated reserves (around $5 trillion), and much smaller than the amounts that were deployed by Asian governments for their own self-protection in response to the crisis, (for example, the PRC's domestic stimulus package, announced in November 2008 in response to the global financial crisis, was valued at $586 billion), significant steps were being taken to further expand the regional safety net.

Commentators have overlooked the fact that the advances in the CMIM emergency fund entailed significant diplomatic breakthroughs. The PRC and Japan in particular, but also the Republic of Korea, reached new political consensus in the sensitive area of financial and monetary cooperation as "co-equal contributors." It was agreed that Japan and the PRC (including Hong Kong, China) would each contribute 32 % of the total to the CMIM, or $38.4 billion of the $120 billion pool.[2] In this equation, the PRC and Japan share the status of the largest co-equal contributors, and the Republic of Korea secured a diplomatic gain with the next largest contribution at $19.2 billion (16 %), followed by ASEAN's combined $24 billion contribution (20 %).[3]

Some analysts see the CMIM co-equal agreement as symbolizing the PRC's eclipse of Japan's influence inside the region (Rathus 2009). However, this is short-sighted. The co-equal agreement arguably provides the PRC with an amount of status in the regional financial system that exceeds its actual financial contributions to date, or its existing capabilities when compared to the current reach of Japanese finance across the region. The co-equal agreement does not reflect Beijing eclipsing Tokyo's influence as such, but rather the two sides reaching a breakthrough in shared leadership. This outcome is the result of unprecedented political compromises between the governments of Japan and the PRC; "regional economic-security nexus" calculations that reach beyond short- to medium-range nationalist calculations, to encompass long-range and broader geo-strategic and geo-economic considerations. For a region that has been marred by deeply held and long-standing interstate tensions, the necessity of such geo-economic preconditioning cannot be overlooked (see also Chap. 2). Japan's decision to support the co-equal agreement is tantamount to conceding sole financial leadership in the Asian region, and accepting co-leadership. This was a significant short- to medium-term concession from Japan, given its actual financial capabilities (relative to the PRC); an act of far-sighted regional diplomacy and leadership, to secure longer-term economic stability within the region.

Not to overlook the major political stumbling blocks that could impede further progress in multilateralizing the CMI, it is questionable whether neighboring Asian economies would agree to the conditionality of peer review and surveillance of their individual macroeconomic policy and national budgetary decisions that is required to access the CMIM funds. It was, therefore, a significant development when the ASEAN+3 (ASEAN countries, plus the PRC, Japan, and the Republic of Korea)

[2] The PRC's contribution consists of $34.2 billion and $4.2 billion from Hong Kong, China.

[3] Within ASEAN, Indonesia, Malaysia, Singapore, and Thailand contributed $4.77 billion each, the Philippines $3.68 billion, Brunei Darussalam $30 million, Cambodia $120 million, Lao People's Democratic Republic $30 million, Myanmar $60 million, and Viet Nam $1 billion.

members agreed to create the ASEAN+3 Macroeconomic Research Office (AMRO). The AMRO was opened in Singapore in May 2011 to serve as an independent regional surveillance unit.[4] The creation of the AMRO, and the progress on its staffing and technical competencies could be the important "second step" in Asian regional financial cooperation, and could further pave the way toward a further loosening of the CMIM's link to the IMF, wherein the release of more than 30 % of a country's CMIM funds requires IMF support.

The need to drive more demand from within the region—since the global crisis—has also translated into more interest in developing regional bond markets. Local currency bond market development, seen as key to strengthening the resilience of national financial systems to economic shocks, has been a policy priority since the 1997–1998 Asian financial crisis. Asian countries made progress before the global crisis with the Asian Bond Markets Initiative (ABMI) and two Asian Bond Funds (ABF1 and ABF2). The deployment of the region's large reserves for regional investment had started before the global crisis. As the subprime mortgage crisis worsened in the US, ASEAN+3 finance ministers in May 2008, launched renewed efforts to develop deeper and more liquid local currency debt markets. Once the global response had coalesced heading into the G20 London meeting, ASEAN+3 finance ministers reconvened in May 2009 in Bali, Indonesia, and approved the creation of a Credit Guarantee and Investment Facility (CGIF) mechanism—as an ADB trust fund—with an initial capital of $700 million (ADB 2010).[5]

The CGIF supports the further development of Asian bond markets by providing guarantees for investors to make it easier for investment firms to issue local currency bonds with longer maturities. My discussions with investment bankers in Hong Kong, China, whose banks are involved in the funds, confirmed that ADB's role in providing such risk mitigation support is key to the experimentation.[6] The longer-term local currency bonds are expected to help channel Asia's savings to finance longer-term investment in local currencies for regional infrastructure and other key areas. The encouragement of the growth of these investment products, and their accompanying institutional infrastructure, are aimed at supporting the formation of more liquid, deeper, and regionally integrated financial markets. Such an outcome would arguably make Asia less vulnerable to external shocks, as well as boost long-term growth potential from within, by recycling capital within the region, rather than have it flow to New York or London.

From the standpoint of the politics of regional integration, it was equally important that the most economically powerful economies in the region reached agreement in

---

[4] AMRO will (i) monitor, assess, and report on the macroeconomic situation and financial soundness of the ASEAN+3 countries, (ii) assess macroeconomic and financial vulnerabilities in any of the ASEAN+3 countries and provide assistance in timely formulation of policy recommendations to mitigate such risks, and (iii) ensure compliance of swap requesting parties with the lending covenants under the CMIM agreement (ASEAN Secretariat website. http://www.asean.org/25193.htm).

[5] The CGIF was approved by ADB's Board of Directors in April 2010.

[6] Author's discussions in Hong Kong, China, November 2010.

Bali that Japan and the PRC would each contribute $200 million to the CGIF fund, ADB $130 million, the Republic of Korea $100 million, and the ten ASEAN countries $7 million each (ADB 2010). The establishment of the CGIF trust fund is another important advance in regional multilateral cooperation between the most powerful economies in the region. The growth prospects for Asian bond markets are tremendous, as emerging East Asia currently accounts for less than 7 % of local currency bonds outstanding globally. Government bonds account for 70 % of the total bonds outstanding, and corporate bond markets remain small (except in the Republic of Korea), but have been growing rapidly in the wake of the global crisis. Primary bond markets have grown rapidly, however secondary markets have grown more slowly. There is much to be done to improve the institutional infrastructure to support the development of bond markets in Asia.

3.3 Preconditioning the Post–2007 Regionalism

Capannelli's (2011) comparison of the results from the ADB surveys (in 2008 and 2010) of opinion leaders in Asia and the Pacific on the international architecture shows that Asia's opinion leaders (including government representatives) have become increasingly supportive of further regional economic integration. The post–2007 advances in Asian regionalism build on a pattern of rising regional intergovernmental cooperation that preceded the global financial crisis. Capannelli et al. (2009) note that the forms of regional cooperation have varied across and within world regions, "ranging from formal agreements designed to lead the integration process, to informal measures to manage the consequences of integration." It has entailed increasingly frequent consultations on regional issues, across all levels of government. That, increasingly, most heads of state have multiple, regularly scheduled opportunities to meet regionally, each year, and their ministers and other leading officials of national agencies also meet frequently at various forums. In Asia, this growing pattern of regional policy cooperation can be seen at forums at the regional level, such as the Executives' Meetings of East Asia Pacific Central Banks (EMEAP), to more formal organizations such as ASEAN, ASEAN+3, Asia–Europe Meeting (ASEM), or Asia–Pacific Economic Cooperation (APEC), and in regional dialogue arrangements that are embedded within global institutions such as United Nations (UN) agencies and the Bank for International Settlements (BIS).

Other sources of momentum for growing regionalism in Asia—that preceded the global crisis—were the ASEAN Free Trade Area discussion, the PRC–ASEAN Free Trade Agreement (CAFTA, discussed below), and the regional connectivity programs involving infrastructure projects that were initiated to link subregions in Asia.[7] Some of the initiatives, such as the GMS, the CAREC forum, and BIMSTEC,

[7] One other factor that has also reinforced the trend toward to increased regional cooperation in Asia has been the effective regionalized coordination on health crises and containing transboundary diseases such as avian influenza and SARS, over the past decade. I thank Giovanni Capannelli and Sabyasachi Mitra for highlighting this point.

were launched over the past two decades by member governments, and then received additional support from multilateral development banks, including ADB. Infrastructure investment facilitates regional integration that in turn, further encourages regional cooperation, including cooperation on infrastructure development. The work of the ADB Institute found that investment in infrastructure for regional cooperation can create a "virtuous cycle" that supports development (Bhattacharyay 2010). Development banks have played a particularly active role in supporting the building of Asia infrastructure, especially infrastructure that promotes regional growth, trade, and investment cooperation, ranging from transport infrastructure to the governance and financing of infrastructure.

Whereas the GMS is a more established program of regionalism, the CAREC forum and BIMSTEC are at the frontline of expanding regionalism between East and Central Asia, and East and South Asia, respectively. The CAREC program, started in 2005, is a partnership of eight countries (Afghanistan, Azerbaijan, the PRC, Kazakhstan, Kyrgyz Republic, Mongolia, Tajikistan, Uzbekistan, Turkmenistan, and Pakistan) and six multilateral institutions (ADB, European Bank for Reconstruction and Development, IMF, Islamic Development Bank, United Nations Development Programme, and the World Bank). CAREC works to promote "development through cooperation, leading to accelerated economic growth and poverty reduction" (ADB CAREC website). It promotes subregional cooperation in the priority areas of transport, trade facilitation, trade policy, and energy, and especially in transport cooperation that is seen as crucial to promoting sustainable economic growth and rapid poverty reduction among the member countries. CAREC also aims to help its members and neighboring countries realize their potential in an increasingly integrated Eurasia. In 2009, the program mobilized $3.9 billion for projects in the transport, trade, and energy sectors.

ADB has been a key coordinating force behind the CAREC program, and has provided guidance and support to its development. ADB research has indicated that improved connectivity, efficient sharing of natural resources, shorter transit times, and clear, consistent trade regimes will bring large dividends. An ADB Policy Brief for CAREC suggests that increased regional cooperation, along with key economic reforms, could help double per capita incomes in the CAREC region and reduce poverty from more than 40 % to less than 25 % by 2015 (ADB 2005). These research findings have provided momentum for subregional integration.

The other case of subregional collective action—BIMSTEC—covers Bangladesh, India, Sri Lanka, Thailand, Myanmar, Bhutan, and Nepal. BIMSTEC was initiated in 1997 to:

> …create an enabling environment for rapid economic development, accelerate social progress in the sub-region, promote active collaboration and mutual assistance on matters of common interest, provide assistance to each other in the form of training and research facilities, cooperate more effectively in joint efforts that are supportive of, and complementary to national development plans of member states, maintain close and beneficial cooperation with existing international and regional organizations, and cooperate in projects that can be dealt with most productively on a sub-regional basis and which make best use of available synergies (BIMSTEC website).

The foreign policy goal of BIMSTEC was to link the "Look West" policy of the Southeast Asian members of BIMSTEC and the "Look East" policy of the South Asian members. BIMSTEC thus bills itself as a "link between ASEAN and SAARC" (BIMSTEC website). The seven members of BIMSTEC cover 14 priority sectors, which are led by member countries in a voluntary manner: trade and investment; technology; energy; transport, and communication; tourism; fisheries; agriculture; cultural cooperation; environment and disaster management; public health; people-to-people contact; poverty alleviation; counter-terrorism and transnational crimes; and climate change. BIMSTEC provides an institutional link between South Asia and Southeast Asia that encapsulates 1.3 billion people, or 21 % of the world population, a combined GDP of $750 billion, and a considerable number of complementarities. A study commissioned by BIMSTEC shows the potential for $43 billion to $59 billion trade under a BIMSTEC free trade agreement (FTA). The priority at the 16th meeting of the BIMSTEC Trade Negotiating Committee (TNC), held from 17 to 21 March 2008 in India, was the negotiation of the "List of Goods" related to the Framework Agreement of the BIMSTEC TNC that was signed in 2004. These negotiations aim to culminate in an FTA (BIMSTEC website).

Both the CAREC and BIMSTEC subregional initiatives make the case for the importance of institutions for Asian connectivity. The idea is that economies in the region need to be rebalanced toward regional demand- and trade-driven growth through increased regional connectivity, in order for Asia to be more economically sustainable and resilient against external shocks (Bhattacharyay 2010).

The effectiveness of connectivity, according to Bhattacharyay, depends on the quality of hard and soft infrastructure. In terms of soft infrastructure—which supports hard infrastructure—the facilitating institutions that ensure connectivity are appropriate government policies, systems, and procedures, and effective regulatory coordination and cooperation. Asia currently has numerous overlapping subregional institutions involved in national and regional energy, transport, and telecommunications infrastructure connectivity; however their effectiveness appears constrained. They lack clear and binding system of rules and policies, and are overly informal.

Seamless connectivity within the region requires reforms to foster a more effective, formal, and rules-based institutional framework. ADB has put concerted efforts into institutional reforms for Asian connectivity and meeting the financing challenges including developing institutional options for regional infrastructure financing.

3.4 Emerging Faces of Asian Regionalism

The global financial crisis has resulted in adjustments in the mindset, calculations of national interest, and policy preferences of government leaders of the key economies in the region. On the one hand, the crisis has encouraged authorities in the PRC to give more support to regional arrangements, both for meeting emergency liquidity needs, and for providing medium-term national developmental support. On the other hand, the crisis has encouraged Asian countries to consider how to foster further

Pan–Asian synergies, stretching the outreach from East Asia to India, and vice versa. Foremost is growing recognition across Asian capitals that achieving sustained growth of the economies inside the region will also require Asia to provide greater developmental support ("benefit-sharing") to economies beyond the region.

Regional Activism of the PRC

For Asia, the PRC is key for diversifying growth options. The call from the US to reduce reliance on the US market means that Asian countries need to find alternative options for driving demand, diversifying their export markets, and fostering new sources of growth from within the region. The PRC realizes it must take policy measures to adjust its own growth model, by increasing domestic demand (Wang 2007; Zhang 2011). The PRC can play a greater role in driving demand and growth for economies in the Asian region, by absorbing more exports of final goods where the PRC is the consumer of finished goods, rather than processing trade. Such a shift would signal the PRC's evolution into more of a consumer, and less of an assembler, and that would provide grounds for optimism that the PRC can serve as a source of resilience against exogenous demand shocks in the short to medium run, and be a sustained source of growth in the long run (Park and Shin 2010). However, many countries in the region already enjoy significant trade surpluses with the PRC, and for some economies in Northeast Asia, their interests will continue to be closely bound with producing within the PRC via production networks, for export to the rich end-markets of the US and Europe, and now elsewhere, even with growing demand from the PRC. But, East Asian policymakers, including those of the PRC, recognize that they cannot simply wait for a US and EU recovery, and must think about helping to stimulate market-oriented solutions involving the PRC, and also a growing India; that some coordinated action is necessary at the regional level across Asia, but also in other regions of the South.

The PRC, Japan, the Republic of Korea, and some other Asian economies have amassed large foreign currency reserves, which have recently shown their value for national economic security when deployed to insulate their economies in a time of global financial volatility and currency instability (Chin 2011). Reserve accumulation is, however, inherently inefficient, and Asian authorities are increasingly aware of the need for regional solutions that are integrated with national and global initiatives. Already established regional trade mechanisms such as ASEAN's separate trade agreements with the PRC, Japan, and the Republic of Korea provide an institutionalized platform for increasing intra-regional trade links, to further expand regional production networks, and to stimulate growth from within the region.

As other scholars have correctly pointed out, the current momentum behind enhanced trade regionalism is also bound up with the global level, with problems of the global multilateral trading regime, with the ongoing impasse of the Doha Round of world trade negotiations (Chin and Stubbs 2011). Regardless, indications are that "negotiated liberalization" is increasingly the preferred path for market opening.

Asia is setting precedents for creating new regional and potentially global norms and rules, with its managed opening, and controlled liberalization via preferential trade agreements. The PRC–ASEAN Free Trade Agreement (CAFTA) reflects such an approach to trade and investment liberalization (Chin and Stubbs 2011). CAFTA is calibrated to the differing levels of development of countries in the region, and allows for controlled opening, by allowing countries to open gradually without having to face competition immediately from powerful external corporate actors. Zhang Yunling, a leading expert on the PRC's Asian regional relations at the Chinese Academy of Social Sciences writes that: "For [the PRC], CAFTA is more than just a trade agreement. It helps to provide a comprehensive framework for cooperation between [the PRC] and the ASEAN countries. [The PRC] is now the largest market for ASEAN exports, but relations go well beyond trade to include infrastructure, connectivity and capacity building for human development" (Zhang 2012).

Beyond trade integration, the global financial crisis and the extended downturn in key developed economies have also altered national interests in the realm of finance and money, and spurred a succession of changes in the international behavior of Asian economies in regional financial and monetary cooperation. Since the start of the crisis, as mentioned earlier, the bilateral swaps under the CMI have been multilateralized, enlarged to $120 billion, and operationalized since December 2009. However, the percentage of funds from this regional facility that can be immediately accessed is still limited to 30 %, and the rest still requires IMF sanctioning. My own research has mapped how the previous limits in the regional emergency mechanisms led some vulnerable economies in the region to access national reserves, quickly establish a new set of bilateral currency swap arrangements with non-regional and regional governments, and work at the global (G20) level to prevent the contagion effects of the global financial fallout.[8]

The PRC is one of the countries where changes in national interests, and important breakthroughs on international financial and monetary behavior can be observed. The PRC's policy researchers have called for more regional cooperation within Asia as one line of response to the global financial crisis and the turbulence that has come in its wake (Zhang 2011, 2012). Huang Ping, head of the American Studies Institute at the Chinese Academy of Social Sciences suggested that the PRC should play a more constructive role in many cooperative frameworks, including regional networks: "For [the PRC], opening up to the world should mean to seek a constructive role in both global and regional cooperation. The financial crisis has also provided [the PRC] with a wider choice in working with various regional partners" (Huang 2009). Prior to the global crisis, the PRC authorities had already given their support to regional bond market development (ABMI, ABF1, and ABF2), although there continued to be some caution on the part of Beijing, if not hesitation, during this period. At the height of the 2008–2009 global financial crisis,

[8] For example, the Republic of Korea arranged a one-year $30 billion swap with the US in October 2008, and followed up with a three-year currency swap of CNY180 billion ($26.3 billion) with the PRC, and a two-year $20 billion swap with Japan. Singapore signed a $30 billion currency swap with the US in October 2008 and followed up with another swap with Japan (Chin 2010a).

Beijing supported the previously noted Indonesian proposal to enhance ADB's role in crisis prevention countercyclical financing. At the Boao Forum for Asia in April 2009, the PRC's central bank governor stated that the IMF had failed in its crisis prevention responsibilities, and that "regional institutions such as the Asian Development Bank, could also alleviate the impact of financial crisis through increasing spending and boosting regional activities" (Xinhua Net (online) 2009).

After global financial markets were stabilized, the PRC's finance ministry turned back to the development of regional bond markets. In the wake of the global financial crisis, the PRC's finance ministry focused on supporting information and communication technology (ICT) infrastructure development that is crucial to providing the enabling infrastructure that is needed for the CGIF, as well as the ongoing efforts to foster regional local currency bond markets in Hong Kong, China, via corporate bond guarantees that have their origins in a 1997 APEC-led initiative.[9] Beijing has grown more comfortable with this aspect of regional financial policy cooperation, and endorsed moving ahead with building the institutional underpinnings, or key blocks for the emerging regional financial architecture.

These observations regarding the evolution in the PRC's thinking on regional interdependence appear to run counter to the predictions of a number of prominent analysts prior to the crisis, that the PRC would be unlikely to readily endorse moves toward financial and monetary integration. On the sensitive issue of monetary cooperation, it is likely that Beijing is not ready to endorse the creation a regional currency basket, the immediate formation of an Asian currency unit that might serve as an index for measuring exchange rate deviations or, more ambitiously, to move toward a regional peg (Yu 2007). Decision makers in the PRC have to decide whether the PRC is ready to make the yuan a part of a regional currency basket. But research in the PRC is being directed at this theme, including on cost-benefit analyses, and next steps. In brief, the PRC authorities have continued to take a gradualist approach to supporting financial regionalism, that starts not from "grand" architecture but from the "bottom-up", in "bits and pieces", building new international consensus along the way, and eventually connecting the pieces.

The PRC leaders have given the "green light" in their official statements to proceed further—though incrementally—with regional financial and monetary cooperation. The central bank governor, Zhou Xiaochuan's speech that was published prior to the April 2009 London G20 meeting gave a key signal of the priority that Beijing was attaching to experimentation on alternative reserve asset options, including pursuing increased regional financial and monetary cooperation, and internationalization of the yuan (Zhou 2009). Support from the most senior levels followed in remarks by the PRC President Hu Jintao on Asian regional cooperation in his speech to the General Assembly of the United Nations in September 2009, that since the outbreak of the global financial crisis, the PRC has "actively contributed to the building of an East Asian foreign currency reserve pool," and would "continue with its efforts to promote regional monetary and financial cooperation, maintain financial

[9] Author's discussions. Beijing, September 2010.

and economic stability, and push forward financial cooperation and trade within the region" (Hu 2009).

Jintao's and Wen Jiabao's official announcements in 2009 that the PRC would support an enlarged and multilateralized CMI gave indication that the PRC leaders had made a shift toward the idea of an Asian currency unit. Influential new research groupings were directed to analyze the prospects for an Asian currency unit, and for greater regional financial and monetary cooperation more broadly, including the new "super think tank" (created in March 2009), the China Center for International Economic Exchanges (CCIEE), chaired by former Vice Premier Zeng Peiyan, a political heavyweight of state economic planning.[10]

Beijing's increased support to regional financial and monetary innovation is rooted in concerns over what it deems is over-reliance on the dollar—and the inherent vulnerabilities in holding over $2 trillion in currency reserves, on the one hand; and a desire to lay alternative monetary foundations for stable future growth over the longer-term, on the other (Wang 2007; Chin and Helleiner 2008; Chin and Wang 2010).

India's Outreach

India's continuing economic rise, and its growing interest in pursuing regional cooperation with East Asia is an emerging motor of Asian regionalism and of pan-Asian economic integration. Recently, Delhi expanded its strategic vision, most noticeably in Asia, and Indian authorities are giving greater priority to their "Look East" policy, and to strengthening ties with East Asia (Rajamohan et al. 2008). The PRC has become a major trading and economic partner to India. But as a hedge against the PRC's rise, India has also broadened its security agenda, and strengthened ties with Japan, ASEAN, and the Republic of Korea. These bilateral advances also provide momentum for India's increased involvement in regional multilateralism. The negative effects of the 2008–2009 global financial crisis on India's exports gave Delhi a clear warning about the need to strategize about alternative options, of which further stimulating Indian's links with intra-Asian growth would be optimal (Chin 2011). The ongoing downturn in EU and US markets only make the point more obvious.

The question though, is how deep or sustained is India's interest in linking to East Asia, as it entails some economic and political risks for India? India and the ASEAN countries have entered into a framework agreement on comprehensive economic cooperation. India is not (yet) a full-fledged member of the ASEAN+3 network, but does hold regular summits with ASEAN. Some analysts envisage that, in

---

[10] Zeng Peiyan is the PRC's former leading state planner, and the CCIEE officially operates under the purview of the National Development and Reform Commission, the powerful planning organ of the PRC party-state. The CCIEE also has several current or former ministerial-level officials, prominent business leaders, and leading academics appointed as vice-chair to its board (Li 2009).

The CCIEE reportedly formed a research partnership with influential Japanese counterparts to investigate the Asian currency unit. The author's discussion with a senior representative of a leading Japanese international policy think tank. Rome, May 2009.

the years ahead, India's ties with the ASEAN network will strengthen via an ASEAN+3+3 (ASEAN+3 countries and India, Australia, and New Zealand) (Sinha and Pradhan 2008). They moreover suggest that such a regional network would help India to cooperate in regional financial programs, similar to the present network of ASEAN+3 (the feasibility of such developments is addressed below). For now, India is becoming increasingly engaged in the institutionalized policy dialogue and some programs of East Asian regionalism.

Delhi has also recently worked on FTA-type arrangements with the Republic of Korea, and is currently negotiating economic partnership agreements (EPAs) with Japan and the PRC. Such EPAs have been consciously pursued by Delhi and Tokyo (and Beijing) as a strategic goal, as building blocks for an even larger regional economic integration. At the same time that India has been reaching more toward the East, Delhi has also been driving intra-regional trade and investment links within South Asia, via its South Asian Association for Regional Cooperation (SAARC) arrangements. It has recently added building more ties with Central Asia to its expanding international agenda. India was the primary driver behind the SAARCFINANCE, established in September 1998, as a regional network of the SAARC central bank governors and finance secretaries. The goal is to give further momentum to the SAARC by elevating the cooperation to international finance and monetary issues. Unlike its recent outreach to East Asia, which at times has been partial and cautious despite the increased priority, India has participated actively in SAARCFINANCE activities (Sinha and Pradhan 2008).

Sinha and Pradhan argue that it is important for India to forge a closer relationship for mutual trade and investment within the Asian region and also to adopt a proactive role vis-à-vis the ASEAN economies. They suggest that India has already demonstrated its strength in the services sector, especially software. If this can be complemented by the hardware and manufacturing base of East Asia, then India and the region can "prosper together in the new global scenario." According to these two Indian analysts, the rapid change that has taken place in Asia provides new opportunities that "must be seized" by each side (Sinha and Pradhan 2008). The BIMSTEC arrangements (discussed above) are one institutional platform for forging such regional linkages.

The reality is that India's share of exports to the Asian region have remained somewhat sluggish and below optimal projections. India's FDI openness, despite increasing, is still much lower than that of other Asian emerging economies. As India's services exports are increasing at a rapid pace, the country is confronting challenges emanating from the uncertainty of access to cross-border exports of services and barriers to the movement of people. At the same time, it is useful to note that the latest wave of Indian integration into East Asian regionalism is being driven by the activities of Indian companies, which have come to recognize their complementary strengths, and have become increasingly linked with East Asian production networks. In turn, East Asian companies have also begun to utilize India's strengths in research and development (R&D), and software and design, and some have relocated their global R&D centers to India. Several Indian companies have also begun to take advantage of lower manufacturing costs for hardware in the PRC, and have invested there in order to rationalize their production.

The above trends may become more entrenched as the emerging free trade arrangements between India and Southeast Asian countries come into effect. The BIMSTEC arrangements may serve to support the crucial micro-decisions at firm level. ADB became a development partner with BIMSTEC in 2005, to undertake a study that helps promote and improve transport infrastructure and logistics among the BIMSTEC countries. ADB completed an initial scoping and feasibility project called the BIMSTEC Transport Infrastructure and Logistic Study (ADB 2006). The project issued an initial report in August 2006 that was conveyed to all members. ADB then commissioned a more extensive technical assistance report for BIMSTEC in August 2006, and the team of consultants delivered a final report in January 2008 (ADB 2008). The final report included: (i) a review of present trade patterns and identification of the main transport and logistics constraints and their impact on transaction costs and trade; (ii) a framework of policies and strategies to overcome the constraints; and (iii) an outline of possible financing modalities and sources.

It is also possible that India could eventually assume a greater role in helping to forge financial cooperation in the Asian region. Such a move would likely be motivated not only by trade integration, but as well by the structural shift that is resulting from India's co-integration with stocks markets in Hong Kong, China and Singapore (though less with the Japanese stock market) (Raj and Dhal 2008). The prospects for India's cooperation with East Asia on monetary policy are more complicated. It is unsure whether Delhi would support the fundamental reform of the global reserve scenario that is entailed in the creation of an Asian currency unit.

In terms of central banking cooperation, India attends the informal meetings of the Asia Cooperation Dialogue, attended by participant central banks. The Government of India has committed to participating in the ABF2 for a total of $1 billion. While these moves are promising, one would want to be mindful that India may have a different set of national interests than other key emerging economies in Asia, specifically with respect to the international monetary system. Delhi and Indian business appear more willing to work within the dollar order despite the volatility in the value of the dollar.[11] This speaks to more fundamental differences in exchange rate regimes as the starting point for regional monetary cooperation. An interesting question is whether India would be in a similar position relative to a future East Asian monetary union, as the UK and the European Monetary Union. Such distinctions are alluded to in Suman Bery's analyses (Bery 2010).

3.5 Conceptual and Policy Implications

The above findings reconfirm the theoretical proposition in historical institutionalism that financial crises have a catalytic effect in stimulating regional innovation, as seen after the 1997–1998 Asian financial crisis (Calder and Ye 2004; MacIntyre

[11] The author thanks Manmohan Agarwal, former dean of the School of International Studies and professor at the Centre for International Trade and Development at Jawaharlal Nehru University in India, for highlighting this point.

et al. 2008; Chin and Stubbs 2011; Henning 2002). The discussion above suggests that the global financial crisis did trigger advances in regional integration in Asia from 2008 onwards, especially in the realm of financial and monetary cooperation, but also with the growing regional activism of the PRC, and the integration outreach between East Asia and India. The analysis further shows the importance of disaggregating the international response of Asian states to the global crisis along both temporal and spatial dimensions (differentiating varying temporalities and "levels of analysis"), with the first order response being Asian states responding initially to the global financial crisis at national, bilateral, and global levels; and then followed by their second order response, of giving more attention to regional cooperation.

The central collective action challenge for the Asian economies is figuring out how to pursue inclusive forms of regionalism, which attempt to strike a balance between helping themselves and supporting balanced and sustainable growth of the global economy. Asia is searching for modes of regional cooperation that are complementary with current global macroeconomic rebalancing efforts, such as the G20. However Asian countries should also consider other options, including innovative South–South and South–North cooperation initiatives (outside the "G20 box"), that are also broadly supportive of global economic integration and openness, and most important, the amelioration of North–South developmental imbalances. This chapter shows that Asian economies are responding to the impact of the global crisis, in part, by pushing ahead, incrementally, with regional cooperation.

Asian countries are also responding to endogenous distribution tensions by taking gradual steps particularly to strengthen regional financial cooperation, and to share the benefits of development, more evenly, across the region. A key channel for enhanced burden/benefit sharing within the Asian region, and increased Asian financial cooperation through coordinated use of accumulated foreign exchange reserves (over $5 trillion), is the financing of infrastructure development and modernization. Modernizing physical connectivity, and the accompanying soft infrastructure that supports transport and transit facilitation for the smooth movement of people, capital, and knowledge, should remain an important priority for Asian countries—and more collective action is needed. ASEAN has developed a master plan on connectivity (adopted at ASEAN's Hanoi Summit on 28 October 2010) with the support of ADB and ESCAP. Nagesh Kumar notes that the deficit for investment in infrastructure in the less developed parts of Asia runs into trillions of dollars (see Chap. 8). Zhai (2010) estimates that the annual investment needed to close the infrastructure gaps in Asia is $800 billion, and that this amount cannot be met by existing arrangements. New collective mechanisms are needed to marshal Asian currency reserves to finance infrastructure development on this scale.[12]

But Asian countries need to consider how they can share the benefits of their growth with other developing regions, especially through their support to infrastructure modernization. Asian countries are responding to growing exogenous pressure from deficit- and debt-ridden countries to undertake fundamental structural, financial, and monetary reforms (Adams et al. 2010), and through ADB for instance,

[12]Author's notes for the presentation by Nagesh Kumar, ADBI Annual Conference, Tokyo, 3 December 2010.

have commenced "developmental benefit-sharing" discussions with other regions of the South, and of the North. For example, ADB was approached by the Inter-American Development Bank in 2010–2011, on how the economies of Latin American and the Caribbean could draw best practices and lessons-learned from the Asian experience in establishing regional production networks. Equally important, Asia has much to offer to help other regions of the South, in terms of the financing, engineering, and managerial expertise related to highway and trans-regional railway development, port networks, and so-called "soft infrastructure." For example, Africa's infrastructure faces a critical deficit. Absolute shortfalls are observed across all sectors. The African Development Bank (AfDB) notes that only about a third of the continent's rural population has access to roads, less than 40 % of Africans have access to electricity, only 5 % of agriculture is under irrigation, only 34 % of the population has access to improve sanitation, and about 65 % to clean water. AfDB estimates that it will cost at least $93 billion per year until 2020 to bring infrastructure in Africa on par with that of other low- and middle-income countries (Kaberuka 2011).

Such "global rebalancing" measures within and beyond the Asian region, and the advances in the regional emergency financing arrangements and financial markets development, hold the potential to cumulatively reshape economic globalization, over the medium-term. The main policy recommendation is that Asia must play a greater role in reshaping economic globalization, as we shift towards an increasingly multicentered world economy. Much will depend on Asia's ability to help the global community to navigate a less-centralized and more multilayered global economic governance system, which Asia itself is helping to create with CMIM and CGIF. At the same time, if Asia is to remain on the path of dynamic growth, and in order for growth to remain stable, then moves toward greater de facto and de jure coordination are necessary. In terms of a shared vision for emerging Asian regionalism, it is realistic to suggest that Asian countries should—to the maximum extent possible—ensure that emerging Asian regionalism is complementary to, rather than competitive with, global multilateral initiatives. In so doing, Asian countries need to identify their common interests, forge a shared strategic vision, and advance their shared solutions at regional meetings, and at the global level—which will necessarily include strengthening their shared voice, and advancing innovative benefit-sharing initiatives via the G20 process, the IMF, World Bank, and regional development banks, the Financial Stability Board, the Basel Committee, and the World Trade Organization. The feasibility of Asia making greater global governance contributions will depend significantly on Asia's willingness to make serious advances in regional collective action and global leadership.

The future role of the rising economic giants—the PRC and India—and their willingness and ability to work with the traditional drivers of regional cooperation in Asia, is thus pivotal. In light of the Indian Prime Minister's words at the Chinese Academy of Social Sciences (January 2008), "with optimism to the future and the role which India and [the PRC] are destined to play in the transformation of Asia and the world" (Singh 2008), one can appreciate ADB Vice President Zhao Xiaoyu's statement that "as Asia moves toward economic integration, the PRC and India will undoubtedly be central in its evolution" (Zhao 2010). At the same time, the PRC and India "need to take steps to help forge an integrated pan-Asian free trade zone, which is free of restrictions on regional flows of goods, services, and capital"; and "need to provide deep and liquid financial markets" (Zhao 2010) that are open to cross-border financial flows and services—and with strong oversight standards and effective protection for national and foreign investors.

If India and the PRC can cooperate and work together with the traditional drivers of Asian regionalism to forge the necessary institutional frameworks for greater regional coordination, they would likely do so by making breakthroughs on achieving balances between meeting their differing national, regional, and global developmental needs and challenges, simultaneously. Such cooperation would have a transformative impact for the world economy.

References

Adams, C., Jeong, H. Y., & Park, C-Y. (2010). Asia's contribution to global rebalancing. Asian Development Bank Working Papers on Regional Economic Integration Series. No.58. September.

Asian Development Bank (ADB). CAREC website. CAREC program. http://www.adb.org/countries/subregional-programs/carec. (accessed 25 November 2012).

Asian Development Bank (ADB). (2005). Central Asia in 2015. CAREC Policy Brief No.1. http://www.adb.org/Carec/Policy-Briefs/CAREC-Policy-Brief-01-2005.pdf.

Asian Development Bank (ADB). (2006). BIMSTEC transport infrastructure and logistic study. ADB technical assistance report, Project number 38396. August. http://www.adb.org/documents/tars/reg/38396-reg-tar.pdf.

Asian Development Bank (ADB). (2008). Technical Assistance completion report, BIMSTEC transport infrastructure and logistic study, Project Number TA-6635 REG. http://www.adb.org/Documents/TACRs/REG/38396-01-reg-tcr.pdf.

Asian Development Bank (ADB). (2009). Enhancing ADB's response to the global economic crisis: Establishing the countercyclical support facility. ADB Policy Paper. May.

Asian Development Bank (ADB). (2010). *Institutions for Asian regional integration: Toward an Asian economic community*. Manila: Asian Development Bank.

Bery, S. (2010). Does Asia have common interests in global monetary system reforms? *East Asia Quarterly*. October–December. 38–39.

Bhattacharyay, B. (2010). Institutions for Asian connectivity. ADBI Working Paper No. 220. Tokyo: Asian Development Bank Institute. http://www.adbi.org/working-paper/2010/06/25/3915.institutions.asian.connectivity/.

BIMSTEC website. http://www.bimstec.org/about_bimstec.html (accessed 25 November 2012).

Calder, K., & Ye, M. (2004). Regionalism and critical junctures: Explaining the 'organization gap' in Northeast Asia. *Journal of East Asian Studies, 4*, 191–226. Spring.

Capannelli, G. (2011). Institutions for economic and financial integration in Asia: Trends and prospects. ADBI Working Paper No. 308. Tokyo: Asian Development Bank Institute.

Capannelli, G., Li, J-W., & Petri, P. (2009). Developing indicators for regional economic integration and cooperation. Manila: ADB Working Paper Series on Regional Economic Integration. No. 33.

Chin, G. (2010a). Remaking the architecture: The emerging powers, self-insuring and regional insulation. *International Affairs, 86*(3), 693–715.

Chin, G. (2010b). The emerging countries and China in the G20: Reshaping global economic governance. *Studia Diplomatica, LXIII*(2–3), 105–124.

Chin, G. (2011). Mediating financial instability: China, the BRICs and continuing rise. In P. Savona, J. Kirton, & C. Oldani (Eds.), *Global financial crisis: Global impact and solutions* (pp. 89–108). Aldershot: Ashgate.

Chin, G., & Helleiner, E. (2008). China as a creditor: Rising financial power? *Journal of International Affairs, 62*(1), 87–102.

Chin, G., & Stubbs, R. (2011). China, regional institution-building, and the China-ASEAN Free Trade Area. *Review of International Political Economy, 18*(3), 277–298.

Chin, G., & Wang, Y. (2010). Debating the international currency system: What's in a speech? *China Security, 6*(1), 3–20.

G20 Working Group 4. (2009). *Final report: The World Bank and other multilateral development banks.*

Henning, R. (2002). *East Asian financial cooperation*. Washington, DC: Institute for International Economics.

Hu, J. (2009). China to further assist developing countries. Speech cited in *China Daily*. 24 September. http://www.chinadaily.com.cn/china/2009-09/24/content_8730895.htm.

Huang, P. (2009). Quoted in You Nuo, Fu Jing, and Wang Bo. Nation should play greater role in G20, Expert says. *China Daily.* 9 March 2009. http://www.chinadaily.com.cn/bizchina/2009-03/19/content_7594063.htm.

Kaberuka, D. (2011). Boosting infrastructure investments in Africa. *World Economics, 12*(2), 7–24.

Kuroda, H., & Kawai, M. (2002). *Strengthening regional financial cooperation in East Asia.* Asia Pacific Economic Papers No 332. Canberra: Australia-Japan Research Center, Australia National University. http://www.crawford.anu.edu.au/pdf/pep/pep-332.pdf.

Li, C. (2009). China's new think tanks: Where officials, entrepreneurs and scholars interact. *China Leadership Monitor*. Number 29.

MacIntyre, A., Pempel, T. J., & Ravenhill, J. (2008). *Crisis as catalyst: Asia's dynamic political economy*. Ithaca: Cornell University Press.

Obama, B. (2010). Quoted in Obama warns nations not to rely on exports to US. *BBC News* (Asia-Pacific). 13 November. http://www.bbc.co.uk/news/world-asia-pacific-11748433#story_continues_1.

Park, D., & Shin, K. (2010). Can trade with the People's Republic of China be an engine of growth for developing Asia? *Asian Development Review, 27*(1), 160–181.

Raj, J., & Dhal, S. (2008). Integration of India's stock market with global and major regional markets. In: *Bank for International Settlements. Regional finance and integration in Asia.* Paper No. 42. pp. 202–236.

Rajamohan, P. G., Rahut, D. B., & Jacob, J. T. (2008). Changing paradigms of Indo-Japan relations: Opportunities and challenges. ICRIER Working Paper No. 212.

Rathus, J. (2009). The Chiang Mai initiative: China, Japan and financial regionalism. *East Asia Forum*. http://www.eastasiaforum.org/2009/05/11/the-chiang-mai-initiative-china-japan-and-financial-regionalism/.

Singh, M. (2008). Cited in Indian PM confident of bigger roles India, China to play in world affairs. *People's Daily.* 15 January. http://english.people.com.cn/90001/90776/90883/6338755.html.

Sinha, C., & Pradhan, N. C. (2008). India's financial openness and integration with Southeast Asian Countries: An analytical perspective. In *Regional Finance and Integration in Asia*. Bank for International Settlements. Paper No. 42. pp. 181–201.

Summers, L. (2009). Quoted in lunch with the FT: Larry Summers. *Financial Times*. 9 July. http://www.ft.com/intl/cms/s/2/6ac06592-6ce0-11de-af56-00144feabdc0.html#axzz1fgAnKeEZ.

Wang, X. (2007). China as a net creditor: An indication of strength or weakness. *China and World Economy, 15*(6), 22–36.

Xinhua Net (online). (2009). China's central bank governor says IMF needs improvement. 18 April. http://news.xinhuanet.com/english/2009-04/18/content_11210468.htm.

Yu, Y. (2007). *The Asian financial crisis and the rise of Asian regionalism.* Paper presented at the Asian Development Bank Conference. Japan: Kyoto.

Zhai, F. (2010). The benefits of regional infrastructure investment in Asia: A quantitative exploration. ADBI Working Paper No. 223. Tokyo: Asian Development Bank Institute.

Zhang, Y. (2011). Emerging force: China in the region and the world. *Global Asia 6*(4). Winter. http://www.globalasia.org/Issue/ArticleDetail/241/emerging-force-china-in-the-region-and-the-world.html.

Zhang, Y. (2012). China's regional and global power. *East Asia Forum*. 6 February. http://www.eastasiaforum.org/2012/02/06/chinas-regional-and-global-power/.

Zhao, X. (2010). Monetary and currency cooperation across emerging Asia. Speech in Kunming, People's Republic of China. 27 July. http://www.adb.org/Documents/Speeches/2010/ms2010066.asp.

Zhou, X. (2009). Reflections on reforming the international monetary system. Speech given on 23 March. http://www.pbc.gov.cn/detail.asp?col=4200&ID=279 (Chinese); http://www.pbc.gov.cn/english/detail.asp?col=6500&id=178 (English).

Chapter 4
Managing Asia's Free Trade Agreements

Shujiro Urata

Abstract Asia has seen a proliferation of free trade agreements (FTAs) in the twenty-first century. Unlike the cases in Western Europe or North America, no region-wide FTAs have been established in Asia. To minimize the spaghetti bowl effect from many FTAs, two region-wide FTAs have been proposed and studied. One is the East Asia FTA (EAFTA) comprising the Association of Southeast Asian Nations (ASEAN)+3 countries (10 ASEAN countries, plus the People's Republic of China, Japan, and the Republic of Korea). The other is the Comprehensive Economic Partnership in East Asia (CEPEA) comprising ASEAN+6 countries (10 ASEAN countries, plus the PRC, Japan, the Republic of Korea, India, Australia, and New Zealand). CEPEA leads to larger benefits with greater trade creation and smaller trade diversion, but EAFTA is easier to manage because of smaller membership. Faced with these issues, the best approach may be that the concerned governments do not choose one over the other but continue the processes in tandem. When the desire of governments toward the establishment of either EAFTA or CEPEA reaches a critical point, a framework agreement should be negotiated and the process of establishing a region-wide FTA should begin. ASEAN is likely to play a central role and ASEAN's experiences of a region-wide FTA (AFTA) should provide useful lessons. Construction of a region-wide FTA should be flexible in that in addition to EAFTA and CEPEA other formulations such as ASEAN+3+2 (10 ASEAN countries, plus the PRC, Japan, the Republic of Korea, Australia, and New Zealand) should be allowed if India is not ready to participate in the project. New members should be allowed to join the existing FTA such as EAFTA if the conditions for entry are satisfied.

Keywords ASEAN • Asian trade • Exports • Free trade agreements • Imports

---

S. Urata (✉)
Waseda University, Tokyo, Japan
e-mail: surata@waseda.jp

G. Capannelli and M. Kawai (eds.), *The Political Economy of Asian Regionalism*,
DOI 10.1007/978-4-431-54568-2_4,

4.1 Introduction

Asia joined other regions of the world in a free trade agreement (FTA) frenzy in the first decade of the twenty-first century.[1] Several regions in the world other than Asia began actively to look at FTAs as a means for promoting trade liberalization around the 1990s, when the Uruguay round of multilateral trade negotiations under the auspices of the GATT (General Agreement on Tariffs and Trade) was making little progress (Fig. 4.1). A strong interest in FTAs has continued to exist and it increased even more after the establishment of the World Trade Organization (WTO) in 1995, which succeeded the GATT with a more comprehensive coverage and stronger legal foundation, as the new multilateral trade negotiations (the Doha Development Agenda) under the WTO entered into the deadlock. Indeed, the number of FTAs reported to the GATT started to increase rapidly in the 1990s and the pace has accelerated since the mid-1990s.

Around 2000 Asia began to negotiate FTAs with economies in and outside the region. The pace of starting FTA negotiations by Asian economies sped up as the domino effect for signing FTAs was set off. Indeed, the number of FTAs in effect was only one in 1976 in Asia, but it increased rapidly to 92 by 2010 (ADB 2011). One of the concerns that have arisen from the proliferation of FTAs is a possible increase in trade costs. A firm that is interested in enjoying the benefits of using FTAs has to satisfy certain conditions, which differ among the FTAs, leading to an

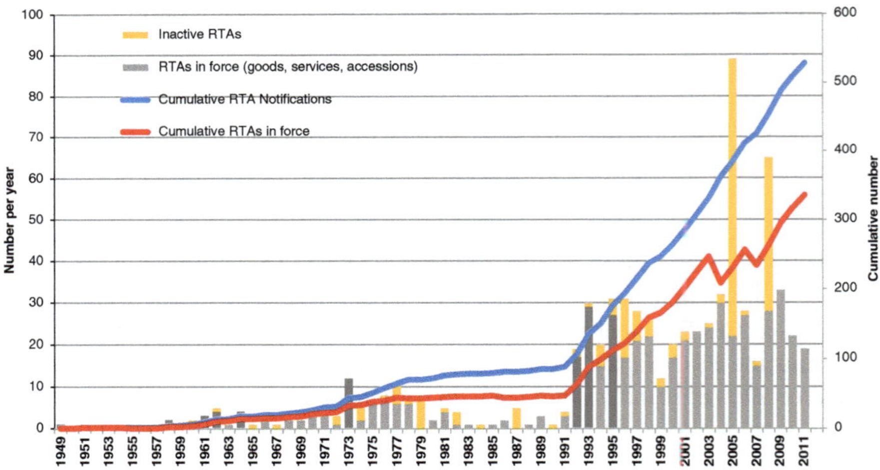

Fig. 4.1 Evolution of FTAs in the world. *FTA* free trade agreement, *RTA* regional trade agreement
Note: The figures indicate the number of RTAs, which include FTAs and customs unions. Because a dominant proportion of RTAs is FTAs, we use the expression "FTA" rather than "RTA" in the text and the headline of this figure.
Source: WTO website. http://www.wto.org/english/tratop_e/region_e/regfac_e.htm

---

[1]Unless otherwise indicated, Asia in this chapter represents ASEAN+6 countries, that is, ten Association of Southeast Asian Nations (ASEAN) countries plus the People's Republic of China (PRC), Japan, the Republic of Korea, India, Australia, and New Zealand.

increase in cost of using FTAs. Faced with this situation, countries in Asia began to examine the possibility of establishing a region-wide FTA, which would promote economic growth of the region by creating a large unified market. The realization of the need to establish a region-wide FTA in Asia on the part of policymakers and business people also comes from the fact that region-wide FTAs have been set up in North America and Western Europe making Asia the only region without a unified market among the three major regions in the world.

In light of these developments, this paper discusses ways to construct a region-wide FTA in Asia. The structure of the paper is as follows. Section 4.2 reviews FTA developments in Asia, while Sect. 4.3 examines the factors, both economic and political factors, behind the rapid expansion of FTAs. Section 4.4 analyzes the utilization of FTAs and Sect. 4.5 attempts to find ways to establish a region-wide FTA in Asia by examining the similarities and differences of existing major FTAs. Some concluding comments are presented in Sect. 4.6.

4.2 Proliferation of FTAs in Asia

Asia was not active in the formation of regional trade agreements (RTAs), which include FTAs and customs union, until the twenty-first century (Table 4.1).[2] The ASEAN Free Trade Area (AFTA), which was established in 1992, was the only major FTA until 2002, when the number of FTAs started to increase rapidly.[3]

Table 4.1 FTAs in Asia (cumulative)

	Framework agreement						Types of FTAs	
	Proposed	Signed/under negotiation	Under negotiation	Signed	In effect	Total	Bilateral	Plurilateral
1989	1	0	0	1	3	5	3	2
1995	1	0	0	16	14	31	26	5
2000	3	0	6	20	25	54	46	8
2005	45	18	28	28	51	170	133	37
2010	55	19	45	27	92	238	180	58

FTA free trade agreement
Note: Asia in this table includes the Asian Development Bank members
Source: Asian Regional Integration Center website http://aric.adb.org/1.php (accessed 15 April 2011)

[2] In the GATT/WTO, regional trade agreements (RTAs), which violate one of its basic principles of non-discrimination, are permitted under GATT Article XXIV with several conditions, which include liberalization of substantially all the trade of the members, not increasing trade barriers on non-members, and completing the RTA process within 10 years. For developing members, more lenient conditions are applied under the enabling clause. An FTA is considered to be a shallow form of regional integration, because it only removes tariff and non-tariff barriers among the members, while a customs union is a deeper integration, as it adopts common external tariffs on non-members, in addition to the removal of tariff and non-tariff barriers on trade among the members. All the RTAs established so far in Asia are FTAs.

[3] For discussions on FTAs in East Asia, see for example, Aggarwal and Urata (2006), Urata (2005), Pangestu and Gooptu (2004), Soesastro (2006), Sally (2006), and Kawai and Wignaraja (2010; 2011).

Faced with increasing competitive pressure from the emerging PRC and with a rising regionalism in Europe and other parts of the world, the members of ASEAN started the ASEAN Free Trade Area (AFTA) process in 1992 to make ASEAN a competitive region for exports and for attracting foreign direct investment (FDI).[4] The 1992 agreement provided for the liberalization of tariff and non-tariff measures under the common effective preferential tariffs. The target year for achieving tariff and non-tariff liberalization was originally set for 2008, but was later moved forward to 2002. AFTA has been in effect among the original six ASEAN members—Brunei Darussalam, Indonesia, Malaysia, the Philippines, Singapore, and Thailand—since January 2002 when tariff rates were reduced to 0–5 %, though the exclusion list was long and individual country circumstances varied. The AFTA process was completed for the original members in January 2010, when all the tariffs for intra-ASEAN trade were removed with some exceptions. New AFTA members, Viet Nam, Lao People's Democratic Republic, Myanmar, and Cambodia have lowered tariff rates for their intra-ASEAN trade and they are expected to complete tariff removal by 2015.

Compared to tariff liberalization, non-tariff barriers including border barriers such as import quotas and anti-dumping actions as well as behind-the-border measures such as technical, administrative, and safety regulations are more difficult to be dealt with. In order to minimize trade costs that have arisen from these regulations, ASEAN countries have attempted to either harmonize or mutually recognize standards and other regulations. Although some progress has been made in this area, substantial non-tariff barriers still remain.

ASEAN has pursued liberalization of trade in services under the 1995 ASEAN Framework Agreement on Services (AFAS). AFAS aims to go beyond commitments in the General Agreement on Trade in Services (GATS), in order to improve the efficiency and competitiveness of ASEAN service providers. Services trade liberalization has proceeded through several rounds of negotiations, but there still remain substantial barriers to service trade. Among the four modes of supply of services trade—(i) cross-border supply, (ii) consumption abroad, (iii) commercial presence, and (iv) movement of natural persons—modes (iii) and (iv) are most sensitive. ASEAN adopted a flexible approach of "ASEAN minus X" to accommodate ASEAN member countries that are unable to move at the same pace.

FDI liberalization in ASEAN has been underway through the 1998 ASEAN Investment Area (AIA) and the 2009 ASEAN Comprehensive Investment Area (ACIA) that provide coordinated investment cooperation and facilitation programs, market access, and national treatment of all industries. The AIA had long exclusion lists, but there have been improvements. As with services liberalization, the ASEAN minus X formula has been introduced in the AIA. Under the ACIA, in addition to the AIA provisions including investment liberalization and facilitation, investment protection that has provisions on investor-state dispute settlement mechanisms, transfer, and repatriation of capital, and others, was included.

[4] Chia (2011) gives a detailed account of ASEAN's programs for promoting its economic integration including those related to trade in goods and services and foreign direct investment.

In 2003 the ASEAN leaders agreed to set the target year of 2020 for the establishment of an ASEAN Community, which is composed of the ASEAN Security Community, the ASEAN Economic Community (AEC) and the ASEAN Socio-cultural Community. Under the ASEAN Economic Community, free flow of goods, services, investment, and capital is to be established. The target date for the establishment of an ASEAN Community was later moved forward to 2015. ASEAN countries introduced the AEC Blueprint in 2007 to achieve the AEC. The Blueprint sets out the measures to be taken and the schedule for their implementation. In order to monitor the progress by ASEAN members for the Blueprint, ASEAN ministers and officials adopted a "scorecard". According to the scorecard for 2008–2009, 82 % of the goals have been achieved on the objective of a single market and production base (Chia 2011).

Besides AFTA, ASEAN as a group as well as its members individually became active in FTA discussions with other countries in the early 2000s. ASEAN has enacted five ASEAN+1 FTAs (with PRC, the Republic of Korea, Japan, India, and Australia–New Zealand, that is the Closer Economic Relations (CER) Trade Agreement), making ASEAN an FTA hub for East Asia (Table 4.2). ASEAN and the PRC enacted an FTA in goods trade in July 2005 and they completed the liberalization process in January 2010. ASEAN and the PRC enacted an FTA in services trade in July 2007 and they signed an ASEAN–PRC Investment Treaty in August 2009. ASEAN excluding Thailand enacted an FTA with the Republic of Korea in August 2006 and tariff reduction began in June 2007. Thailand signed the ASEAN–Republic of Korea FTA in February 2009. ASEAN and the Republic of Korea signed an FTA in services in November 2007 and an Investment Treaty in June 2009. ASEAN and Japan enacted an FTA in goods in December 2008. ASEAN enacted FTAs with India and Australia–New Zealand in January 2010. The ASEAN–Australia–New Zealand FTA includes trade in services and investment, while the ASEAN–India agreement does not.

Many ASEAN members have become active in establishing bilateral FTAs (Table 4.3). Singapore has enacted FTAs with countries such as New Zealand, Japan, Australia, the United States (US), the European Free Trade Association (EFTA), and India and it is currently negotiating FTAs with other countries. It is important to note that Singapore established an FTA called P4 (later changed to Trans-Pacific Strategic Partnership Agreement, or TPP) with Brunei Darussalam, New Zealand, and Chile in 2006. Thailand has implemented FTAs with Australia, New Zealand, and Japan and is currently under negotiations with the US and others. Malaysia enacted an FTA with Japan and it joined the negotiations of the expanded TPP. Indonesia, the Philippines, and Viet Nam each enacted an FTA with Japan.

Compared to ASEAN countries in Southeast Asia, the economies in Northeast Asia including the PRC, Japan, the Republic of Korea, and Taipei,China had not been active in FTAs until the end of the 1990s. Since 2000, the PRC has implemented 11 FTAs including those with ASEAN; Hong Kong, China; Macau, China; New Zealand; and Taipei,China, and is negotiating FTAs with several other countries. Japan has enacted 10 bilateral FTAs with Singapore, Mexico, Malaysia, Chile, Thailand, the Philippines, Indonesia, Brunei Darussalam, Viet Nam, and Switzerland,

Table 4.2 FTAs in East Asia and trade between FTA partners in intraregional trade, 2008(%)

Exporter \ Importer	PRC	Japan	Korea, Rep. of	Australia	New Zealand	India	ASEAN	Brunei Darussalam	Cambodia	Indonesia	Lao PDR	Malaysia	Myanmar	Philippines	Singapore	Thailand	Viet Nam	D	E	F
PRC	–	7.8	4.3	1.9	0.2	2.0	7.3	0.0	0.1	1.2	0.0	1.4	0.1	0.6	2.0	1.1	0.9	23.6	7.5	31.9
Japan	8.2	–	3.5	0.9	0.1	0.5	6.0	0.0	0.0	0.7	0.0	1.0	0.0	0.6	1.6	1.7	0.5	19.3	6.0	31.3
Korea, Rep. of	6.0	1.5	–	0.4	0.1	0.6	3.1	0.0	0.0	0.6	0.0	0.4	0.0	0.3	1.0	0.4	0.5	11.6	3.7	32.0
Australia	2.5	2.2	0.9	–	0.5	0.9	1.2	0.0	0.0	0.2	0.0	0.2	0.0	0.1	0.3	0.2	0.1	8.1	1.4	17.0
New Zealand	0.2	0.1	0.1	0.4	–	0.0	0.2	0.0	0.0	0.0	0.0	0.0	0.0	0.0	0.0	0.0	0.0	1.0	0.7	73.9
India	0.7	0.3	0.2	0.1	0.0	–	1.0	0.0	0.0	0.2	0.0	0.2	0.0	0.0	0.4	0.1	0.1	2.3	1.2	52.2
ASEAN	5.9	5.9	2.4	2.4	0.3	1.9	15.3	0.1	0.3	3.0	0.1	3.5	0.2	1.0	3.9	2.1	1.2	34.0	33.6	98.9
Brunei Darussalam	0.0	0.2	0.1	0.0	0.0	0.0	0.2	–	0.0	0.2	0.0	0.0	0.0	0.0	0.0	0.0	0.0	0.6	0.6	100.0
Cambodia	0.0	0.0	0.0	0.0	0.0	0.0	0.0	0.0	–	0.0	0.0	0.0	0.0	0.0	0.0	0.0	0.0	0.1	0.1	99.7
Indonesia	0.6	1.5	0.4	0.3	0.0	0.3	1.8	0.0	0.0	–	0.0	0.3	0.0	0.1	1.0	0.3	0.1	5.0	4.7	93.9
Lao PDR	0.0	0.0	0.0	0.0	0.0	0.0	0.0	0.0	0.0	0.0	–	0.0	0.0	0.0	0.0	0.0	0.0	0.1	0.1	100.0
Malaysia	1.3	1.1	0.5	0.5	0.0	0.5	3.2	0.0	0.0	0.4	0.0	–	0.0	0.2	1.8	0.6	0.1	7.0	7.0	100.0
Myanmar	0.0	0.0	0.0	0.0	0.0	0.1	0.2	0.0	0.0	0.0	0.0	0.0	–	0.0	0.0	0.2	0.0	0.3	0.3	84.1
Philippines	0.4	0.4	0.2	0.0	0.0	0.0	0.6	0.0	0.0	0.0	0.0	0.1	0.0	–	0.3	0.1	0.0	1.6	1.6	99.2
Singapore	2.0	0.9	0.9	0.8	0.1	0.7	6.1	0.1	0.1	2.0	0.0	2.3	0.1	0.4	–	0.8	0.5	11.6	11.6	100.0
Thailand	1.2	1.2	0.2	0.6	0.0	0.2	2.4	0.0	0.1	0.3	0.1	0.6	0.1	0.2	0.6	–	0.3	5.9	5.9	100.0
Viet Nam	0.3	0.5	0.1	0.2	0.0	0.0	0.7	0.0	0.1	0.1	0.0	0.1	0.0	0.1	0.2	0.1	–	1.8	1.8	100.0
A	23.4	17.8	11.5	6.2	1.1	5.8	34.2	0.1	0.4	5.9	0.2	6.6	0.4	2.7	9.1	5.6	3.3	100.0	54.3	
B	6.0	5.9	2.7	2.6	0.9	2.4	33.8	0.1	0.4	5.6	0.2	6.6	0.4	2.6	9.1	5.6	3.3	54.3		
C	25.7	33.0	23.3	41.7	80.4	40.8	99.0	100.0	99.2	95.1	99.7	100.0	96.6	98.3	100.0	100.0	100.0			

AFTA, ASEAN+1 FTAs, FTA in effect, FTA in negotiation

A, imports from ASEAN+6 countries as a share of total intraregional trade; B, imports from FTA partners as a share of total intraregional trade; C, imports from FTA partners as a share of country's total intraregional imports (B/A); D, exports to ASEAN+6 countries as a share of total intraregional trade; E, exports to FTA partners as a share of total intraregional trade; F, exports to FTA partners as a share of country's total intraregional exports (E/D) ASEAN Lao PDR Lao People's Democratic Republic, PRC People's Republic of China

Notes: Figures except those under B, C, E, F indicate the shares in intraregional trade (ASEAN+6)

Source: Adopted and modified from Shiino and Mizuno (2010)

Table 4.3 FTAs for selected Asian economies (as of January 2011)

Economy	Proposed	Under negotiation A	Under negotiation B	Conclusion Signed	Conclusion In effect	Total
ASEAN						
Brunei Darussalam	4	1	1	0	8	14
Cambodia	2	0	1	0	6	9
Indonesia	6	1	2	1	7	17
Lao People's Democratic Republic	2	0	1	0	8	11
Malaysia	3	2	6	2	9	22
Myanmar	2	1	1	0	6	10
Philippines	4	0	1	0	7	12
Singapore	4	1	9	3	18	35
Thailand	6	4	3	0	11	24
Viet Nam	4	1	2	0	7	14
East Asia						
China, People's Republic of	8	2	3	1	11	25
Japan	7	0	3	1	11	22
Korea, Republic of	12	2	5	3	6	28
Hong Kong, China	1	1	0	0	2	4
Taipei,China	1	1	1	0	5	8
Mongolia	2	0	0	0	0	2
Australia–New Zealand						
Australia	4	2	7	0	8	21
New Zealand	4	1	4	0	9	18
South Asia						
Bangladesh	0	2	1	1	2	6
India	9	4	8	1	11	33
Pakistan	10	5	3	2	6	26
Sri Lanka	2	1	0	1	4	8

ASEAN Association of Southeast Asian Nations, *FTA* free trade agreement
A framework agreement, *B* free trade agreement
Source: ADB (2011)

and one regional FTA with ASEAN. It is currently in negotiations with Australia, the Gulf Cooperation Council (GCC), India, Peru, and the Republic of Korea.[5] The Republic of Korea has implemented six FTAs including those with Chile, Singapore, India, the EFTA, and ASEAN and it has signed agreements with the US and the European Union (EU). The Republic of Korea is actively pursuing FTA policies as it is currently in negotiations with countries including Canada and Mexico.

Taipei,China is very keen on having FTAs with many countries but political sensitivities with the PRC have precluded it from achieving this objective. However, the situation is likely to change as Taipei,China enacted an FTA with the PRC in 2010. In addition to the PRC, Taipei,China has enacted four FTAs with small countries in Central America including Nicaragua and El Salvador.

[5] Japan's FTAs with India and Peru have been concluded and signed while the negotiations with the Republic of Korea were suspended in December 2004.

India has enacted five FTAs with Sri Lanka, Singapore, ASEAN, the Republic of Korea, and the South Asian Association for Regional Cooperation (SAARC) and it finished negotiations and signed agreements with Japan and Malaysia. India is currently negotiating five FTAs including with the Bay of Bengal Initiative for Multi-Sectoral Technical and Economic Cooperation (BIMSTEC),[6] the EU, GCC, Mauritius, and Thailand.

As a result of increasing FTAs in Asia, the share of trade that is covered by FTAs in overall trade (FTA coverage ratio) has increased for Asian countries. Among the Asian countries, ASEAN registers the highest FTA coverage ratio amounting to 56.5 %.[7] The FTA coverage ratios for the PRC, Japan, and the Republic of Korea are much lower compared to those for ASEAN. Specifically, the values for the PRC are 21.9 %, for Japan 16.5 %, and for the Republic of Korea 36.0 %.[8] The values rise to 28.3, 36.5, and 61.1 %, if the FTAs under negotiation are considered in the computation. These values indicate that there is room for further FTA expansion for Asian countries, especially for those in Northeast Asia. Confining the scope of analysis to ASEAN+6 countries, one finds that the FTA coverage ratio for intraregional trade is 54.3 % (Table 4.2). The limited FTA coverage ratio in East Asia is mainly due to the absence of an FTA covering the PRC, Japan, and the Republic of Korea.

Unlike Europe or North America, both of which have established region-wide FTAs, East Asia so far has established a number of bilateral and minilateral FTAs and not a region-wide FTA. Recognizing the economic benefits of region-wide FTAs such as a large unified market, several ideas have been floated for establishing region-wide FTAs. However, differences in opinions about region-wide FTAs among East Asian economies have so far precluded them from establishing a region-wide FTA.

At the 1998 ASEAN+3 leaders' summit meeting, the leaders set up the East Asia Vision Group to study long-term vision for economic cooperation. The group has presented the leaders with recommendations including the establishment of an East Asia FTA (EAFTA). The Joint Expert Group, which was set up at the recommendation of ASEAN+3 economic ministers to study the feasibility of an EAFTA, presented recommendations to the economic ministers in 2006 to start the process in 2007 toward the establishment of an EAFTA. The recommendations by the Joint Expert Group were not adopted and the Joint Expert Group was asked to conduct further study. The Joint Expert Group undertook phase two of the project and recommended to start the process toward the establishment of an EAFTA in 2009. Responding to those recommendations, the leaders ordered the government officials to set up four working groups: rules of origin (ROOs), tariff nomenclature, customs procedure, and economic cooperation, as steps toward achieving an EAFTA.

---

[6] BIMSTEC includes Bangladesh, Bhutan, India, Myanmar, Nepal, Sri Lanka, and Thailand.

[7] FTAs used for the computation of FTA coverage ratios include enacted and signed FTAs. FTA coverage ratios that are reported in the text are for 2009. The trade statistics used for the computation of the FTA coverage ratios are taken from IMF's *Direction of Trade Statistics*.

[8] For comparison, the FTA coverage ratios for the US and the EU are 38 % and 74.8 %, respectively.

Japan proposed the Comprehensive Economic Partnership in East Asia (CEPEA), which is an agreement including an FTA covering ASEAN+3+3 (India, Australia, and New Zealand) or ASEAN+6, at the ASEAN+6 economic ministers' meeting in 2006. ASEAN+6 are also members of the East Asia Summit, which was held for the first time in 2005. It has been argued that behind the CEPEA idea lies Japan's strategy of taking a leadership role in setting up a regional institution in East Asia, as it was the PRC that took the initiative in the EAFTA discussions. A similar course of events to those for EAFTA evolved for CEPEA. As is the case for EAFTA, government officials are engaged in the discussions under the four working groups.

The PRC, Japan, and the Republic of Korea (CJK) began an official joint study on their FTA involving government officials, academics, and businesspersons in 2010. A feasibility study of a tripartite FTA by the private sector involving government related research institutes began in 2003. The study has continued by changing the focus of research topics over time. The joint study, scheduled to finish by the end of 2012, will present recommendations on a CJK FTA to the leaders. Since these three North East Asian countries account for a dominant share of gross domestic product (GDP) in East Asia, either defined as ASEAN+3 or ASEAN+6, the establishment of EAFTA or CEPEA crucially depends on the establishment of a CJK FTA. In addition to economic issues such as increased competition, non-economic issues such as historic and social problems have made it difficult for discussing tripartite cooperation such as a CJK FTA. However, economic and non-economic environment surrounding the three countries have changed, as we discuss in Sect. 3, and therefore, positive steps toward the establishment of a CJK FTA have been adopted.

One FTA that has attracted enormous attention recently is the TPP. The TPP was originally established in 2006 under the name of Pacific 4 (P4) by Brunei Darussalam, Chile, New Zealand, and Singapore. The TPP started to draw attention because the United States (US) along with Australia, Peru, Viet Nam, and Malaysia joined negotiations on the expanded TPP. The TPP, ASEAN+3, and ASEAN+6 FTAs were recognized as pathways toward a Free Trade Area of the Asia-Pacific (FTAAP), covering 21 Asia–Pacific Economic Cooperation (APEC) member economies, by APEC leaders at their summit in 2010. Behind the US 2006 proposal of an FTAAP is a concern that the US would be excluded from East Asia to result in the decline in its economic activities in East Asia. It should be noted that the differences in the members between ASEAN+6 and APEC give rise to important implications of the groupings. Taipei,China and the Russian Federation, important economic players, are included in an FTAAP, while India, a member of ASEAN+6, is excluded. Besides, Cambodia, Lao PDR, and Myanmar are ASEAN members and thus included in ASEAN+3 and ASEAN+6, but they are not included in APEC. Because of this, APEC and more significantly the TPP are regarded as frameworks that may weaken ASEAN cohesiveness. Another important characteristic of TPP is its high liberalization requirement in that practically all the tariffs on intra-FTA members' trade are to be removed within 10 years after its enactment.

It is important to point out that the US does not seem to be interested in promoting economic development of ASEAN countries as a group. Unlike the PRC, Japan, the

Republic of Korea, Australia–New Zealand, and India, which enacted FTAs with ASEAN, and the EU, which is negotiating an FTA with ASEAN, the US has not discussed the possibility of a US–ASEAN FTA. Instead, the US enacted bilateral FTAs with Singapore and began discussions with selected ASEAN countries within the framework of TPP. This reflects the view that the US is interested in high-level FTA with comprehensive coverage including labor, environment, competition policy, intellectual property rights, and trade facilitation with a focus on supply-chain management. To the eyes of the US, some ASEAN countries are not ready to participate in such a high-level FTA.

4.3 Characteristics and Motives of FTAs in East Asia

One notable characteristic of FTAs in East Asia is their comprehensive coverage. As such, some of the FTAs established in East Asia are named as Economic Partnership Agreements (EPA) (for example, Japan–Singapore EPA), or Closer Economic Partnership Arrangement (for example, PRC–Hong Kong, China), and others. These new types of FTAs typically include facilitation of foreign trade, liberalization, and facilitation of FDI, and economic and technical cooperation, in addition to trade liberalization, which is included in traditional FTAs. It is worth noting that the contents of these new types of FTAs are similar to those of the APEC forum, whose three pillars are (i) liberalization of foreign trade and foreign investment, (ii) facilitation of foreign trade and foreign investment, and (iii) economic and technical cooperation.

Among the three pillars, economic and technical cooperation is given special attention in Asian FTAs because the narrowing gap between the high-income and low-income countries is considered very important for achieving economic prosperity and social and political stability of the region that consists of countries with very different levels of economic development. One of the cooperation programs that can be found in many FTAs in Asia is the promotion of small and medium-sized enterprises (SMEs), which would contribute not only to the construction of competitive and resilient economic structure but also to the improvement of the livelihood of people. These objectives may be achieved because SMEs have important positions in many economies in terms of production and employment. It is important to note that economic assistance has been used to gain support for FTAs from FTA partners by the PRC and Japan, which are eager to play a leadership role in regional integration.

Having noted a common characteristic of comprehensiveness of FTAs in Asia, specific contents do differ among the FTAs, reflecting different motives of the countries concerned. Japan emphasizes the importance of liberalization and facilitation of investment and service trade, as such measures would provide a free, transparent, and stable business environment for Japanese firms, which have invested heavily in Asia. In particular, Japan is interested in setting up a well functioning intellectual property rights protection system. By contrast, developing countries such as ASEAN and the PRC do not have equally strong interests in these measures. Indeed, ASEAN and the PRC have adopted a gradual and sequential approach by dealing with trade in goods and services and investment separately with different timing, as liberalization in trade in goods is followed by liberalization in service trade and investment. India is interested in liberalization of services trade such as IT software, legal, financial, and medical services, while it is not keen on opening up goods' trade.

Another notable characteristic of FTAs in Asia in recent years is the high degree of trade liberalization in goods. As noted earlier on the discussions of AFTA, trade liberalization rate, defined as the share of products subject to zero tariff rates in total number of products, under AFTA has risen, indicating gradual trade liberalization. Reflecting the recognition of the importance of high-level FTA in terms of trade liberalization to gain benefits from FTAs, trade liberalization rates adopted for the enacted FTAs in Asia have become very high exceeding 95 %. Noticeable exceptions are those FTAs involving Japan and India. Because of the difficulty in opening up agriculture sector due to strong opposition, Japan has excluded agricultural products from trade liberalization in its FTAs. As a consequence, trade liberalization rates for Japan's FTAs are quite low around 85 %, while those for Japan's FTA partners are significantly higher around 95 %.[9] Because of strong opposition from protectionists, India has difficulty opening up its market via FTAs, resulting in low trade liberalization for its FTAs. Indeed, India's trade liberalization rate for the India–Singapore FTA is as low as 43.8 %.

There are various common motives of East Asian countries behind their FTA strategies, despite the differences in their importance among the countries. First, rapid expansion of FTAs in other parts of the world has made Asian economies realize the importance of establishing FTAs in order to maintain and expand their export opportunities (Urata 2010). FTAs with this kind of market seeking objective are largely defensive in nature. A case in point is Japan's FTA with Mexico. Japanese firms were in a disadvantageous position vis-à-vis US firms or EU firms in the Mexican market because the US and the EU had FTAs, giving their firms duty-free access to Mexico. In order to overcome this disadvantage, Japanese firms put pressure on the Japanese government to negotiate an FTA with Mexico. It should be noted here that a stalemate of the Doha Development Agenda negotiations under the auspices of the WTO turned the attention of the WTO members with an interest in trade liberalization to FTAs. The market seeking motive played a role for FTAs between and among Asian economies, as trade barriers are still substantial for many sectors in Asian economies.

Second, countries interested in promoting structural domestic reform to achieve economic growth use FTAs as external pressure on the opposition to structural reform, in order to implement domestic structural reform. The motive of promoting domestic reform was important for the Republic of Korea in pursing an FTA with the US. Being sandwiched between the PRC, a rapidly catching up economic giant, and Japan, a highly competitive economic giant, the Republic of Korea needed to carry out structural reforms to maintain and improve competitiveness.

[9] Information on trade liberalization rates is provided by Japan's Ministry of Economy, Industry, and Trade (METI).

Third, rivalry among Asian economies over gaining a leadership role in the region has activated their FTA strategies. Both the PRC and Japan, which are competing to become a "leader" in the region, are keen on using FTAs to strengthen their relationships with ASEAN, the Republic of Korea and other countries. In November 2002 Japan proposed an economic partnership framework to ASEAN one day after the PRC agreed to start FTA negotiations with ASEAN. It should also be noted that ASEAN, the Republic of Korea, and other countries consider FTAs as a means to maintain and increase their influence in Asia. ASEAN has been rigorously pursing FTAs with major countries in order for them to take a "driver's seat" in regional integration in Asia, while the Republic of Korea is moving ahead of other countries such as Japan and the PRC to take a lead in the FTA race.

Fourth, countries with active outward foreign direct investment would like to use FTAs to improve the business environment in FDI recipient countries, so that multinational corporations (MNCs) can perform efficiently. This motive is sought by including FDI liberalization and facilitation in FTAs. As was pointed out earlier, this is one of the most important motives for Japan as many Japanese MNCs have invested in East Asia. This motive is likely to be more important for other Asian countries in the future, as the number of countries in East Asia with active outward FDI is bound to rise.

So far, we have discussed the motives behind bilateral and plurilateral FTAs. We now turn to the motives behind region-wide FTAs such as EAFTA or CEPEA. Many countries in the region realize the importance of establishing a large region-wide, unified market to promote economic growth and reduce development gaps as firms can expect benefits from achieving scale economies. Besides, economic and technical cooperation may be provided efficiently under one region-wide framework by consolidating separate programs provided by individual countries.

The crises contributed to the discussions on the promotion of region-wide FTAs. The 1997–1998 financial crisis in East Asia increased the awareness among East Asian countries of the need for regional cooperation such as a region-wide FTA to avoid another crisis and to promote regional economic growth. The immediate concern about financial problems resulted in regional cooperation in financial areas. Specifically, bilateral currency swap arrangements to deal with the shortage in foreign exchange under the name of the Chiang Mai Initiative (CMI) were set up by ASEAN+3 countries in 2000, and it was expanded to become multilateral currency swap arrangement in 2009 under the name of CMI Multilateralization. Furthermore, ASEAN+3 countries are developing the Asian Bond Market, in order to establish efficient and liquid bond markets in East Asia, with a view to better utilize East Asian savings for East Asian investments. It is also expected to contribute to the mitigation of currency and maturity mismatches in financing, which was one of the factors that led to the Asian financial crisis.

The global financial crisis that started in 2008 also increased interest among the East Asian countries for the establishment of a region-wide FTA. Unlike the case of the Asian financial crisis for which financial linkage with the US and Europe was a problem, it was East Asia's dependence on the US and Europe for its exports that caused a sharp decline in East Asia's economic activities. A collapse of the housing bubble in the US led to the subprime mortgage crisis in 2008, which in turn spread to Europe. As a result of the crisis, US and EU economies experienced a sharp decline in their economic activities, leading to a huge decline in their demand for imports. This decline in import demand in turn caused a decline in East Asia's exports to the US and EU, triggering a downward spiral. In order to avoid such negative impacts caused by factors outside the region, East Asian countries started to argue for the need to increase intraregional dependence by establishing a region-wide FTA.

4.4 FTA Utilization

It is needless to repeat that the objective of an FTA is to promote foreign trade between and/or among FTA members. It is therefore important to assess the utilization of FTAs. Such a study would reveal the obstacles in using FTAs, thereby providing important policy implications for the construction of a meaningful region-wide FTA. With this in mind, we examine the utilization of FTAs by firms. Since the availability of the information required for such an analysis is limited, we can examine only some selected cases.

Two kinds of information have been used to assess the utilization of FTAs. One is trade data that are covered by FTA preferences. The FTA utilization rate can be obtained by dividing FTA trade data by overall trade. The computed FTA utilization rate is likely to be undervalued if trade subject to a zero tariff rate is not excluded from the overall trade. Although this FTA utilization rate is the ideal measure, such measure may be computed for very few countries in Asia because of data unavailability.

The other information to assess FTA utilization that previous studies used is that obtained from a firm survey. A typical survey on FTA usage asks if a firm used FTA or not. FTA utilization is measured by dividing the number of FTA using firms by the number of surveyed firms. Some of the problems of the information obtained from this kind of firm survey include the followings, limited coverage, no information on traded value, and difficulty in determining the denominator. Surveys are generally conducted by sending out a questionnaire to selected firms or by conducting an interview with a small number of firms. Their coverage is naturally limited. The computed FTA utilization rate is based on the number of firms rather than the value of trade, as such it should be denoted as firm-level FTA utilization rate. Generally, one uses the number of surveyed firms as the denominator for the computation of the FTA utilization rate, but one should be careful not to include firms without trading relationships with the countries under question. Specifically, to compute Japan's FTA utilization rate for the Japan–Singapore FTA, one should include only the firms trading with Singapore. In general, FTA utilization surveys try to obtain the information on the use of several FTAs, and thus it becomes difficult to isolate the information that is appropriate only for a particular FTA in question. Having indicated some possible problems in using the information obtained from

Table 4.4 FTA utilization rate (%)

ADBI study (exports)					
Japan	PRC	Korea, Rep. of	Singapore	Thailand	Philippines
29.0	45.1	20.8	17.3	24.9	20.0
RIETI study (by destinations)					
Exports					
	Japan		Korea, Rep. of		Thailand
Mexico	32.9	Chile	96.9	Indonesia	61.5
Malaysia	12.2	ASEAN	2.6	Malaysia	25.2
Chile	23.7			Philippines	46.9
				Viet Nam	46.6
				Australia	62.5
				Japan	22.7
Imports					
	Korea, Rep. of		Australia	adjusted for 0 tariff	
Chile	90.5	New Zealand	50.5	95.19–97.60	
Singapore	29.8	South Pacific	3.2	99.32–99.35	
EFTA	42.5	Singapore	2.9	90.99–91.44	
ASEAN	43.3	Thailand	42	75.97–73.86	
		US	23.2	69.42–82.51	
		Chile	6.5	96.05–96.33	

ADBI Asian Development Bank Institute, *ASEAN* Association of Southeast Asian Nations; *EFTA* European Free Trade Association, *RIETI* Research Institute of Economy, Trade, and Industry, *US* United States

Note: ADBI Study and Japan for RIETI Study use information obtained by firm surveys, while others in the RIETI Study use trade (customs) data

Source: Kawai and Wignaraja (2010) for the ADBI study; Takahashi and Urata (2010) for the RIETI study; Cheong et. al (2010) for the Republic of Korea; Pomfret et al. (2010) for Australia; Kohpaiboon (2010) for Thailand

firm surveys, it has to be emphasized that firm surveys provide important information for deriving policy implications. For example, firm surveys can provide the properties of firms using or not using FTAs.

Table 4.4 presents FTA utilization ratios for selected FTAs in East Asia. FTA utilization rates vary widely among different FTAs, ranging between 99 % after adjusting for zero tariff rates for Australia and 2.6 % for exports from the Republic of Korea to ASEAN. As one would expect, the FTA utilization rates derived from the firm survey tends to be lower than those computed by using trade data.

Analyses of the firm responses to the questionnaire reveal several interesting observations. One common finding from both the ADBI and Japan's Research Institute of Economy, Trade, and Industry (RIETI) studies is that the size is an important factor for the use of FTAs. Large firms tend to use FTAs more than small firms because large firms can afford costs required to obtain the certificate of origin that is needed to use an FTA. Such costs include learning about FTA provisions and obtaining information such as the sources of inputs to be submitted with the application for the certificate of origin. Small firms with limited human and financial resources cannot afford such costs.

The ADBI study (Kawai and Wignaraja 2010) showed the firms with larger foreign equity participation tend to use FTAs. This finding indicates that firms with extensive foreign networks can take advantage of tariff-free opportunities arising from FTAs. Product based studies on Japan and Thailand for the RIETI study confirmed the expected positive relationship between high FTA preferential tariff margin (difference between applied most favored nation (MFN) tariff rate and FTA tariff rate) and high use of FTAs.

The ADBI and RIETI studies found similar impediments to FTA utilization. They include lack of information (knowledge) about FTAs, small FTA preferential tariff margin, and administrative costs associated with obtaining certificate of origin. As indicated above, these costs are particularly high for small firms. These findings indicate the need to reduce costs for the use of FTAs by simplifying the procedures.

The ADBI study investigated the views of firms concerning the "noodle bowl" effect or "spaghetti bowl" effect or multiple ROOs and found that large and old firms with multiple FTA markets tend to have negative views. Unexpectedly, small firms are found not to be concerned with the noodle bowl effect. It may be that large firms are engaged in trade with many countries and therefore they face the problems of multiple ROOs. By contrast, small firms tend to trade with a small number of countries, and thus do not face the multiple ROO problems. These findings appear to show that resolving the problem due to the noodle/spaghetti bowl effect, or multiple ROOs, would expand trade among FTA partners, contributing to the increase in FTA utilization rate.

4.5 Establishment of a Region-Wide FTA

Asia has seen rapid increase of FTAs since the beginning of the twenty-first century. Many of these FTAs are bilateral or plurilateral and unlike the situations in North America or Europe, a region-wide FTA has not been established yet in Asia. Recognizing the benefits of a region-wide FTA with larger market, Asian countries have been examining the ways to establish a region-wide FTA, as was discussed in Sect. 2. Two region-wide FTA proposals have been under study. One is an East Asia FTA (EAFTA) comprising ASEAN+3 (ASEAN members plus PRC, Japan, and the Republic of Korea) and the other is a Comprehensive Economic Partnership in East Asia (CEPEA) comprising ASEAN+6 (ASEAN members plus PRC, Japan, the Republic of Korea, India, Australia, and New Zealand). In addition to these two region-wide FTAs, the TPP has become a possible FTA covering some countries in Asia and the other side of the Pacific.

In the discussions of region-wide FTAs, it is useful to know the benefits and costs of such FTAs. Tables 4.5 and 4.6 show the impacts of EAFTA and CEPEA on GDP and economic welfare, respectively, for their members and other selected countries. The figures are taken from the simulation exercise using the Global Trade Analysis Project (GTAP) model conducted for Phase II of the CEPEA study. Two types of simulation were conducted for EAFTA and CEPEA. One considers tariff elimination only (scenario 1 for CEPEA and scenario 4 for EAFTA), and the other takes

Table 4.5 The impacts of FTAs on GDP (% change)

	ASEAN+6			ASEAN+3	
	Scenario 1	Scenario 2	Scenario 3	Scenario 4	Scenario 5
PRC	−0.03	4.65	4.64	−0.05	4.49
Japan	0.04	0.64	0.56	0.02	0.63
Korea, Rep. of	0.38	2.67	2.28	0.34	2.64
Indonesia	0.13	4.35	4.13	0.11	4.15
Malaysia	0.62	9.53	8.95	0.57	9.24
Philippines	0.12	5.95	5.51	0.11	5.77
Singapore	−0.02	3.83	3.65	−0.02	3.63
Thailand	0.59	7.46	7.17	0.56	7.21
Viet Nam	1.61	11.04	10.17	1.60	10.79
Cambodia	0.38	8.59	7.17	0.29	8.38
Myanmar	0.07	6.15	5.36	0.07	6.00
Lao PDR	0.40	5.99	4.69	0.40	5.94
Brunei Darussalam and Timor-Leste	1.86	6.98	6.14	1.86	6.92
Australia	0.11	1.27	1.20	−0.03	−0.03
New Zealand	0.08	1.94	1.77	−0.04	−0.02
India	0.45	3.40	2.70	−0.03	−0.07
Hong Kong, China	0.00	0.02	0.02	0.00	0.02
Taipei,China	−0.10	−0.18	−0.15	−0.11	−0.17
NAFTA	0.00	−0.02	−0.02	0.00	−0.02
EU25	−0.03	−0.09	−0.09	−0.02	−0.08
Latin America	−0.02	−0.05	−0.05	−0.02	−0.04
Rest of the world	−0.03	−0.08	−0.09	−0.03	−0.07

ASEAN Association of Southeast Asian Nations, *EU* European Union, *FTA* free trade agreement, *GDP* gross domestic product, *Lao PDR* Lao People's Democratic Republic, *NAFTA* North American Free Trade Area, *PRC* People's Republic of China

Notes: Scenario 1 = ASEAN+6: tariff elimination; Scenario 2 = ASEAN+6: tariff elimination, trade facilitation, cooperation; Scenario 3 = ASEAN+6: tariff elimination (excluding agriculture and food products), trade facilitation, cooperation; Scenario 4 = ASEAN+3: tariff elimination; Scenario 5 = ASEAN+3: tariff elimination, trade facilitation, cooperation

Source: CEPEA (2009)

into account of comprehensive nature of the FTA by including trade facilitation and economic cooperation (scenario 2 for CEPEA and scenario 5 for EAFTA). In addition, one more scenario, in which agriculture and food products are excluded from tariff elimination, is adopted for CEPEA simulation (scenario 3). The data used for the analysis are for 2004.

Three general patterns can be identified from the simulation results. First, both in terms of GDP and economic welfare, FTA members gain while non-members lose. These results are expected because FTA members can improve the use of existing resources such as labor and capital by exploiting newly emerged export opportunities from the formation of FTA, while non-members lose export opportunities as a result of discrimination. Second, the larger the FTA membership, the larger are the benefits obtained by FTA members. This relationship is also expected because a larger group provides greater business opportunities so that use or allocation of existing resources can be improved. This observation comes from a comparison of

Table 4.6 The impacts of FTAs on welfare (equivalent variation, % of GDP)

	ASEAN+6			ASEAN+3	
	Scenario 1	Scenario 2	Scenario 3	Scenario 4	Scenario 5
PRC	−0.03	4.37	4.30	−0.05	4.22
Japan	0.18	0.92	0.92	0.17	0.92
Korea, Rep. of	0.68	3.27	3.02	0.64	3.23
Indonesia	0.68	5.13	4.57	0.17	4.51
Malaysia	2.08	13.23	12.45	1.51	12.35
Philippines	−0.06	6.18	5.80	0.01	6.08
Singapore	0.97	7.40	6.82	0.86	6.86
Thailand	2.35	10.01	9.08	2.43	9.84
Viet Nam	1.99	11.30	9.74	2.14	11.18
Cambodia	−0.06	7.08	6.02	−0.05	7.04
Myanmar	−0.47	6.01	5.48	−0.59	5.55
Lao PDR	−0.92	4.69	4.60	−0.84	4.72
Brunei Darussalam and Timor-Leste	5.74	13.35	12.68	5.55	12.84
Australia	0.84	2.49	1.87	−0.17	0.06
New Zealand	0.24	2.61	2.05	−0.21	−0.02
India	−0.19	2.77	2.44	−0.10	−0.09
Hong Kong, China	−0.48	−0.83	−0.76	−0.42	−0.72
Taipei,China	−0.92	−2.52	−2.45	−0.85	−2.39
NAFTA	−0.05	−0.15	−0.13	−0.04	−0.12
EU25	−0.07	−0.18	−0.18	−0.06	−0.15
Latin America	−0.07	−0.19	−0.14	−0.05	−0.15
Rest of the world	−0.10	−0.46	−0.47	−0.07	−0.36

ASEAN Association of Southeast Asian Nations, *EU* European Union, *FTA* free trade agreement, *Lao PDR* Lao People's Democratic Republic, *NAFTA* North American Free Trade Area, *PRC* People's Republic of China

Notes: Scenario 1 = ASEAN+6: tariff elimination; Scenario 2 = ASEAN+6: tariff elimination, trade facilitation, cooperation; Scenario 3 = ASEAN+6: tariff elimination (excluding agriculture and food products), trade facilitation, cooperation; Scenario 4 = ASEAN+3: tariff elimination; Scenario 5 = ASEAN+3: tariff elimination, trade facilitation, cooperation

Source: CEPEA (2009)

the impacts of CEPEA and EAFTA that shows CEPEA provides larger benefits to the members compared to EAFTA. Obviously India, Australia, and New Zealand gain from CEPEA, but they lose from EAFTA. For the countries that are neither CEPEA nor EAFTA members, the impacts of these two types of FTAs are very similar. Third, the more comprehensive the FTA, the greater is the benefit. A comparison of the results of scenarios 1 and 2 for CEPEA and scenarios 4 and 5 for EAFTA reveals that trade facilitation and economic cooperation increase the magnitude of benefits substantially. Moreover, a comparison of scenarios 2 and 3 shows that exclusion of agriculture and food products lower the benefits for the CEPEA members. The decline in the magnitude of the benefits is large for developing members with large agricultural sectors.

The simulation results brought out the importance of trade facilitation for achieving benefits from FTAs. In the simulation exercise the impact of trade facilitation is considered by assuming import-augmenting technical progress, leading to import

Table 4.7 Trading across borders: trade facilitation (2010)

	Ranking (out of 183 countries)	Documents to export (number)	Time to export (days)	Cost to export ($ per container)	Documents to import (number)	Time to import (days)	Cost to import ($ per container)
PRC	50	7	21	500	5	24	545
Japan	24	4	10	1,010	5	11	1,060
Korea, Republic of	8	3	8	790	3	7	790
Australia	29	6	9	1,060	5	8	1,119
New Zealand	28	7	10	855	5	9	825
India	100	8	17	1,055	9	20	1,025
Brunei Darussalam	52	6	25	630	6	20	708
Cambodia	118	10	22	732	10	26	872
Indonesia	47	5	20	704	6	27	660
Lao PDR	170	9	48	1,860	10	50	2,040
Malaysia	37	7	18	450	7	14	450
Myanmar	NA	NA	NA	NA	NA	NA	NA
Philippines	61	8	15	675	8	14	730
Singapore	1	4	5	456	4	4	439
Thailand	12	4	14	625	3	13	795
Viet Nam	63	6	22	555	8	21	645

Lao PDR Lao People's Democratic Republic, *NA* data not available, *PRC* People's Republic of China
Source: World Bank, Doing Business 2010. http://www.doingbusiness.org/ (accessed 15 April 2011)

expansion. It is of interest to investigate the current conditions concerning trade facilitation for ASEAN+6 countries. The World Bank's *Doing Business* database reports time and cost associated with trading activities, which are affected by the efficiency, reliability, stability of government administration. Their findings, which are shown in Table 4.7, reveal wide variations in trading costs among the sample countries. In terms of ranking, which summaries the situations for six different categories, Singapore is ranked top among 183 countries. The Republic of Korea (8th) and Thailand (12th) are ranked high, while Lao PDR (170th), Cambodia (118th) and India (100th) are ranked low. Compared to the situation in Singapore, time, documents, and costs required for trading in some countries are twice as much. Reducing time, documents, and costs for trading promotes trade and attracts foreign direct investment, which in turn contribute to economic growth. This observation is important in designing FTAs.

We saw earlier that ASEAN+6 FTA, or CEPEA, will bring large benefits to East Asian countries. Suppose the creation of CEPEA is a tentative goal for a region-wide FTA in East Asia, what should be a roadmap toward achieving this goal. Outright negotiation for CEPEA is one possibility and sequential negotiations beginning with EAFTA and then CEPEA is another possibility. Regardless of the choices, negotiations should be built on existing ASEAN+1 FTAs, because starting from scratch would be too complex as it involves either 13 or 16 countries.

With this observation in mind, we compare the contents of ASEAN+1 FTAs to identify similarities and differences. Such an analysis would reveal the challenges

Table 4.8 Tariff concessions in ASEAN+1 FTAs (%)

	AANZFTA	ACFTA	AIFTA	AJFTA	AKFTA
Brunei Darussalam	99	99.9	82.6	96.1	97.8
Cambodia	86	86.7	84.1	NA	85.5
Indonesia	93	89	50.4	88.1	90.3
Lao PDR	91	96.4	77.5	NA	85.4
Malaysia	96	99.9	79.6	93.6	93.5
Myanmar	86	86.9	73.6	NA	87.5
Philippines	95	86.5	75.8	96.8	97.9
Singapore	100	100	100	100	100
Thailand	99	88.3	74.3	96.9	93.7
Viet Nam	91	NA	69.7	NA	83.8
Australia	100	–	–	–	–
New Zealand	100	–	–	–	–
PRC	–	94.6	–	–	–
India	–	–	74.3	–	–
Japan	–	–	–	86.5	–
Korea, Rep. of	–	–	–	–	92.2

AANZFTA ASEAN–Australia/New Zealand FTA, *ACFTA* ASEAN–People's Republic of China FTA, *AIFTA* ASEAN–India FTA, *AJFTA* ASEAN–Japan FTA, *AKFTA* ASEAN–Republic of Korea FTA, *ASEAN* Association of Southeast Asian Nations, *FTA* free trade agreement, *Lao PDR* Lao People's Democratic Republic, *NA* data not available, *PRC* People's Republic of China

Note: Figures indicate the proportion of tariff elimination in terms of tariff lines

Source: Kuno (2011)

that policy makers have to overcome to establish a region-wide FTA. Let us begin with the agreements on trade in goods. Kuno (2011) undertook a detailed analysis and he first found that ASEAN+6 countries use different tariff classification for their tariff concessions, making it difficult to construct a rather straightforward and simple tariff schedules. It is not only that different countries use different tariff schedules but also that the same countries use different schedules for their FTAs with different countries. An example of the former case can be found in ASEAN–Japan FTA, in which Japan uses HS2002 with 9-digit classification, while Singapore uses HS2002 with 8-digit classification. An example of the latter case may be found for Singapore, which uses HS2002 with 8-digit classification for ASEAN–Japan FTA but uses HS2007 with 8-digit classification for ASEAN–Republic of Korea FTA.

Tariff concessions of the same country differ depending on FTAs. Table 4.8 shows the level of tariff concessions (liberalization) by countries for five ASEAN+1 FTAs. Except for Singapore, which eliminated all the tariffs in all three FTAs, other ASEAN countries have different levels of tariff elimination for different FTAs. For example, Thailand eliminated 99 % of tariffs in ASEAN–Australia/New Zealand FTA, but its tariff elimination rates for other FTAs are lower. The tariff elimination rate is particularly low at 74.3 % for ASEAN–India FTA. The level of tariff elimination committed by a country depends on various factors including its relative competitiveness of the sectors vis-a-vis FTA partners. A lack of common tariff elimination schedule among different FTAs makes it difficult to consolidate these different FTAs.

Table 4.9 Commonality of ROOs across 5 ASEAN+1 FTAs

	Frequency distribution of HS lines (6-digit HS2002)	
Degree of commonality	No.	%
At least one common ROO in all 5 FTAs	3,318	64.0
In only 4 FTAs	766	14.8
In only 3 FTAs	825	15.9
In only 2 FTAs	255	4.9
No common ROOs	23	0.4

ASEAN Association of Southeast Asian Nations, *FTA* free trade agreement, *HS* harmonized standard, *ROO* rules of origin
Source: Medalla (2011)

On the tariff elimination rates, it should be noted that +1 countries, or Australia, New Zealand, PRC, India, Japan, and the Republic of Korea, have different rates in their FTAs with ASEAN. Among them, Australia and New Zealand are most open as they committed to remove tariffs on all products, while India is most closed as it committed to remove tariffs on 74.3 % of the products. Among CJK, the countries with more to fewer open commitments are indicated in the order of the PRC, the Republic of Korea and Japan.

In FTAs, the rules of origin (ROOs) play a very important role to ensure that preferential treatment is accorded to FTA members by avoiding trade deflection.[10] There are four major ROOs that are adopted by ASEAN+1 FTAs—wholly obtained or produced (WO), regional value content (RVC), change in tariff classification (CTC) and specific process rule (SPR). A general rule is applied to all the products except those products that are subject to product specific rules (PSRs).

Except for ASEAN–PRC FTA and ASEAN–India FTA, the basic rule is a co-equal rule: RVC(40) or a change in tariff heading (CTH). RVC(40) requires a minimum 40 % regional value content. CTH is equivalent to CTC at (harmonized standard) HS 4-digit level. For the ASEAN–PRC FTA, the general rule is RVC(40). In the case of the ASEAN–India FTA, the general rule is RVC(35) and a change in tariff sub-heading (CTSH). In other words, regional content requirement at 35 % is less restrictive compared to other ASEAN+1 FTAs, but it has an additional requirement of a change in tariff classification, albeit at a higher-6 digit level.

Differences in the ROOs adopted by five ASEAN+1 FTAs pose an obstacle in establishing a region-wide FTA, in which unified ROOs by product should be adopted. Medalla (2011) compared ROOs adopted by five ASEAN+1 FTAs at 6-digit HS lines. The figures in Table 4.9 show the number of HS lines that have common ROOs. According to Medalla's computation, all five FTAs have at least one common ROO in 64 % of all HS lines. Moreover, in 90 % of the time, three or more FTAs share a common ROO. These findings seem to indicate that harmonization of ROOs may not be a far-fetched idea among five ASEAN+1 FTAs.

[10] The discussions on ROOs draw on Medalla (2011).

Table 4.10 Correlation coefficients of services trade liberalization commitments among ASEAN+1 FTAs

	AFAS	AANZFTA	ACFTA	AKFTA
AFAS	1			
AANZFTA	0.718	1		
ACFTA	0.615	0.826	1	
AKFTA	0.704	0.87	0.83	1

AFAS ASEAN Framework Agreement on Services, *AANZFTA* ASEAN–Australia/New Zealand FTA, *ACFTA* ASEAN–PRC FTA, *AKFTA* ASEAN–Republic of Korea FTA, *ASEAN* Association of Southeast Asian Nations, *FTA* free trade agreement
Source: Ishido (2011)

Turning to trade in services and investment, agreements have not been included in all ASEAN+1 FTAs. Agreements on service trade are included in ASEAN–Australia/New Zealand FTA, ASEAN–PRC FTA, and ASEAN–Republic of Korea FTA, but not in ASEAN–Japan FTA or ASEAN–India FTA.[11] Ishido (2011) investigated the liberalization levels of the commitments by sectors under these three ASEAN+1 FTAs and ASEAN Framework Agreement in Services (AFAS). He found similarities in the level of liberalization commitments among them, as correlation coefficients, which are computed using country-average liberalization level by sector, between the pair of FTAs are greater than 0.615 (Table 4.10). Indeed, the correlation coefficient between ASEAN–Australia/New Zealand FTA and ASEAN–Republic of Korea FTA is as high as 0.870. These findings indicate that the sectoral patterns of liberalization and/or protection for trade in services under ASEAN+1 FTAs are similar and thus consolidating these FTAs into one FTA may be possible. However, it is important to note that consolidation of FTAs does not mean liberalization of trade in services.

An agreement on investment is included in the ASEAN–PRC FTA, the ASEAN–Republic of Korea FTA and the ASEAN–Australia/New Zealand FTA. The contents of agreement on investment in these FTAs, the ASEAN Comprehensive Investment Area, and the Japan–Singapore EPA (FTA) are shown in Table 4.11.[12] A comparison of these contents reveals that the ASEAN–PRC FTA's investment regime is restrictive as it does not ensure national treatment before the establishment, while other FTAs and Japan–Singapore FTA provide it. Differences can be found in the level of liberalization concerning performance requirements. The ASEAN–PRC FTA is most lenient in the application of performance requirements, while the Japan–Singapore FTA is most strict. Wide variations are found in terms of market access given to foreign investment among ASEAN+3 countries. Table 4.12 shows the number of restricted sectors to foreign firms. Singapore, Japan, Indonesia, and Brunei Darussalam are open to foreign firms as the number of restricted sectors is

[11] An agreement on trade in services is included in a chapter in Japan's bilateral FTAs with Brunei Darussalam, Indonesia, Malaysia, the Philippines, Singapore, Thailand, and Viet Nam.

[12] An agreement on investment is included in a chapter in Japan's bilateral FTAs with Brunei Darussalam, Indonesia, Malaysia, the Philippines, Singapore, and Thailand.

Table 4.11 Elements of investment agreement/investment chapter in FTAs

			ACIA	ACFTA	AKFTA	JS EPA
	National treatment (pre-establishment)		◎	△	◎	◎
	Most-favored-nation treatment (pre-establishment)		◎	◎	◎	△
	Prohibition of performance requirement (PR)		◎	△	◎	◎
Liberalization of investment	○ = Absolutely prohibited ● = Permitted if required as a condition for granting interest × = no mention	Export requirement	×	×	×	○
		Export restriction	○	×	○	○
		Local content requirement	○	×	○	○
		Local procurement requirement	○	×	○	○
		Export and import balance requirement	○	×	○	○
		Domestic sale restriction requirement	×	×	×	○
		Technology transfer requirement	×	×	×	●
		Head office establishment requirement	×	×	×	●
		Research and development requirement	×	×	×	●
		Specific region supply requirement	×	×	×	●
		Local citizen employment requirement	×	×	×	×
		Officers' nationality requirement	×	×	○	○
	Reservations		Negative	–	Negative	Negative
Protection of investment	National treatment (post establishment)		◎	◎	◎	◎
	Most-favored-nation treatment (post establishment)		◎	◎	◎	◎
	Treatment of investment		◎	◎	◎	◎
	Umbrella clause		△	◎	△	△
	Expropriation and compensation		◎	◎	◎	◎
	Compensation in cases of strife		◎	◎	◎	◎
	Transfers		◎	◎	◎	◎
	Subrogation		◎	◎	◎	◎
	Investment dispute between an investor and a member state		◎	◎	◎	◎
	Disputes between or among member states		◎	◎	◎	◎

ACIA ASEAN Comprehensive Investment Area, *ACFTA* ASEAN–PRC FTA, *AKFTA* ASEAN–Republic of Korea FTA, *EPA* economic partnership agreement, *FTA* free trade agreement, *JS EPA* Japan–Singapore EPA,

Notes: For items other than performance requirement, ◎indicates the presence of provision concerning the item and; △ indicates otherwise

Source: Ministry of Economy and Trade, Industry (METI) (2011)

Table 4.12 Number of sectors under foreign ownership restriction (out of 89 ISIC 2-digit industries)

Brunei Darussalam	18	Myanmar	23	PRC	40
Cambodia	23	Philippines	50	Japan	12
Indonesia	15	Singapore	10	Korea, Rep. of	21
Lao PDR	29	Thailand	63		
Malaysia	59	Viet Nam	45		

Lao PDR Lao People's Democratic Republic, *PRC* People's Republic of China
Source: EAFTA (2009)

lower than 20 (out of 89 sectors), while Thailand, Malaysia, and the Philippines are relatively closed as the number of restricted sectors exceeds 50.

We have examined the liberalization frameworks concerning trade in goods, services, and foreign direct investment adopted by ASEAN+5 FTAs. It is important to identify the commonalities and differences in order to make progress towards achieving a region-wide FTA. Having conducted an analysis on the liberalization frameworks, it should also be emphasized that trade and FDI facilitation measures such as customs procedures for the case of trade in goods and screening and appraisal procedures for the case of FDI play important roles in creating one unified market under a region-wide FTA.

4.6 Concluding Remarks

Asia has seen a proliferation of FTAs in recent years. However, unlike the cases in Western Europe or North America, no region-wide FTAs have been established in Asia. Accordingly, concerns for a possible noodle/spaghetti bowl effect have arisen. To promote foreign trade by avoiding the negative impacts of the noodle/spaghetti bowl effect, Asian governments have begun studying the feasibility of establishing region-wide FTAs. Two region-wide FTAs have been proposed and studied. One is EAFTA comprising ASEAN+3 countries, and the other is CEPEA comprising ASEAN+6 countries. Currently, for both EAFTA and CEPEA working groups comprising government officials are conducting stocktaking exercises on four issues: rules of origin, tariff nomenclature, customs procedure, and economic cooperation in ASEAN+1 FTAs with a view to set up unified rules that are necessary for the establishment of a region-wide FTA.

Between EAFTA and CEPEA, CEPEA is preferable as far as economic impacts are concerned, because CEPEA leads to larger benefits with greater trade creation and smaller trade diversion because of its broader membership compared to EAFTA. On the contrary EAFTA is preferable from the practical point of view concerning negotiation, as EAFTA negotiations involve smaller number of participants than CEPEA. Faced with these issues, the best approach may be that the concerned governments do not choose one over the other but continue the processes in tandem. As has been the case since the beginning of the discussions, the PRC should take a lead in the EAFTA process while Japan should do so in the CEPEA process. In the meantime, the PRC, Japan, and the Republic of Korea should pursue the establishment of a CJK FTA, which is an important missing link in both EAFTA and CEPEA. While the PRC and Japan should make efforts to play constructive roles for the establishment of region-wide FTAs and a trilateral CJK FTA, they also should support ASEAN in achieving the ASEAN Economic Community (AEC). Without the AEC, a region-wide FTA, either EAFTA or CEPEA, will not be constructed, because ASEAN plays a central role in the construction of regional architecture in Asia.

When the desire of the stakeholders toward the establishment of either EAFTA or CEPEA reaches a critical point, the framework agreement should be negotiated and the process of establishing a region-wide FTA should begin. For this process, ASEAN's experiences of gradualism and differential treatment between developed and less developed members by setting the targets should provide useful lessons. Construction of a region-wide FTA should be flexible in that in addition to EAFTA and CEPEA other formulations such as ASEAN+3+2 should be allowed if India is not ready to participate in the project. Similarly, new members should be allowed to join the existing FTA such as EAFTA and CEPEA after their establishment, if the conditions for entry are satisfied.

While Asian countries work earnestly to set up a region-wide FTA in Asia, those Asian countries that are ready to join the TPP should do so. This is because the characteristics of the TPP on the one hand and an Asia-wide FTA on the other hand are different and they can complement each other. The TPP is a very high-level FTA with a number of high-standard rules on behind-the-border issues such as competition and intellectual property rights. As such, only countries with developed economic systems can join the TPP. By contrast, a region-wide FTA in Asia, either EAFTA or CEPEA, places an emphasis on economic cooperation to reduce development gaps. Those EAFTA or CEPEA countries that cannot join the TPP yet may join it after achieving economic growth and building a relevant economic system with necessary rules on policies.

Finally, governments are expected to provide temporary safety nets to people who are negatively affected by FTAs in order to successfully negotiate FTAs. Increased competition from increased imports that result from FTAs, could reduce production and employment. Faced with potential threat of reduced income and/or job opportunities, workers in non-competitive sectors oppose FTAs. Recognizing that trade liberalization would promote economic growth but at the same time generate potential negative impacts on certain groups of people, governments should be ready to provide such assistance as temporary income compensation and training and education to those negatively impacted people so that they can upgrade their skills to obtain higher paying jobs. A combination of trade liberalization with appropriate structural adjustment assistance would improve the welfare level of the people.

References

Aggarwal, V. K., & Urata, S. (Eds.). (2006). *Bilateral trade agreements: Origins, evolution, and implications*. New York: Routledge.

Asian Development Bank (ADB). (2011). *FTA trends, FTAs by status*. Manila: Asia Regional Integration Center. Asian Development Bank. http://aric.adb.org/1.php (accessed 15 April 2011).

CEPEA. (2009). *Phase II Report of the Track Two Study Group on Comprehensive Economic Partnership in East Asia (CEPEA)*.

Cheong, I., Kim, H., & Cho, J. (2010). Business use of FTAs in Korea. RIETI Discussion Paper Series 10-E-038. Tokyo: Research Institute of Economy, Trade and Industry.

Chia, S. Y. (2011). Association of Southeast Asian Nations economic integration: Developments and challenges. *Asian Economic Policy Review, 6*(1, June), 43–63.

EAFTA. (2009). *Desirable and feasible option for an East Asia FTA*. A Report by Joint Expert Group on EAFTA Phase II Study.

Ishido, H. (2011). Liberalization of trade in services under ASEAN+n: A mapping exercise. Paper prepared for ERIA Project Comprehensive Mapping of FTAs in ASEAN and East Asia.

Kawai, M., & Wignaraja, G. (Eds.). (2010). *Asia's free trade agreements: How is business responding?* Cheltenham and Northampton: Edward Elgar.

Kawai, M., & Wignaraja, G. (2011). Asian FTAs: Trends, prospects and challenges. *Journal of Asian Economics, 22*(1), 1–22.

Kohpaiboon, A. (2010). Exporters' response to FTA tariff preferences: evidence from Thailand. RIETI Discussion Paper Series 10-E-039. Tokyo: Research Institute of Economy, Trade and Industry.

Kuno, A. (2011). Constructing the Tariff dataset for the ERIA FTA database. Paper prepared for ERIA Project Comprehensive Mapping of FTAs in ASEAN and East Asia.

Medalla, E. M. (2011). Taking stock of the ROOs in the ASEAN+1 FTAs: Toward deepening East Asia integration. Paper prepared for ERIA Project Comprehensive Mapping of FTAs in ASEAN and East Asia.

Ministry of Economy, Trade, and Industry (METI). (2011). The 2011 Report on compliance by major trading partners with trade agreements: WTO, FTA/EPAs, BITs [Fukosei Boeki Hokokusho: WTO Kyotei oyobi Keizairenkeikyotei/Toshikyotei karamita Shuyoukoku no Boeki Seisaku] (in Japanese).

Pangestu, M., & Gooptu, S. (2004). New regionalism: Options for China and East Asia. In H. Kharas & K. Krumm (Eds.), *East Asia Integrates* (pp. 79–99). Washington, DC: World Bank.

Pomfret, R., Kaufmann, U., & Findlay, C. (2010). Use of FTAs in Australia. RIETI Discussion Paper Series 10-E-042. Tokyo: Research Institute of Economy, Trade and Industry.

Sally, R. (2006). Free trade agreements and the prospects of regional integration in East Asia. *Asian Economic Policy Review, 1*(2, December), 306–321.

Shiino, K., & Mizuno, R. (2010). *New Era of FTAs—Asia being the core in broadening FTA network*. Tokyo: JETRO (in Japanese).

Soesastro, H. (2006). Regional integration in East Asia: Achievements and future prospects. *Asian Economic Policy Review, 1*(2, December), 215–234.

Takahashi, K., & Urata S. (2010). On the use of free trade agreements by Japanese firms: Further evidence. *Business and Politics, 12*(1), Article 2.

Urata, S. (2005). Free trade agreements: A catalyst for Japan's economic revitalization. In T. Ito, H. Patrick, & D. E. Weinstein (Eds.), *Reviving Japan's economy* (pp. 377–410). Boston: MIT Press.

Urata, S. (2010). Exclusion fears and competitive regionalism in East Asia. In M. Solis, B. Stallings, & S. N. Katada (Eds.), *Competitive regionalism: FTA diffusion in the Pacific Rim* (pp. 27–53). New York: Palgrave MacMillan.

World Bank. Doing Business. (2010). http://www.doingbusiness.org/ (accessed 15 April 2011)

Chapter 5
Regional Financial Architecture Beyond the Global Financial Crisis

Soyoung Kim and Doo Yong Yang

Abstract This chapter examines recent developments in and future prospects for regional financial and monetary cooperation and integration in East Asia and suggests some issues that could contribute to more constructive development of the regional financial architecture. The regional financial architecture has faced new challenges because Asia's regional economic development is a real factor of the global economy. The global financial crisis and global imbalances are good examples. This implies that the regional financial architecture is no longer regional-only. The authors also argue that rigorous multilateral surveillance on a regional basis, consistently applied and with associated peer pressure, can help build the domestic financial architecture and ultimately mitigate the excessive macroeconomic volatility. Furthermore, a regional financial institute could be a venue for building consensus and reflecting regional views in the negotiation process of setting global financial standards.

Keywords Asian bond funds • Asian bond markets • Chiang Mai Initiative • International financial cooperation • Regional cooperation

5.1 Introduction

The 1997–1998 Asian crisis brought about many structural changes including structural reforms in banking and corporate sector and more liberalized capital markets in crisis hit-countries. East Asia; one of them is regional monetary and financial

S. Kim
Department of Economics, Seoul National University, Seoul, Republic of Korea
e-mail: soyoungkim@snu.ac.kr

D.Y. Yang (✉)
College of International Studies, Kyung Hee University, Seoul, Republic of Korea
e-mail: yangdy@khu.ac.kr

G. Capannelli and M. Kawai (eds.), *The Political Economy of Asian Regionalism*,
DOI 10.1007/978-4-431-54568-2_5, © Asian Development Bank Institute 2014

cooperation. Before the Asian crisis, no one would have seriously argued for the creation of a system of regional financial integration in East Asia. Most experts believed that a market-led integration process was desirable and in fact was taking root in East Asia because of the heterogeneity in economic and financial development of each economy in the region. The financial crisis that erupted in 1997 changed the region's confidence in such a process because financial liberalization was at least partially responsible for the crisis. Consequently, the Asian financial crisis was a strong impetus to search for a regional mechanism that could forestall future crises. This produced a significant policy-led integration in East Asia (Bergsten 2000; Henning 2002).

Some policymakers proposed a regional self-liquidity support system as evidenced in the Asian Monetary Fund (AMF) and Japan's New Miyazawa plan right after the Asian crisis. However there were fewer consensuses on this proposal both in the region and at the global level. When the proposal to create an AMF was withdrawn in 1997 at the objection of the United States (US) and the International Monetary Fund (IMF), the leaders of the Association of Southeast Asian Nations (ASEAN) responded by inviting the People's Republic of China (PRC), Japan, and the Republic of Korea to join in an effort to seek economic cooperation in the region. The ASEAN+3 (ASEAN members plus the PRC, Japan, and the Republic of Korea) summit in November 1999 released a Joint Statement on East Asian Cooperation that covered a wide range of possible areas for regional cooperation. Recognizing the need to establish regional financial arrangements to supplement the existing international facilities, the ASEAN+3 finance ministers at their meeting in Chiang Mai, Thailand, in May 2000, agreed to strengthen the existing cooperative framework in the region by creating a liquidity support system incorporating bilateral swap arrangements (BSAs) known as the Chiang Mai Initiative (CMI). The CMI was followed by another regional initiative for developing and integrating bond markets of individual countries into a large unified regional market, known as the Asian Bond Markets Initiative (ABMI). However, some economists argue that regional cooperation has not developed far enough to build a regional defense system to cope with the negative effects of global shocks, as evidenced by a huge accumulation of foreign reserves in the region since the crisis.

Two recent important impetuses on new developments in the regional financial architecture are the global imbalances and the global financial crisis in the late 2000s. The global imbalances cast pressure on regional policy dialogue to coordinate macroeconomic policies to deal with regional responses to correct the large current account imbalances between Asia and the US. Moreover, the global financial crisis that is somewhat related to the global imbalances cast new development in the global financial architecture including the emerging Group of 20 (G20), reforms of global financial institutions, and new standards for global financial markets. These developments have also influenced issues of the regional financial architecture. The global financial crisis was indeed different from previous crises in the region—it originated in the US. While it affected Asia, the region recovered far faster than other parts of the world. This awakened the notion that Asia now takes up a crucial part of the world economy as an engine of world economic growth and that cooperation among Asian countries is essential.

This chapter examines recent developments in and future prospects for regional financial and monetary cooperation and integration in East Asia and suggests some issues that could contribute to more constructive development of the regional financial architecture. Section 2 discusses the background of financial and monetary cooperation in East Asia by reviewing the basic theories, arguments, and empirical studies. Section 3 reports on the progress of regional financial and monetary cooperation of East Asia. Section 4 provides suggestions for future developments in regional financial and monetary cooperation. Section 5 provides the conclusion.

5.2 Background of Financial and Monetary Cooperation in East Asia

Economic Crisis and Financial and Monetary Cooperation

Emerging market economies are vulnerable to external shocks. To deal with external shocks, the first line of defense is at the national level. If countries had sound institutions to prevent investor herding, contagion, and speculative attacks, they would have been able to thwart the crisis even while going through cyclically unfavorable macroeconomic conditions. However, this first line of defense is not effective when a country is not mature enough to reduce the negative impact of external shocks. Institutional change and support mechanisms are required to cope with adverse outcomes if and when financial globalization materializes (Bhagwati 2004). In developing countries, institutional distortions and market failures complicate credible inflation targeting, render large exchange rate movements more dangerous, make fixed exchange rates acutely crisis-prone, and reduce the beneficial effects of financial globalization (Obstfeld 2004).

Even for developed countries, it is hard for small open economies to cope with highly volatile capital flows. Eichengreen (2008) suggests that in the presence of highly volatile international capital flows, it is hard for intermediate regimes including soft pegs to survive and the only viable choices are polar regimes such as hard pegs and free floating ("hollow middle hypothesis," "bi-polar view"). However, it is difficult for most countries including most in East Asia to give up exchange rate stability given the importance of international trade and price stability. As a result many countries managed exchange rates tightly despite the fact that they publicly announced free floating (Calvo and Reinhart 2002). But it is hard for these countries to manage the exchange rate tightly in the presence of highly volatile capital flows and therefore face a dilemma.

This is the rationale for establishing a global defense system such as global financial institutions, global financial standards, and policy dialogue in the G20. However, as witnessed, the global financial cooperation system is far from perfect to deal with contagious effects and the spillover of the global or regional scale of external shocks. For example, the global financial architecture did not prevent the financial crisis in East Asia at all. Some people even argued that the IMF program had adverse effects on crisis countries during the Asian financial crisis. In general, heterogeneity in the interests of countries around the world makes it hard to form a perfect global financial cooperation system.

This pessimistic outlook arouses a deep concern in developing countries that they will continue to be vulnerable to future financial crises, even if they faithfully carry out the kinds of reform recommended by the IMF and World Bank. These concerns, coupled with the fundamental dilemma of a small open economy in choosing the proper international monetary frameworks in the face of highly volatile international capital flows, led most Asian countries to pile up large foreign exchange reserves that had not been observed before. This national strategy of having a very large stock of foreign reserves to deal with large capital flight may decrease the probability of crisis, but accumulating, maintaining, and managing huge foreign exchange reserves is extremely costly.

A large body of literature argues that capital flows in different countries, particularly developing countries in the same region, are synchronized through various channels of contagion, including herding behavior and information asymmetry, through finance and trade channels (Calvo and Mendoza 2000; Mendoza 2001; Glick and Rose 1999; Kaminsky and Reinhart 2000). International investors may classify different countries in a single group and make region-based investment decisions. A crisis in a country may change international investors' perceptions of risks of other countries in the same region. The devaluation of a country's currency resulting from a crisis may lead other countries in the region to lose international competitiveness of other countries in the region, which may make other countries more prone to a crisis. In addition, capital flows can be highly synchronized if shocks that determine capital flows are positively correlated or spill over across countries, or if developing countries go through financial liberalization processes at the same time. A regional grouping for support is logical given contagion's geographical concentration. Neighbors have an interest in helping put out a financial crisis before it spreads (Ito et al. 1999). As long as a crisis remains country or region-specific, there is no urgent political need for unaffected countries to pay the significant costs associated with playing the role of firefighter. In addition to providing financial assistance in tandem with international support, a regional financial cooperation mechanism may conduct policy reviews and initiate a dialogue process.

Policy dialogue, including monitoring and surveillance, is the bedrock on which rests coherent policy formation for regional financial arrangements. A monitoring and surveillance process would provide prompt and relevant information for assessing the situation of countries in trouble and the potential contagious effects of a crisis to neighboring countries. Furthermore, a joint exercise based on a region-wide early warning system would facilitate closer examination of financial vulnerabilities. In addition, the regional policy dialogue process would contribute to ensuring the effective implementation of high-quality banking and financial standards, and to promoting financial market development. Building on this insight and from the monetary integration experience of Western Europe, a growing number of East Asian economists are realizing that a regional initiative could be an alternative solution to the deficient international financial architecture. These efforts have resulted in a number of regional cooperative arrangements, including the CMI, the ABMI, an Asian Bond Fund (ABF), and a surveillance mechanism known as the Economic Policy Review and Dialogue (EPRD). We will review the progress of regional financial and monetary cooperation in Sect. 3.

Benefits from International Financial Market Integration

Although most popular arguments on regional financial and monetary cooperation are related to currency and/or financial crises, there are other arguments to support regional financial and monetary cooperation. In this section, we list some other possible benefits from regional financial and monetary cooperation for East Asia.

International financial integration can provide various benefits. First, internationally mobile capital flows can facilitate inter-temporal consumption smoothing. Without any international capital mobility, a country is likely to decrease its consumption under a temporary fall in income. However, each country can smooth its consumption by international lending and borrowing under a temporary change in income. Second, international capital mobility can help to allocate worldwide savings into the most efficient investment opportunity. Without international capital mobility, investment should be fully financed by domestic savings. However, under perfect international capital mobility, investments can be financed from international financial market without enough domestic saving. Third, international trade in risky assets can provide benefits from international risk sharing. Without international trade in risk assets, each country will fully face country-specific risks. However, through international portfolio diversification, each country can hedge country specific risks. Fourth, international portfolio diversification can promote investments with higher return and risks, and may lead to higher long run growth (Obstfeld 1994). Each country can make investments with higher return and risks by diversifying risks internationally and such investments may enhance the long run average return and/or growth rate.

When international financial markets are not fully integrated, international financial cooperation can facilitate international financial integration. In this way, international financial cooperation can help to realize various benefits of international financial market integration. The following empirical studies suggest that international financial markets are not fully integrated and that East Asian economies have not fully exploited the gains from international financial market integration.

There are some studies that report the degree of financial integration based on the size of cross-border assets. Simple theoretical models (such as Lucas 1982 and Obstfeld and Rogoff 1995) suggest that the optimal proportion of foreign assets of domestic investors is close to 100 %. However, they are far from 100 %, in line with many studies on other economies (known as "home bias puzzle" or "portfolio diversification puzzle") (Kim et al. 2008; Kim and Lee 2008). Related to this issue in East Asia, Kim et al. (2007) examine Feldstein and Horioka (1980) type-investigation on savings and investment relationships and find that savings–investment correlation is very high in East Asian economies, and higher than those found in developed countries. This implies that East Asian economies do not fully exploit important aspects of benefits from international financial market integration. Other studies such as Kim et al. (2006, 2008) and Kim and Lee (2008) examine international risk sharing properties of East Asia. These studies show that international risk sharing in East Asian economies is far from perfect, suggesting that countries do not fully exploit one important gain from international financial market integration.

There are some arguments for "regional" financial and monetary cooperation or integration (against "global" financial and monetary cooperation or integration). When global cooperation or integration is not perfect, regional cooperation or integration can provide benefits to countries. In this regard, a number of studies show that global financial integration is far from perfect, supporting the case for regional financial integration, possibly through regional financial cooperation. The success of regional cooperation also depends on regional and global environments. Regional cooperation can receive much attention, when regional interests are different from global interests and when interests of regional members are similar. Regional cooperation can be more successful when regional member countries have similar political and social objectives. When more resources are available in the region, regional cooperation can be facilitated. Regarding international financial integration through regional cooperation, East Asian economies meet at least some criteria. Many Asian countries have enjoyed high domestic savings rates, which exceed domestic investment rates, implying that there are huge resources available for financial cooperation. In addition, many Asian countries share similar experiences such as financial crises, volatile capital flows, and exchange rate instability.

Monetary and/or exchange rate cooperation can help to promote and stabilize international trade flows. Exchange rate uncertainty may hamper international trade in goods and services. In addition, monetary and/or exchange rate cooperation may prevent competitive devaluation, which could lead to worldwide inflation and/or trade wars. In East Asia, a huge volatility in cross exchange rates within the region would make it hard for some countries to maintain international competitiveness. In recent years, East Asian economies have formed production sharing networks and have tight trade linkages with each other (Kim et al. 2011). But too much volatility in cross exchange rates within the region may generate instability in the production sharing networks. In addition, monetary and/or exchange rate cooperation may be needed to mitigate global imbalances.

5.3 Overview of the Regional Financial Architecture in East Asia

This section describes progress on regional financial and monetary cooperation in East Asia since the Asian financial crisis of 1997–1998.

Chiang Mai Initiative and Chiang Mai Initiative Multilateralization

The Chiang Mai Initiative (CMI) was East Asia's response to the IMF-led resolution of the 1997–1998 crisis. The CMI was the first significant effort at Asian financial cooperation to enable member countries to cope with disruptive capital flows and maintain exchange rate stability.[1] Substantial progress has been made in implementing the CMI since then. The ASEAN Swap Arrangement (ASA), one of the main components of the CMI, has increased to $1 billion, effective as of 17 November 2000, and encompasses all ASEAN member countries. Substantial bilateral agreements have been reached regarding the network of bilateral swap agreements (BSAs) under the CMI over the subsequent years. At the 8th ASEAN+3 finance ministers' meeting held on 4 May 2005, developments were taken to strengthen the CMI mechanism. First, the ministers agreed that countries holding BSAs with a certain country in difficulty would make a collective decision in lending money to that country. This agreement is seen as a first step toward multilateralizing the CMI. Since the CMI swap network has not yet been tested, it would be workable only when one or two countries come under pressure. If a number of countries are simultaneously experiencing pressure from capital markets, it would be natural to expect a degree of reluctance to take on any additional obligations in defense of their neighbors. Thus, such joint decisions and action will be required to prevent a free rider problem. Second, the size of the swaps increased. The ASA doubled to $2 billion. At the same time, the current swap amount of any BSA can be expanded by up to 100 % if both sides agree to increase the amount. Consequently, Japan and the Republic of Korea replaced the existing BSA with a new two-way BSA on 24 February 2006. Third, the CMI's autonomy was strengthened in that the autonomous disbursement without IMF involvement increased from 10 % to 20 %. From 2000 to 2006, the size of the CMI reached $83 billion.

Despite these positive developments in the CMI, there were still a number of unresolved issues that cast some doubts as to the efficiency of the CMI as a regional liquidity support system. Most of all, the CMI has not been and is not likely to be activated in the future. This is because the amount of liquidity any country can secure through the currency swaps with other CMI members is relatively small and not necessarily assured. Second, there is no surveillance unit to avoid breach of the swap contract. Although the automatic swap amount was relatively small, the swap-providing countries need to formulate their own assessments of the capacity as well as credibility of the swap-requesting countries to honor their contracts. The operational procedures embodied in the CMI could not effectively resolve the problems

[1] There is nothing new in setting up a regional financial organization. In addition to several institutional inventions observed during the European monetary integration process, there already exists the Arab Monetary Fund and the Latin American Reserve Fund established in 1976 and 1991, respectively. However, such regional funds have not been effectively used for risk management at the regional level, mainly due to lack of the members' strong commitment and operational transparency.

of default on repayment. At the annual meeting of the Asian Development Bank (ADB) in Istanbul, Turkey, in May 2005, the ASEAN+3 finance ministers approved the proposal that doubled the size of the existing individual bilateral swaps ($36.5 billion) with the provision that the actual increase would be decided by bilateral negotiations among the members. In order to avoid this deficiency inherent in the system, it had been proposed to create a secretariat or committee, which would determine joint activation of all swap contracts of the swap requesting countries, so that swap disbursements could be made in a concerted and timely manner. At the Istanbul ADB meeting, the ASEAN+3 finance ministers agreed to adopt in principle a collective decision making mechanism of the network of BSAs to ensure the timely availability of liquidity from the system. At the same time, they also raised the limit of automatic withdrawal to 20 %. A year later at the 2006 ADB annual meeting in Hyderabad, India, the ASEAN+3 finance ministers approved the proposal for adopting a collective decision making mechanism that would activate the swap contracts within 2 weeks to provide liquidity promptly at times of emergency.

In approving the increase in the size and streamlining the operational procedure of the CMI, the ASEAN+3 members also realized that the multilateralization of the BSAs together with the increase in the drawing limit of more than 20 % would not be possible unless a more effective surveillance system was established. Creating a surveillance mechanism for the CMI has been a controversial issue from the beginning. The ASEAN+3 finance ministers, at the 2005 ADB meeting, reaffirmed the need to enhance the ASEAN+3 economic surveillance and integrate it into the CMI, but were not able to make any decision as to the structure, role, and location of a surveillance unit. The joint statement of the ASEAN+3 finance ministers at the 2006 ADB annual meeting reaffirmed their determination in improving the CMI structure and enhancing the regional surveillance capacity, but stopped short of announcing any concrete proposal other than establishing a group of experts and a technical working group on economic and financial monitoring.

This activity led to the creation of a common fund called CMI mutilateralization (CMIM) at the 2007 Kyoto finance meeting. In Madrid in 2008, the ASEAN+3 finance ministers meeting announced progress toward the CMIM where ASEAN+3 countries agreed to mutilateralize the CMI in such a way that any member country can utilize liquidity support from the total fund of $120 billion under the single agreement. The PRC, Japan, and the Republic of Korea would contribute 80 % of the total while ASEAN countries would contribute 20 % of the rest (see Table 7.2 in Chap. 7). The CMIM came into effect in March 2010.

The Asian Bond Markets Initiative and Asian Bond Funds

Since the Asian financial crisis in 1997–1998, there has been consensus among Asian policymakers and economists that the development of Asian bond markets is one of the most important policy goals in the region as a means of preventing future financial crises and promoting regional economic growth. Regional bond markets can be beneficial in preventing a financial crisis by decreasing the dependence on short-term funds and facilitating the recycling of regional savings. One of the reasons for the necessity of developing regional bond markets is that they can provide a complementary channel of finance that will grant long-term financing, and reduce the financial dependence on banks. Immature bond markets in the region resulting in excessive dependence on bank-intermediated financing and foreign short-term financing were major causes of the Asian financial crisis, and these can be mitigated through the regional bond markets. Another reason for the necessity of developing regional bond markets is the realization that through the bond market, extensive amounts of accumulated Asian capital can be recycled directly back into the region. Since the financial crisis, surges in exports and high personal savings resulted in Asian countries accumulating vast foreign exchange reserves. However, most of the accumulated reserves have been invested in the developed markets, including the US and Europe, and only later recycled back into the region in the form of risky assets, such as equities and foreign direct investments. Thus, through the development of Asian bond markets, it may be possible to meet the needs of regional borrowers, who are currently relying on the international financial markets. Well-established regional bond markets will encourage Asian accumulated reserves being invested within the region, facilitating recycling of regional savings and preventing recurrences of financial crises.

At the informal ASEAN Finance and Central Bank Deputies' Meeting (AFDM+3) in Tokyo in November 2002, the Republic of Korea proposed a study on the feasibility of creating new and improving existing Asian bond markets under the ASEAN+3 framework. This proposal received broad support among the thirteen members, and a month later, Japan introduced a plan for the development of regional bond markets in Asia, and the Asian Bond Markets Initiative (ABMI) was born. At the AFDM+3 meeting, the member countries agreed to organize six working groups on a voluntary basis to conduct detailed studies on the construction of market infrastructure and the creation of new debt instruments including bonds denominated in local currencies.

A progress report of the six ABMI working groups, presented to the Istanbul meeting of the ASEAN+3 finance ministers in May 2005 showed that the working groups had not made any substantial progress in advancing the ABMI. The best the finance ministers could do was to introduce a roadmap that would guide the gathering and sharing of information on bond market developments among the member economies. They also launched new studies on Asian bond standards, which would identify necessary market infrastructure and introduce market procedures comparable to those of global bond markets, and the possible issuance of Asian currency basket bonds. Few substantial issues such as the deregulation of cross-border transactions in financial instruments in the region were on the agenda of the 2005 ASEAN+3 finance ministers' meeting.

The joint ministerial statement at the 2006 ADB annual meeting notes that concrete progress has been made in promoting the Asian Bond Market. As evidenced, it cites the rapid regional growth in the local currency bond market, which more than quadrupled in size since 1997, although the growth may have little to do with the ABMI itself. It also stated that "the study on the issuance of the asset-backed

Asian currency-backed bonds and cross-border local currency bonds would contribute to further development." On the development of the bond market infrastructure that included regional credit guarantee and investment mechanisms, settlement systems, credit ratings, and Asian Bond Standard, the joint statement is rather subdued by saying that it recognizes "a noticeable progress made in discussions." (ASEAN+3 Finance Ministers 2006).

While ASEAN+3 has been primarily engaged in constructing regional infrastructure for Asian bond markets and harmonizing various financial standards, regulatory systems, and tax treatments throughout the region, another regional institution has taken initiative in establishing Asian bond funds that will invest in bonds issued by Asian governments and corporations. The 11 central banks of East Asia and Pacific[2] belonging to Executive Meetings of East Asia and Pacific Central Banks (EMEAP) launched the Asian Bond Funds (ABF) I and II. ABF I invests only in dollar denominated Asian sovereign bonds whereas ABF II is structured to invest in local currency denominated Asian bonds.

The establishment of ABF I was announced in June 2003. All 11 EMEAP central banks invested in ABF I at its launch, which had a capitalization of about $1 billion. The initial subscription has been fully invested in US dollar-denominated bonds issued by sovereign and quasi-sovereign issuers in eight EMEAP economies (the PRC; Hong Kong, China; Indonesia; the Republic of Korea; Malaysia; the Philippines; Singapore; and Thailand).

Building on the momentum of developing ABF I, EMEAP also launched ABF II on 16 December 2004, which consists of two components: a Pan-Asian Bond Index Fund (PAIF) and a Fund of Bond Funds (FoBF).[3] The PAIF is a single bond index fund invested in local currency denominated bonds in EMEAP economies. The FoBF is a parent fund investing in a number of country sub funds, which in turn invest in local currency bonds issued in EMEAP economies. ABF has invested in sovereign and quasi-sovereign bonds denominated in local currencies. The total amount of EMEAP investment is $2 billion, which is allocated to the PAIF and the FoBF equally. The ABF II funds are intended to passively manage against a set of transparent and pre-determined benchmark indices, covering local currency bonds issued by sovereign and quasi-sovereign issuers in EMEAP economies.

In view of its small size, market participants believe that ABF I may have had little effect on the market for East Asian sovereign dollar bonds. Instead, ABF I investment may have crowded out private investors. ABF II has been more controversial as there is no shortage of the demand for high quality Asian bonds denominated in Asian currencies. Managers of the FoBF have invested in Asian local

[2] They are the Republic of Korea; the PRC; Japan; Hong Kong, China; Singapore; Thailand; Malaysia; the Philippines; Indonesia; Australia; and New Zealand.

[3] The PAIF will act as an investment fund and new asset class for regional and international investors who wish to have a well-diversified exposure to bond markets in Asia. The FoBF is a two-tier structure with a parent fund investing in a number of country sub-funds comprising local currency denominated bonds issued in the respective EMEAP economies. While the parent fund is confined to EMEAP investment, the country sub-funds are intended to provide local investors with low-cost and index-driven investment vehicles and at the same time give regional and international investors the flexibility to invest in the Asian bond markets of their choice. (Park et al. 2004).

currency bonds with a rating below the minimum investment grade that private and institutional investors would not normally invest in. This investment strategy raises the question of whether it is prudent for central banks to invest in non-investment grade bonds and, if it is, what should be the desirable share of these speculative bonds in their total reserves.

There are also two other concerns on the viability of ABF II. One is that since ABF II is likely to invest in East Asian sovereign bonds denominated in local currencies, it may serve as a mutual scheme of financing fiscal deficits among the member countries belonging to EMEAP. In such a case, the investment policy of ABF II cannot solely be dictated by profit motives alone, even though a private institution manages it. If these local currency sovereign bonds can be issued and traded in global bond markets, then ABF II is adding to the demand for these debt instruments. If these bonds are not readily marketable to private and institutional investors in global bond markets, then one can argue that the EMEAP central banks are subsidizing the issuers depending upon the prices they pay for these bonds.

It is also argued that the ABF II initiative has served as a catalyst for the deregulation and opening of local bond markets (Ma and Remolona 2005). Although many pieces of evidence have been presented in support of this development, given the small amount of ABF II investment in designated countries, it is indeed difficult to determine whether and to what extent the observed implementation of the reform measures have been influenced by the ABF II initiative. Furthermore, ABF II contains the possible signaling problem. If ABF II is of considerable size, then it is also possible to imagine that its investment operations could affect the foreign exchange and interest rate policies of the EMEAP member countries whose bonds are purchased or sold by ABF II. Even if the amount of a sale or purchase is relatively small, ABF II's operations may send the wrong signals to the financial markets against the wishes of the EMEAP central banks. This signaling problem is likely to remain even if a private institution manages ABF II insofar as EMEAP central banks have a controlling stake in it. Despite these concerns, the EMEAP member central banks could contribute to the development of Asian bond markets, if they were to use the ABF II leverage to strengthen the regional financial infrastructure and to remove institutional constraints on the supply of high-grade Asian corporate and sovereign bonds.

In May 2010 at the 13th ASEAN+3 finance ministers' meeting, a new regional institution was established. The Credit Guarantee and Investment Facility (CGIF) is a trust fund of ADB—with an initial capital of $700 million—with the objective of supporting the issuance of corporate bonds in the region and contributing to the development of regional bond markets.

Regional Surveillance Mechanism

One important element of regional financial architecture is the establishment of a regional financial surveillance mechanism (Park et al. 2008; Kawai and Houser 2008).

There are several functions of a regional surveillance mechanism that would contribute to the regional financial architecture.

First, a regional monitoring and surveillance system should be constructed to stabilize and strengthen domestic financial systems as a supporting instrument and mechanism for regional financial arrangements. Most crisis-prone developing countries suffer from inadequate economic and legal infrastructure resulting in an inefficient allocation of high savings, inordinately large short-term debt markets, and a general absence of arm's length transactions. The regional policy dialogue process should therefore pay particular attention to the root problems of such countries' weak domestic financial systems. Besides strengthening prudential supervision, risk management, and corporate governance, financial authorities in the region must also actively promote long-term capital markets. This is a case where financial cooperation can deepen and enhance regional financial markets.

Second, improved monitoring and surveillance are also useful in identifying emerging issues and potential problems, thus enabling countries to take collective action at the national level or jointly at the regional level. As often observed in the IMF surveillance process, symptoms of a crisis and economic vulnerabilities have not been captured effectively. Regional initiatives could complement the IMF surveillance process in that regional economies have become much more interdependent through trade and financial channels over the last decade. There is a pressing need to engage in regional monitoring and surveillance precisely because spillover effects in the region are insidious.[4]

The above discussion points to the need for establishing an independent monitoring and surveillance unit for the purpose of providing prompt and relevant information to any regional cooperative group. Its monitoring activities would cover (i) macroeconomic trends and policy changes in the region, (ii) financial market developments, and (iii) structural and institutional changes. This unit is also required to develop a policy dialogue and surveillance mechanism to enforce (i) the implementation of common standards agreed among the members, (ii) policy changes and reforms required of those countries in need, and (iii) economic policy coordination agreed among the members. Such a unit would evolve over time as the participating countries build trust and accumulate experience in policy dialogue.

Although structured regional surveillance initiatives provide a potentially meaningful and substantive value-added contribution to the current ASEAN+3 policy dialogue, East Asian economies have not yet specified common policy objectives. Crisis prevention and management is rather ambiguous as a policy objective for

[4] The IMF is expected to play the role of an insurance firm that has its own monitoring and surveillance device. However, the presence of a regional fund as a cooperative partnership fund will complicate the welfare consequences, depending on whether the regional fund is in a better position to monitor the effort than the IMF. If the regional fund cannot effectively harness its monitoring capabilities to reduce the moral hazard problem, countries may become less cautious; the IMF will tend to provide less insurance. The regional fund may crowd out the more effective insurance provided by the IMF, thus becoming completely dysfunctional. In this regard, peer monitoring is essential for controlling the moral hazards involved in the partnership fund, and may even improve welfare by enhancing the countries risk sharing. For a similar logic, see Kandel and Lazear (1992).

surveillance. Surveillance mechanisms should come along with other pillars of monetary and financial cooperation. In the case of European integration, a more effective and structured surveillance process started only when the European countries sought monetary integration in the 1990s.

After the Asian crisis, a rudimentary surveillance mechanism was established by the ASEAN+3 Economic Policy Review and Dialogue (EPRD) under the CMI. EPRD however has not developed at all as a means of actually coordinated policy even though it is useful as a means of ongoing communication and information exchange (Kawai and Houser 2008).

An important development regarding a surveillance mechanism is the establishment of a new regional surveillance unit under the CMIM—the ASEAN+3 Macroeconomic Research Office (AMRO). AMRO was established in Singapore in April 2011. Its purposes are to monitor and analyze regional economies and contribute to the early detection of risks, swiftly implement remedial actions, and effective decision making of the CMIM. AMRO prepares consolidated reports on the overall macroeconomic and financial assessment of the ASEAN+3 region and the individual ASEAN+3 members.

It is not certain whether the CMIM will effectively function as a regional liquidity support in the region, but it has served as an important forum for policy dialogue and exchange of information on regional as well as country specific problems. The importance of the CMIM is not so much a liquidity support system as it is a framework of policy dialogue. Its recent consolidation is a measure of how far ASEAN+3 members have moved forward in forging regional financial cooperation and facilitating policy dialogue if not coordination.

5.4 Issues on Future Regional Financial Architecture

CMIM: Size, IMF Conditionality, Moral Hazard, and Surveillance

The size of the CMIM should increase to meet regional needs. Despite these recent developments, the CMIM still has several limitations. One important remaining issue is links of the CMIM to the IMF. As long as the CMIM is a source of financial resources supplementary to the IMF, the size of the swap borrowing does not necessarily need to be large enough to meet potential needs, because there exists another deep pocket of financial resources provided by the IMF. However, the conventional IMF program during the Asian financial crisis had been very tight, sometimes very costly, and subject to a "stigma effect," so by now many East Asian economies are reluctant to involve the IMF.

The swap amount a country can draw from the CMIM without IMF involvement is still insignificant. For instance, Thailand can draw $11.925 billion. Since 20 % of the swap arrangements can be disbursed without IMF involvement, the available amount, \$2.385 billion is too small. The size of the IMF package for Thailand was \$16.2 billion, which is far larger than the CMIM amount. At present, the CMIM cannot be a meaningful regional defense mechanism independent of the IMF. Thus, it's crucial to increase the size of CMIM to meet the regional needs.

Although the CMIM is not allowed to design its own conditionality at this point, it does need to establish its own surveillance mechanism. Under the CMIM framework, 20 % of the swap arrangements can be disbursed without IMF involvement. But because this 20 % can be disbursed only with the consent of swap-providing countries, they need to formulate their own assessments about the swap-requesting country. At present, the current practices under the ASEAN+3 process cannot effectively capture emerging problems. For the use of the remaining 80 % of the swap arrangements that is linked with the IMF, the stigma effect may work and things may worsen by using it as it sometimes did for the conventional IMF program. On the other hand, by relaxing the conditions for supports and/or dropping the IMF conditionality, "moral hazard" problems may emerge. This is another reason that the CMIM needs its own surveillance mechanism.

Links with Global Financial Architecture

Regional financial architecture should be more closely linked with the global financial architecture. The 2007–2009 global financial crisis led to new developments in the global financial reforms, such as an extension of international financial institutions, reallocation of IMF quotas, and creation of the Financial Stability Forum. Especially, the reform of the IMF is closely related with the development of the regional financial and monetary cooperation. There are several reform measures of the IMF, which may influence the regional financial arrangement in East Asia. The first is the newly emerged Flexible Credit Line (FCL) that enhanced member countries lending activities by making the IMF lending programs more flexible, streamlining conditionalities. The second is the Precautionary Credit Line (PCL) that requires even a lower standard than FCL and is available for all countries. Moreover, the IMF works with regional institutions more closely in time of crisis. It is worth noting that the European Union (EU) has cooperated closely with the IMF in recent programs for Central and Eastern European countries. The 2010–2011 Greek crisis is also a typical example of cooperation between regional and international institutions.

Since 2008, the development of international and regional financial institutions and provides significant implications for East Asia. When the Asian crisis broke out, there was no regional institution to cooperate with the IMF. As a result, the IMF solely decided the programs and amount of the liquidity support in the region. However, East Asia has created a regional institution that might be capable of providing liquidity supports in time of crisis: CMIM. Therefore, the detailed ways of linking regional architecture, that is, CMIM, with global architecture, that is, various programs of the IMF, need to be developed in the future. Practically, the AMRO

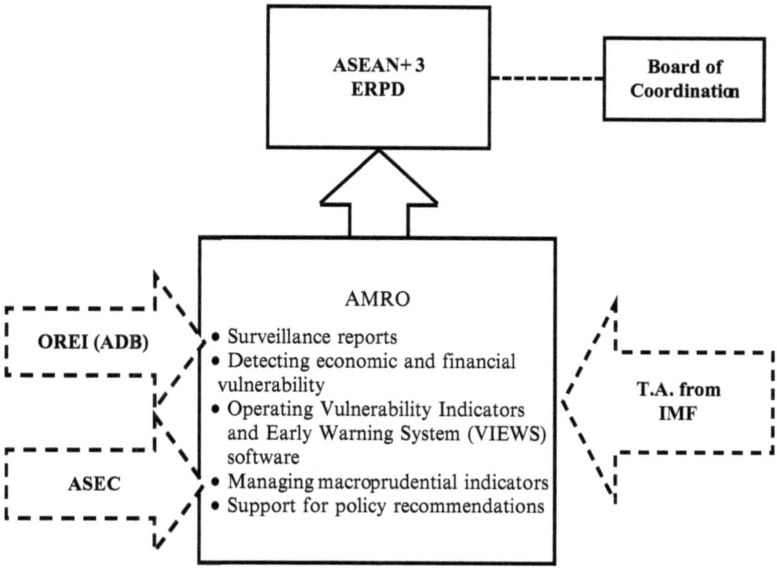

Fig. 5.1 Proposed ASEAN+3 surveillance mechanism. *AMRO* ASEAN+3 Macroeconomic Research Office, *ASEAN* Association of Southeast Asian Nations, *ASEC* ASEAN Secretariat, *EPRD* Economic Policy Review and Dialogue, *IMF* International Monetary Fund, *OREI* Office of Regional Economic Integration, *TA* technical assistance
Source: Park and Oh (2010)

should be an institution that would cooperate closely with the international financial institutions to deal with the provision of liquidity support and design of the program. This implies that the capacity of the AMRO is crucial to perform this kind of cooperative arrangement.

Development of the AMRO

The AMRO will become the first effective regional surveillance mechanism in the region (Fig. 5.1). In order to do that, the AMRO will function not only under the CMIM, but also as the leading institution of the regional financial architecture.

First, AMRO should serve as an institution that leads the policy dialogue mechanism in the region. Given limited financial and human resources inside the unit, a network of government research institutions could be established and the unit could serve as a coordinating agency. It is also expected to serve as a warehouse of information and a provider of warning signals for both individual member countries and the group as a whole. By conducting extensive early warning exercises at the national and regional levels, this unit will identify problems and prepare independent surveillance reports for the members. To avoid duplication of the IMF's Article IV consultation, the unit may participate in IMF surveillance jointly with IMF staff. Combined with country reports submitted by all member countries, this unit's surveillance report will be a compendium report based on its own assessment.

AMRO should also be entitled to conduct preparatory research on future cooperative issues such as exchange rate policy coordination and financial market integration. Macroeconomic volatilities are closely related to inappropriate exchange rate management and fragile financial systems. It therefore cannot be overemphasized that the regional surveillance unit must not only be a watchdog of national macroeconomic and exchange rate policies, but also an overseer of national financial markets, and the links between them and the rest of the world (Wang and Woo 2004).

AMRO will also serve design the activation of CMIM. A proper design of conditionality would be a point of debate. It would be useful to distinguish between technical assistance and financial assistance. There is no reason to discourage competition in the market for technical assistance. Governments should be free to choose the source of technical assistance with the best track record. However, if multiple monetary funds were available, governments facing an imminent crisis would have an incentive to shop around for the most generous assistance and the least onerous conditionality. If the regional monetary fund (or financial arrangement) does not attach IMF-like conditionality, the international financial community might raise the issue of moral hazard. In this regard, relevant but binding policy recommendations should be imposed on borrowing countries. Without an appropriate lending discipline in place, regional financial arrangements would likely be dysfunctional due to the lax supervision of financial assistance.

East Asian economies presently appear to be pursuing financial cooperation in the absence of exchange rate coordination. It is not yet clear whether East Asia will emulate the European experience by adopting some form of monetary integration. However, if East Asia starts monetary integration in the future, the regional surveillance mechanism would have to be structured and managed in order to support the coordinated exchange rate mechanism. As the EU Commission and European Monetary Institute (EMI) served as facilitators to promote economic and monetary integration, East Asia should establish politically independent institutions along with an official policy dialogue process (Table 5.1).

The professionals working at this independent institution should be able to follow up on the decisions of policymakers on integration, and advance common policy objectives and related modalities more adequately by adding their own creative ideas to the policy dialogue group. It is desirable that AMRO will serve as a full-scale regional surveillance mechanism as we discussed in the previous section. This implies that the capacity of AMRO should be close to the par level of the IMF surveillance unit. Moreover the size of liquidity support in the CMIM should be increased since more liquidity supports by the CMIM means higher leverage in the negotiation process of the crisis period with the IMF by designing a crisis-resolution program. A simple and possible way to cooperate in time of regional crisis would be for the CMIM and PCL or FCL to be jointly activated with pre-consultation by AMRO and the IMF. The IMF conditionality in the CMIM should be reduced or

Table 5.1 Historical development of monitoring and surveillance mechanisms in Europe

System	Period	Objects	Monitoring and surveillance institutions	Characteristics
EPU	1950–1958	Trade expansion by securing payment system	Managing Board	Bilateral payment system Multilateral payment system The Board monitors and gives directives
Bretton Woods System & Treaty of Rome	1959–1972	Supporting economic integration by securing fixed exchange-rate system	Monetary Committee Committee of Governors	IMF was more active than regional institutions
Snake System	1973–1978	Maintaining common market and common agricultural policy by reducing bilateral fluctuations and joint-floating against dollar	European Monetary Cooperation Fund Monetary Committee Committee of Governors	National interests were greater than regional interests
EMS	1979–1992	Securing internal stability of exchange rates	Same institutions, but more active	Countries with a strong currency shared the burden of intervention
EMU	1993–present	Introducing single common currency	EMI in the transition period ECB after introduction of the euro	National competences are transferred to the community Binding rules introduced

ECB European Central Bank, *EMI* European Monetary Institute, *EMS* European Monetary System, *EMU* European Monetary Union, *EPU* European Payments Union, *IMF* International Monetary Fund
Source: Park (2004)

eliminated in an appropriate manner, thus enhancing the leverage power of the CMIM. However, this does not mean that two liquidity-supporting programs activate separately. In case of a cooperative program by the CMIM and the IMF, the effectiveness of the liquidity support will increase and the stigma effect of both liquidity supports will be sterilized.

Benefits of International Financial Market Integration

Developments of regional financial and monetary cooperation in East Asia have been mostly related to the objective of crisis prevention. As regional financial and monetary cooperation was initiated after the Asian financial crisis, it is natural for the region to stick to such an objective, not to mention that preventing future crises is vital for all countries in the region. However, as regional financial safety nets become more concrete and complete, other possible objectives of financial and monetary cooperation can be pursued in the future. As discussed in Sect. 2.2, financial and monetary cooperation can make member countries be more accessible to various benefits of international financial market integration. In the long run, Asian economies can substantially enhance welfare levels by pursuing this objective through regional financial and monetary cooperation.

Further developments and deepening of Asian bond market integration through ABMI would naturally work to finance unexploited long-term investment opportunities within the region by recycling saving that will contribute to long run economic growth. Other important benefits of international financial market integration were not previously pursued. Further developments of portfolio diversification within the region or further deepening of cross-border financial assets (especially risky assets) within the region can contribute to diversification of country-specific risks of each member country and to faster long-term growth by promoting more profitable, though riskier, investments. However, the current proposal of regional financial and monetary cooperation of East Asian economies does not deal with such an aspect. This objective should be applied to the global level since current levels of global financial and monetary integration are not enough to provide full benefits of financial and monetary integration to the global economy. While East Asian economies are making an effort to extract more benefits from global integration, we can also pursue regional cooperation to exploit more benefits from regional integration.

5.5 Conclusion and Policy Implications

There have been several developments that have encouraged the formation of a regional financial arrangement in East Asia since the Asian crisis. One development has been the slow progress of the international financial architecture reform. The slow progress has been further complicated by the perception that a new architecture, as it is designed, may not be effective in sustaining global financial stability, nor would it safeguard financial stability in the emerging market economies and developing countries. Thus, it is in the interest of East Asia and other regions to work together to set up its own system of mitigating macroeconomic volatility. In particular, policy dialogue could serve as a vehicle for promoting coherent policy formation at the regional level and at the same time ensuring effective implementation of high quality banking and financial standards.

The three pillars of liquidity assistance, monitoring and surveillance, and exchange rate coordination are essential elements for regional financial and monetary cooperation. However, its development and related institutions will be evolutionary. There has been an emerging consensus that East Asians must join forces to establish regional financial arrangements that will help fend off speculative attacks and, in so doing, stabilize the East Asian financial markets. In order to cope effectively with the instability of capital movements and manage the excess macroeconomic volatility, further efforts are required. At the same time, exchange rate coordination would be required for mitigating the adverse impact of global imbalances and stable international trade of the region. Moreover the financial regulations and prudential measures in the region should be discussed by policymakers in order to reduce the regulation arbitrage. Other initiatives for promoting financial market infrastructure will contribute to financial market development and integration that can provide further benefits to East Asia.

Creating a regional financial institute with a permanent secretariat would help to cultivate support for deeper cooperation on the various issues of financial institution and infrastructure building. Such an institute, made up of a body of experts with agenda setting powers, could promote the process of regional cooperation. Rigorous multilateral surveillance on a regional basis, consistently applied and with associated peer pressure, can help build the domestic financial architecture and ultimately mitigate the excessive macroeconomic volatility. Furthermore, such an institute could be a venue for building a consensus and reflecting regional views in the negotiation process of setting the global financial standards. We believe that the new AMRO will become such an institution that will silence the previous critics of the regional financial arrangement.

References

ASEAN+3 Finance Ministers. (2006). Joint Ministerial Statement. http://www.asean.org/news/asean-statement-communiques/item/the-joint-ministerial-statement-of-the-9th-asean3-finance-ministers-meeting-hyderabad-india-2.

Bergsten, C. F. (2000). A Shanghai Asia Pacific Financial Institute. Unpublished. Washington, DC: Institute for International Economics.

Bhagwati, J. (2004). *In defense of globalization.* New York: Oxford University Press.

Calvo, G., & Mendoza, E. (2000). Rational contagion and the globalization of securitized markets. *Journal of International Economics, 51*, 79–113.

Calvo, G., & Reinhart, C. (2002). Fear of floating. *Quarterly Journal of Economics, 117*, 379–408.

Eichengreen, B. (2008). Exchange rate regime and capital mobility: How much of Swoboda Thesis survives? NBER Working Paper No. 14100.

Feldstein, M., & Horioka, C. (1980). Domestic saving and international capital flows. *The Economic Journal, 90*, 314–329.

Glick, R., & Rose, A. K. (1999). Contagion and trade: Why are currency crises regional? *Journal of International Money and Finance, 18*(4 August), 603–617.

Henning, C. R. (2002). *East Asian financial cooperation. Policy analyses in international economics 68.* Washington, DC: Institute for International Economics.

Ito, T., Ogawa, E., & Sasaki, Y. (1999). Establishment of the East Asian Fund. In: *Stabilization of currencies and financial systems in East Asia and international financial cooperation.* Tokyo: Institute for International Monetary Affairs.

Kaminsky, G. L., & Reinhart, C. M. (2000). On crises, contagion and confusion. *Journal of International Economics, 51*(1), 145–168.

Kandel, E., & Lazear, E. (1992). Peer pressure and partnerships. *Journal of Political Economy, 100*, 801–817.
Kawai, M., & Houser, C. (2008). Evolving ASEAN+3 ERPD: Towards peer reviews or due diligence? In *OECD. Shaping policy reform and peer review in Southeast Asia: Integrating economies amid diversity* (pp. 65–98). Paris: Organisation for Economic Co-operation and Development.
Kim, S., Kim, S. H., & Wang, Y. (2006). Financial integration and consumption risksharing in East Asia. *Japan and the World Economy, 18*(2), 143–157.
Kim, S., Kim, S. H., & Wang, Y. (2007). Saving, investment, and international capital mobility in East Asia. *Japan and the World Economy, 19*(2), 279–291.
Kim, S., & Lee, J-W. (2008). Real and financial integration in East Asia. ADB Working Paper Series on Regional Economic Integration, No. 17. June.
Kim, S., Lee, J.-W., & Park, C.-Y. (2011). Ties binding Asia, Europe, and the USA. *China & World Economy, 19*(1), 24–46.
Kim, S., Lee, J.-W., & Shin, K. (2008). Regional and global financial integration in East Asia. In B. Eichengreen, C. Wyplosz, & Y. Park (Eds.), *China, Asia, and the new world economy* (pp. 168–200). Oxford: Oxford University Press.
Lucas, R. E. (1982). Interest rates and currency prices in a two-country world. *Journal of Monetary Economics, 10*(3), 335–359.
Ma, G., & Remolona, E. (2005). Opening markets through a regional bond fund: Lesson from ABF2. *BIS Quarterly Review*. June. 85–92.
Mendoza, E. (2001). Credit, prices and crashes: Business cycles with a sudden stop. NBER Working Paper No. 8338.
Obstfeld, M. (1994). Risk, diversification, and growth. *American Economic Review, 84*(5), 1310–1329.
Obstfeld, M. (2004). Globalization, macroeconomic performance, and the exchange rates of emerging economies. NBER Working Paper No. 10849.
Obstfeld, M., & Rogoff, K. (1995). Exchange rate dynamics redux. *Journal of Political Economy, 103*(3), 624–660.
Park, Y. (2004). Regional financial integration in East Asia. Unpublished.
Park, Y-J., & Oh, Y. (2010). East Asian financial and monetary cooperation and its prospect: Beyond the CMI. KIEP Working Paper 10-24. Seoul: KIEP.
Park, Y., Park, J., Leung, J., & Sangsubhan, K. (2004). Asian bond market development: rationale and strategies. Unpublished.
Park, Y. C., Wang, Y., & Yang, D. Y. (2008). Regional and multilateral efforts: Institution-building. In J. M. Fanelli (Ed.), *Macroeconomic volatility, institutions and financial architecture, the developing world experience* (pp. 45–72). New York: Palgrave Macmillan.
Wang, Y., & Woo, W. T. (2004). A timely information exchange mechanism, an effective surveillance system, and an improved financial architecture for East Asia. In *Monetary and financial integration in East Asia: The way ahead* (Vol. 2, pp. 426–458). New York: Asian Development Bank and Palgrave Macmillan.

Chapter 6
Promoting Domestic Reforms Through Regionalism

Philippa Dee and Anne McNaughton

Abstract There is a strong presumption among economists that domestic reforms are promoted by regionalism. Yet strong empirical evidence for this proposition is lacking. This chapter examines both the theoretical arguments and empirical evidence on this issue, drawing on the relevant economic, political, and legal literature. The authors argue that in general, the case for reciprocity in domestic reforms is weak. In the one case where a regional agreement appears to have promoted domestic reform—the European Union (EU)—the enforcement mechanisms used by the European Court of Justice played a significant role. But those mechanisms are not unique. Instead, the authors argue that the EU's success was because domestic constituents were empowered to take action against uncompetitive regulation. Thus the EU promoted economic reform in sensitive, behind-the-border areas because it overcame the problem of loss of sovereignty by internalizing the political battle to domestic interests, and yet still provided a non-political frame of reference for the debate.

Keywords ASEAN trade liberalization • EU liberalization • Free trade agreements • Regionalism

P. Dee (✉)
Crawford School of Economics and Government, Australian National University, Canberra, Australia
e-mail: philippa.dee@anu.edu.au

A. McNaughton
Faculty of Law, Australian National University, Canberra, Australia
e-mail: anne.mcnaughton@anu.edu.au

G. Capannelli and M. Kawai (eds.), *The Political Economy of Asian Regionalism*,
DOI 10.1007/978-4-431-54568-2_6, © Asian Development Bank Institute 2014

"This presumption [that international trade is the main vehicle for transmitting reforms and increasing economic freedom] is so ingrained, for economists in particular, that it is hard to know its precise historical origin."

(Gassebner et al. 2008: 1)

"To date, the available, limited, evidence suggests that, with the exception of the European Union, most services policy reform has been unilateral."

(Francois and Hoekman 2010: 678)

6.1 Introduction

As the first quotation above illustrates, there is a strong presumption among economists that trade and economic reform are linked. One particular corollary is that domestic reforms are promoted by regionalism, because regionalism promotes trade. Yet the second quotation above suggests that strong empirical evidence for the second proposition is lacking. The purpose of this chapter is to examine in some detail both the theoretical arguments and empirical evidence on this issue, drawing on the relevant economic, political and legal literatures. It concludes with some proposals on how to use regional institutions to better support domestic reform efforts.

The proposition that domestic reform might be promoted through regionalism can be either a tautology or an impossibility, depending on how the terms are defined. This chapter takes a broad definition of domestic reform, one that is independent of at least some notions of market integration. Domestic reform is defined as behind-the-border reform, and it comprises two key elements:

- contestability—where market competition determines economic outcomes in all circumstances where competition is appropriate; and
- appropriate regulation—where well-designed regulation guides market outcomes in those cases where market forces alone cannot be guaranteed to deliver the best outcomes.

Appropriate regulation is required in cases of market failure, where "natural" monopoly, asymmetric information and/or externalities prevent markets from delivering efficient outcomes. Appropriate regulation may also be required where governments have additional objectives besides efficiency, such as equity, safety, diversity, and so on.

Contestability requires that *market participants* not be able to manipulate the terms of entry into, or operation within, markets to their own advantage by restricting competition. This is the role of competition policy, narrowly defined—to prevent anti-competitive practices by the private sector. But in the Asian region, anti-competitive *government* practices are arguably a much more important impediment to the efficient operation of markets. Thus the objective of domestic reform should be twofold (Dee 2010):

- to remove government legislation, regulation and bureaucratic practice that restricts competition for no good public purpose; and

- to ensure that where government intervention is required to safeguard legitimate objectives (including, but by no means limited to, preventing anti-competitive practices by the private sector), the government intervention is no more burdensome than necessary to achieve those objectives.

This chapter also needs a definition of regionalism. It takes an equally broad definition of this concept—closer regional interaction. In the economic sphere, this closer interaction can be market-driven or institution-driven. Over the last three decades of the twentieth century, Asian economic interaction was primarily market-driven. In the first decade of the twenty-first century, trade agreements have begun to have sufficient "bite" to promote institution-driven economic interaction (Baldwin 2006). But trade agreements are not the only institutions that promote closer regional interaction. There is an alpha-numeric soup of institutional arrangements—Association of Southeast Asian Nations (ASEAN), ASEAN+3, ASEAN+6, East Asia Summit (EAS), ASEAN Regional Forum (ARF), Asia–Pacific Economic Cooperation (APEC)—that are designed to promote closer interaction, not just for economic but also for political and security purposes.

So the question implicit in the title of this chapter has two possible interpretations. The first is whether market-led regionalism creates sufficient dynamics to promote domestic reform, without the assistance of regional institutions. However, in very open economies it may be difficult in practice to distinguish unilateral reform that has been spurred by market-led regionalism from that spurred by other factors (such as purely domestic competitive factors). So this interpretation of the question borders on the tautological. The second interpretation is whether any of the current raft of regional institutions can further promote domestic reform. This chapter concentrates on the second interpretation—whether domestic reform is better promoted by regional institutions, rather than unilaterally by market factors (including market-led regionalism).

The next section of this chapter examines the theoretical arguments on why formal regional agreements might usefully promote reform. The arguments are both political and economic. All have been used at various times to argue that formal regional agreements help to promote trade reform *at* the border. Some of these arguments extend to reforms behind the border.

The following section examines the empirical evidence, including case studies and econometric evidence from both the economic and political/legal literature. Some evidence is circumstantial—looking at what has happened in countries that have entered regional arrangements—and some is more direct—looking in detail at the commitments made in regional agreements. The empirical evidence tends to support the finding in the second quotation above—that few regional arrangements other than the European Union (EU) have successfully promoted domestic reform.

The chapter next examines the reasons for these findings. Various writers have offered a range of reasons why non-EU trade agreements have not promoted domestic reform. This chapter also examines the political and legal literature for the fundamental reasons why the EU has succeeded. Contrary to some popular conceptions, the key is not, or not solely, the existence of a supra-national institutional framework. This is fortunate, since is it widely agreed that the Asian region has no taste for such a framework. But other elements of the recipe for success are transferrable. The final section of this chapter therefore makes suggestions for how Asian regional institutions could internalize some of these lessons on how to promote domestic reform.

6.2 Theoretical Arguments

Political Economy Arguments

One central reason from the political economy literature as to why trade agreements can promote domestic reform is that some binding external mechanism helps to overcome the time-inconsistency problem formalized by Kydland and Prescott (1977). This problem is the inability of political institutions to bind themselves for future periods given that they are exposed to the strategic behavior of private agents (for example, electoral bribes and lobbying by vested interests). So what governments say now that they will do may not be what they actually do in the future—they cannot make credible commitments. In these circumstances, governments may agree *ex ante* to restrict their powers in the public interest. This explains why governments agree, for example, to delegate monetary policy to independent central banks.

It is also why governments may not rely on unilateral action to achieve either trade reform or behind-the-border reform, but rather bind themselves in a formal treaty with trading partners. This rationale is recognized in the legal literature (for example, Pauwelyn 2005) as well as in the economic and political economy literature (for example, Martin 2001). Legal scholars tend to stress that such arrangements also protect the commitments from the "instability" of "representative democracy"—in other words, the problem of strategic behavior is not just a problem of vested interest groups but a problem of democracy more broadly. Thus, for example, Tallberg (2002) uses the time inconsistency problem to explain why the EU member states have chosen to delegate authority to supranational institutions beyond direct democratic control.

An interesting variant of the commitment argument is that reform can occur within a regional trade arrangement as a precursor to the "main event"—World Trade Organization (WTO) membership. Ethier (1998, 1999, 2001) has formalized variants of this argument. His models are explicit attempts to capture some of the salient features of "third-wave" or "new age" preferential trade agreements (PTAs). These agreements first emerged in the 1990s and were not only about merchandise trade, but also included areas such as services, investment, competition policy, government procurement, e-commerce, labor and environmental standards.

Ethier observes that many new age agreements are between small "outside" countries that are not yet members of the world trading system,[1] and larger "inside" countries that are. The small, outside countries want to reform their internal economies so that they can be accepted as members of the global trading system. Ethier asserts that the sign of successful reform is whether these countries attract foreign direct investment. Their problem is how to signal a credible commitment to reform in advance.

The outside country's solution is to sign a PTA with an inside country involving enough trading concessions to the insider country so that it will in turn have an incentive to act as an enforcer and retaliate if the outside country deviates from its reform commitment. The aim is not necessarily to receive enormous concessions from the inside country in return. All that is required is a small trade concession, so that multinationals have an incentive to locate in the outside country. Ethier (2001) also examines in detail the incentives of the large inside country to accede to such an arrangement, even in preference to pursuing further multilateral reform.

Finally, he shows that a world equilibrium on which small countries compete for investment in this fashion is beneficial, because it internalizes an externality. The global interest calls for successful reform to be as widespread as possible, but if there are agglomeration economies, then multinationals will want to cluster their foreign investments together. A global web of bilateral PTAs, initiated by outside countries' competition for investment, internalizes the externality.

This theoretical framework explains a number of United States (US) bilateral trade agreements as "dress rehearsals" for WTO accession. But note that it is essentially WTO accession that is driving the reform, not the PTA per se. This point is recognized by Lewis (2008), for example, who argues that the Lao People's Democratic Republic (Lao PDR) undertook its domestic reforms unilaterally to link its domestic policies and laws to proposed WTO commitments (despite that fact that Lao PDR also signed a bilateral trade agreement with the US). Hence it was WTO membership, and its protections of a rules-based trading system, that drove the reform.

A second reason often cited by economists, but rooted in political economy, is that concession trading can somehow help to neutralize domestic vested interests. It is difficult for governments to build support for liberalization in the face of pressures from vested interests, particularly those in import-competing industries. Participation in regional arrangements may help to build support for liberalization, because exporters who would gain from greater access into overseas markets can counter the pressure from those in import-competing industries, who would lose from lower import protection at home. This argument is found in World Bank (2000) and in Hoekman and Mattoo (2011), for example.

A third rationale, closely related to the commitment argument, is the "skyhook" argument. Governments may be happy to take decisions in the public interest that upset particular vested interests, but find it convenient to blame third parties so as to

[1] Ethier (2001) identifies these as countries that until recently adopted basically-autarkic, anti-market policies.

escape electoral punishment (for example, Tallberg 2002). The third parties may be trading partner governments (in PTAs) or supranational institutions (in the EU).

A final line of argument is one that stresses the administrative efficiency of taking detailed reform proposals out of the political sphere. Politicians (as principals) assign the detailed rule-making to agents, who then develop and apply their policy-relevant expertise, saving politicians' time for more general policy decisions. This argument has been used to explain the delegation of powers to supranational institutions in the EU (Tallberg 2002), and the delegation of trade negotiation and rule-making to trade officials in Geneva (Pauwelyn 2005). In the context of domestic reform, it begs the question of why delegation to an external agent is preferable to delegation to a domestic bureaucracy that is, in at least some political systems, supposed to be apolitical.

There is at least one political economy argument for why a multilateral or plurilateral forum may be inimical to domestic reform. If the reform takes place multilaterally, the possibility of exchanging concessions across sectors in the future may induce countries to withhold reforms today. Harms et al. (2003) claim that this explains the low level of WTO commitments by some countries in financial services, because the financial services agreement was concluded in a separate single-sector negotiation after the Uruguay Round, and participants must have had a reasonable expectation of future multi-sectoral negotiations. They also note that there is a general incentive to retain negotiation coin, and forgo the benefits of unilateral liberalization, by countries that face high entry barriers (including behind-the-border barriers) into their overseas export markets and have sufficient bargaining power to extract concessions from their trading partners.

Economic Arguments

Bagwell and Staiger (1999) show that multilateral trade commitments can help internalize an externality associated with tariff protection. Countries imposing the tariffs can shift some of the cost of those tariffs onto their trading partners because their tariffs can alter world prices and generate a terms of trade decline for their trading partners. Conversely, unilateral reform can generate a terms of trade decline for the reforming country, preventing it from reaping all of the gains from reform. Bagwell and Staiger show that the WTO principles of reciprocity and non-discrimination help to neutralize the world price implications of tariff negotiations and thus allow efficient outcomes. They also note, however, that exceptions to the most-favored nation principle for the purpose of creating a PTA revive the local-price externality, thus frustrating the ability of a multilateral system governed by reciprocity to deliver an efficient outcome.

It is not clear that this terms-of-trade argument extends beyond tariff reforms. Dee and Sidorenko (2006) point out that empirically, the terms of trade effects of unilateral behind-the-border reforms are likely to be minimal or even positive, so trade agreements may not be necessary to ensure efficient outcomes. In the context of cross-border trade in services (rather than goods), Francois and Hoekman (2010) argue that the WTO, with its principles of reciprocity and non-discrimination, may not be sufficient. They cite the work of Antràs and Staiger (2007), who look at the problem of the relationship-specific investments that might be required between domestic and foreign firms involved in the trade of customized inputs (for example, producer services), and the opportunity for post-contractual opportunism that this provides. If firms cannot credibly commit to a price in advance, the volume of trade will be too low from the perspective of international efficiency when governments set trade policy unilaterally. By expanding the volume of trade in the customized input, trade agreements can potentially move countries toward the international efficiency frontier. But this beneficial outcome only comes about if governments have no political economy (distributional) motives, but are only concerned with maximizing real national income (efficiency).[2]

It is possible to find arguments for why trade may be inimical to domestic reform. Gassebner et al. (2008) argue instead that freer trade may reinforce a *status quo* bias in domestic policies. Freer trade will benefit the specific factor in the exporting sector. But diversity of economic institutions (domestic reform in one country, lack of reform in the other) may be the source of the gains from trade. If the specific factor in the exporting sector is politically influential, they may lobby for trade reform but against domestic reform, even if the two together would generate a higher benefit to the economy as a whole. They cite India as a possible example of this phenomenon. This argument would also explain why many of the regional trade agreements between developing countries in the East Asian region are heavy on merchandise trade reform but (the titles of chapters in the trade agreements notwithstanding) light on other types of reform (Ochiai et al. 2010).

A different kind of economic argument is a "spillovers" argument articulated by Kawai and Wignaraja (2011) and Czaga (2004), among others. Kawai and Wignaraja (2011) argue that East Asia's market-led integration and its development of production networks and region-wide supply chains has begun to require not just further liberalization of trade and foreign direct investment (FDI), but also the harmonization of policies, rules and standards governing trade and investment, as well as the protection of investment and intellectual property rights. Thus liberalization at the border has begun to create pressure for harmonization behind the border. They argue that Asian policy makers view PTAs as vehicles to support this harmonization effort. They are thus part of the policy framework to deepen production networks and supply chains formed by global multinationals and emerging Asian firms. The Japanese support for the development of an ASEAN Economic Community through its funding of the Economic Research Institute for ASEAN and East Asia is consistent with this idea.

Kawai and Wignaraja (2011) also note that the region's response to the Asian financial crisis has demonstrated how Asian economies can cooperate to address common challenges. The key product of that cooperation was the Chiang Mai

[2] The argument of Bagwell and Staiger (1999) in the context of simple tariff reform does not depend on the motives of government.

Initiative—a multilateral currency swap arrangement among ASEAN; the People's Republic of China (PRC); Hong Kong, China; Japan; and the Republic of Korea to manage regional short-term liquidity problems. Nevertheless, this arrangement was not used during the recent global financial crisis. The authors also note that Asian countries have been attracted to PTAs because of slow progress in the WTO Doha negotiations. In those negotiations, developed countries are being asked to liberalize agriculture while developing countries are being asked to liberalize industrial goods and services. To date the negotiations have focused on agriculture and industrials, with not much effort being devoted to behind-the-border issues.

6.3 Case Studies and Broad-Brush Econometric Evidence

Given the variety of theoretical arguments why regional institutions may promote domestic reform, one would expect the empirical evidence to bear them out. The purpose of this section is to canvas the empirical literature.

Case Studies

Individual case studies establish that regionalism is neither necessary nor sufficient for domestic reform. Several examples can be cited to show that formal regional agreements are not necessary.

Martin (2001) shows that while East Asian reformers have successfully made many of the reforms to domestic and trade policies required to secure export and income growth, there has been no single approach to achieving this. The PRC's reform process focused mainly on unilateral reform and WTO accession. Martin argues that several East Asian transition economies (Cambodia, Lao PDR, Myanmar, and Viet Nam) used accession to the ASEAN free trade agreements as part of their reform strategy, though he notes that some of the exceptions allowed under the original liberalization commitments were excessive. He notes that Viet Nam's and Lao PDR's bilaterals with the United States required more extensive reforms. But as noted above, these were essentially dress rehearsal for WTO accession. WTO accession has also been a key driver of unilateral reform in Cambodia. Francois (2005) argues that EU accession would not exert much pressure on Turkey to restructure its transport, because Turkey has to a large extent undertaken the required reforms and put in place the required regulatory frameworks unilaterally.

While these examples show PTA membership or accession is not necessary for domestic reform, the experiences of Canada and Mexico show that it is not sufficient. Barichello (2004) argues that the effect of North American Free Trade Agreement (NAFTA) or its predecessor Canada–US Trade Agreement (CUSTA) on domestic agricultural policy reform in Canada has been minimal. He notes that the negotiations were conducted specifically to avoid sensitive non-tariff barriers. In one instance CUSTA actually led to an increase in protection from non-tariff measures. In contrast, the Uruguay Round Agreement was associated much more closely with actual or potential policy reforms. And there was significant unilateral reform in the form of substantial cuts in budgetary support, driven by the domestic imperative to eliminate budget deficits.

Francois (1997) notes that Mexico's reform process started well before NAFTA. Starting with its WTO accession, Mexico began a major restructuring program in the 1980s. This included reforms of trade, intellectual property rights, foreign exchange restrictions, foreign investment, and privatization. Francois also notes that formal consultation mechanisms with the United States were also in place before the NAFTA negotiations. Graham and Wada (2000) identify a trend break in the pattern of US FDI into Mexico in 1989. Over 1966–1988, the stock of US FDI grew at 3.1 % a year; over 1989–1998 it grew at 5.6 % a year. They argue that this was not caused by NAFTA or the series of bilateral deals between the US and Mexico that preceded it, but as a response to Mexico's unilateral reforms.

More tellingly, Tornell et al. (2004) document how Mexico failed to attain rapid growth in the 1990s, and that after 2001 its gross domestic product (GDP) and exports stagnated. They argue that the lack of growth cannot be blamed on NAFTA or the other reforms that were implemented. The source of the problem was a lack of structural reform after 1995, as well as Mexico's response to the peso crisis—a deterioration in contract enforceability and an increase in non-performing loans.[3] While PTAs may be neither necessary nor sufficient for domestic reform, what is the preponderance of empirical evidence? It comes in two types—broad-brush econometric exercises, and more detailed comparisons of PTA commitments with domestic policies.

Broad-Brush Econometric Evidence

Econometric Evidence from Economic Papers

The empirical findings of Gassebner et al. (2008) are in line with their theoretical arguments. Using a panel of 144 countries over 1995–2006, they find that empirically, economic reforms are not driven by greater trade openness. They also find that reforms are not habit-forming—instead there is a *status quo* bias. But they do find evidence of the importance of reforms in other countries. The important mechanism is not international trade, but geographical and cultural proximity. Countries that are more integrated in the process of the global exchange of information also tend to be more reform-minded. Finally, they find that EU membership also helps.

[3] Francois (1997) notes that the crisis did not lead to the re-imposition of exchange controls or a dramatic increase in protection, in part because of strong intervention by the United States and the International Monetary Fund—in this qualified sense, NAFTA did provide a policy anchor to the reforms already in place. But NAFTA had not led to further structural reforms.

Harms et al. (2003) examine empirically what drives (the lack of) liberalization commitments in financial services trade (an example of a behind-the-border commitment made through a trade agreement). They find empirical evidence to support the idea that members of international trade coalitions in agriculture and textiles held back financial services commitments, possibly to use them as bargaining chips in future negotiations.

Econometric Evidence from Legal and Political Papers

The EU is supposedly the archetypical example of a formal regional agreement that has generated domestic reform. What does the EU-focused literature say? For empirical evidence on this score, we need to turn to the legal rather than the economic literature, for the following reason.

The EU Treaty is a negative list agreement—everything is liberalized unless otherwise stated. This is in contrast to positive list agreements, such as the specific commitments of the General Agreement on Trade in Services (GATS) under the WTO, where nothing is liberalized unless otherwise stated. Furthermore, the EU Treaty covers a wide range of areas and unlike most negative list PTAs, does not have detailed annex lists of exceptions and reservations,[4] though it allows general exceptions on grounds such as public morality, public policy, public security or public health (similar to the Article XX exceptions of the General Agreement on Tariffs and Trade (GATT), though in the EU Treaty the details vary depending on the area covered).

Therefore, one measure of actual reform in the EU is provided by the enforcement of these original broad commitments through dispute resolution, rather than by the gradual accumulation of more ambitious commitments. And in the early years, despite their obligations under the Treaties, Member states were not dismantling trade barriers, either at or behind their borders (McNaughton 2011), so dispute resolution was the key mechanism by which actual reform took place. Seminal empirical work in this area is by Stone Sweet and Brunell (1998).

They conceive of European integration as a response to the demands of those individuals and companies who need European rules (that is, a more reformed regime), and those who are advantaged by European law and practices compared with national law and practices. Thus from a legal perspective, they argue that integration depends on the development of more liberal rules to govern transnational

[4] Becoming a member of the EU is like becoming a member of a club: the state does not get to pick and choose which parts of the treaties it will bind itself to. However, in particular instances—the United Kingdom's and Northern Ireland's refusal to adopt the euro, for example—*all* the Member States agree upon the primary provisions of EU law in relation to the euro *and then* they all agree to a Protocol under which, in this case, the United Kingdom and Northern Ireland can "opt in" at a later stage, upon notifying the Council of Ministers of their intention to do so. So in an EU context, the exercise of state sovereignty and the adoption of treaty provisions operate differently from in "mainstream" public international law, including that of the WTO and regional trade agreements.

activities, the capacity of supranational organizations to respond to those demands, and a stable and effective means of resolving legal disputes.

Furthermore, they argue that to the extent that the legal system actually removed national barriers to exchange within the EU (a process known in legal circles as *negative integration*, and in trade circles roughly equivalent to the adoption of negative list liberalization commitments that immediately require the elimination of all non-conforming measures), it put pressure on governments to adopt EU market regulations (known in legal circles as *positive integration*, and in trade circles roughly equivalent to the development of EU directives and other secondary legislation to provide a reformed behind-the-border regulatory structure, such as through harmonization, to ensure that the benefits of liberalization were realized).[5]

To test this proposition, Stone Sweet and Brunell (1998) undertake regression analysis over the period 1961–1992 to test whether the extent of transnational dispute settlement (measured by the annual number of so-called Article 177 references, whose significance is explained in a later section) is influenced by the level of transnational activity (measured by annual levels of intra-EU trade) and the number of European rules (measured by the annual number of directives and regulations promulgated by the European Commission). Note that according to the European Economic Community Treaty, all national measures restricting trade were required to be abolished by the end of 1969, and by virtue of the doctrine of direct effect initiated in 1963 (the significance of which is also discussed later), traders could then ask national judges not to apply such measures. Given the time period covered by their regressions, it seems that the argument is a twofold one. Where trade was already significant, traders had an incentive to ensure that negative integration actually occurred, and hence mounted dispute action when they perceived that it had not. As the negative integration further spurred trade, this first incentive was strengthened. It also provided pressure to create additional directives and regulations to further promote transnational activity (though econometrically the authors do not correct for the resulting endogeneity of either their measure of intra-EU trade or European rules), and thus further dispute settlement to enforce the additional rules.

They find that both variables have a significant positive effect on dispute settlement. However, adding EU rules to the regression does not explain a great deal more of the variation in dispute settlement activity than trade volumes alone (the adjusted R squared in both cases is 0.92). Thus it might appear that additional rules and directives have not generated much additional reform. This does not mean that behind-the-border reform has not occurred. The original Treaty itself contained commitments across a broad range of behind-the-border matters. In fact, Stone Sweet and Brunell (1998) present data on both the extent and subject matter of dispute resolution activity over time. They show that in the 1971–1975 period, more than half the references concerned just two sectors—the free movement of goods and agriculture. In the 1991–1995 period, these two areas accounted for only 27 % of total references, while areas such as establishment (that is, commercial presence), transport, competition, social provisions, social security, taxes and the environment had grown in relative importance.

[5] See Stone Sweet (2010) for a summary in precisely these terms.

What the finding does suggest is that it was the actions of individuals involved in trade that drove the liberalization. The activity of the European Commission in generating additional directives and regulations was much less important (though still statistically significant). In fact, the use of directives reached its peak between 1986 and 1992, and thereafter the Commission found it increasingly difficult to promote integration through direct legislation (McNaughton and Furlong 2008).

Pitarakis and Tridimas (2003) undertake much more careful econometric analysis, paying particular attention to directions of causality (and hence the endogeneity of intra-EU trade). They confirm that legal challenges to instances of incompatibility between EU law and national law (a process they call legal integration) has significantly boosted EU trade. Interestingly, Carrubba and Murrah (2005) also find that public support for EU integration and public political awareness also boost the use of the legal system to support economic integration.

Not only has the subject matter of challenges to national legislation become broader over time, so too has the legal interpretation of what constitutes a regulatory impediment to economic integration. Because the Treaty obligations are based on the principle of negative integration, (that is, the removal of barriers to trade) and are broad-brush, it has been through judicial interpretation and the accretion of case law that regulatory barriers have been defined. Barnard (2010) documents how a gradual widening of interpretation has occurred across all the key pillars of EU integration—free movement of goods, free movement of services (including establishment), free movement of persons, and free movement of capital. Interpretations initially focused on "non-discrimination", but the case law then widened to include barriers to "market access"—regulatory measures that may not explicitly discriminate against foreign sources of goods, services, people or capital, but which nevertheless impede their access. Most recently, the concept has widened even further to any measure that is a "restriction on" or "obstacle to" free movement.

In the area of goods, under the so-called *Dassonville* formula, for example, "all trading rules" that are "capable of hindering, directly or indirectly, actually, or potentially" intra-EU trade are considered as having an effect equivalent to quantitative restrictions, and are therefore prohibited. The jurisprudence has also tackled the problem of goods having to meet the regulatory requirements of more than one regulator. The *Cassis de Dijon* decision replaces dual regulation of a product (by home and host states) with single (home state) regulation, which the host country is required to respect under the principle of mutual recognition. Under this principle there is a *presumption* of the equivalence of the regulatory measures.

A wide variety of national rules have been judged to be restrictions on the freedom to provide services—authorization requirements, translation requirements, requirements to swear an oath of allegiance, maximum or minimum staffing levels, minimum fees, rules regulating gambling, and advertising restrictions.[6] In the case of people movement, the interpretation is now even wider—there is no longer a requirement for the movement to be linked to economic activity.

[6]Note, however, that with the final version of the recent Services Directive, the EU has stopped short of allowing the regulation in the country of origin to automatically prevail when services are traded cross-border (McNaughton 2011).

The original Treaty provisions on the movement of capital were weaker that those elsewhere, because capital movements were seen to be closely linked to the stability of economic and monetary policy. It was not until 1992 (with the advent of the Single Market) that capital movements were finally liberalized, and not until 1995 that barriers were allowed to be the subject of transnational dispute settlement actions (and thus subject to judicial interpretation) in the same way as barriers to goods, people, or services. But the jurisprudence has developed along similar lines to that for services. The free movement of capital was a condition of entry into the first stage of monetary union.

6.4 Evidence from Examining PTAs

The above econometric evidence is relatively broad-brush—it tests for links between trade and domestic reform, without looking systematically at the influence of regional trade agreements. A great deal of literature examines the effects of having a PTA in place. A relatively small but growing literature looks beyond the existence of PTAs, to examine the effects of their detailed provisions. We now consider each type of evidence in turn.

Econometric Evidence from Looking at the Existence of PTAs

A vast literature examines empirically the link between the existence (or much more rarely, the content) of PTAs and measures of economic performance. The most well-known framework is the gravity model, which explains bilateral flows of merchandise trade, and is often used to test for the influence of having a PTA in place. But to the extent that merchandise trade flows are affected by the presence of PTAs, they are likely to be driven in the first instance by commitments on border trade measures such as tariffs, as much as by any commitments on behind-the-border reforms. So this literature is not the best source of evidence on the existence of behind-the-border reform commitments in PTAs.

The gravity model framework and its successors have also been used to explain bilateral FDI. This evidence is more likely to indicate the presence and effectiveness of behind-the-border reforms, because at least some of the key barriers to FDI, both pre- and post-establishment, operate behind the border. Unfortunately, there is little comparable evidence on bilateral services trade, which is governed by a raft of behind-the-border regulation, because there is little bilateral data available on services trade flows.

The study of FDI that probably comes closest to establishing a link between PTAs and domestic reform is Park and Park (2008). They argue that while PTA membership can be an important factor in attracting FDI, it cannot be a sufficient condition—PTA membership should be accompanied by domestic reform measures. This is essentially an empirical test of Ethier's argument that was summarized above. But they also say that PTA membership works by being a commitment device for the domestic reform, so it is the domestic reform that is attracting the FDI, not the PTA membership. They show that both reform and PTA membership boost FDI, but do not examine empirically the interaction between reform and PTA membership.

Dee (2008) does a careful mapping of PTA provisions on cross-border trade in services, investment and the movement of people, and looks at their impact on FDI. She uses a specification of the behavior of FDI taken from theoretical models that jointly explain patterns of trade and FDI, and allow for complex network patterns of both. She finds evidence that patterns of FDI (and trade by implication) in the Asian region are driven by fundamentals, in a way that makes use of fine divisions of comparative advantage, but is also subject to considerations of economies of scale and transport costs. This is in contrast to investment patterns in some other regions (such as in Latin America, where distance and risk considerations are found to dominate). The resulting network patterns of investment in Asia do not appear to have been driven by the investment and services provisions of PTAs signed with the bilateral providers of FDI. But the network nature of regional investments in Asia means that individual members have been insulated from any investment diversion when their FDI source countries have signed PTAs with third countries. This is because the investment that the sources make in third countries can be a general equilibrium complement to bilateral investment within the overall Asian network. So PTAs are seen as being neither a threat nor a promise to FDI in the region.

Many more such studies of the effects of PTA membership on trade and investment flows can be cited. But most only look at the existence of PTA membership, and do not distinguish the behind-the-border features, as Dee (2008) does. And at best, the evidence these studies provide is only circumstantial.

Evidence from Looking at the Detailed Provisions of PTAs

It is not possible to tell whether PTAs have promoted domestic reforms, simply by looking at the PTA commitments themselves. This is because:

- PTA commitments may simply reproduce commitments made in the WTO; and
- even when they go beyond WTO commitments, they may still lag actual practice.

It is incredibly time-consuming for outsiders (that is, those outside of the trade negotiation fraternity) to compare PTA commitments with WTO commitments. It is not sufficient to look at chapter titles, nor even the broad content of the chapters in each agreement, because the devil is in the detail—particularly in the detailed annexes of reservations and exceptions, as well as in the product classifications used to describe the goods and services for which commitments are being made. Further, in some chapters, such as those on intellectual property, the language is highly technical and legalistic, and difficult for non-specialists to understand. In other chapters, the commitments being made are "soft" (for example on a "best endeavors" basis), so it is not at all clear that they should be counted as substantial commitments. One comprehensive comparison of a single PTA, the Australia–US Free Trade Agreement, with the WTO commitments of its two partner countries confirms that a great deal of the PTA was already committed in the WTO (Dee 2005). A more selective comparison, limited to services commitments, made for a number of East Asian Free Trade Agreements comes to a similar conclusion, particularly for the less developed members (Fink and Molinuevo 2007).

It is even more time consuming to compare PTA commitments with actual practice. The tariff schedules of most countries are publicly available, so it is reasonably straightforward to compare PTA tariff commitments with actual practice. But for virtually all behind-the-border areas, actual practice is defined in a complex web of legislation, regulation, and formal and "informal" bureaucratic practice. Collecting information on all the strands of this web is a truly major undertaking. As will be seen, there is growing evidence that PTA commitments can lag actual practice, sometimes by a considerable margin, particularly in developing countries. Accordingly, it is not possible to take exercises that just look at provisions (for example, Fink and Molinuevo 2007; Kawai and Wignaraja 2011; Plummer 2007) to impute actual reform.

Studies that have made systematic comparisons of PTA commitments with either WTO commitments or actual practice are not yet comprehensive, but are slowly growing in number. This section will concentrate on reporting comparisons that have been made for commitments in services and investment. In part, this is because these areas are where most comparisons have been made to date. Nevertheless, the commitments in services are highly relevant to the broader issue of whether PTAs promote domestic reform. This is because restrictions on trade in services usually take the form of domestic regulation, as services tend to be highly regulated, reflecting a variety of important public policy objectives (Czaga 2004).

The services agenda (broadly defined, and including commercial presence) is also aligns relatively closely with the revealed integration objectives in the East Asian region. The ASEAN Economic Community Blueprint—a document outlining the priorities for economic integration in that region—contains reasonably "hard" targets for services, investment, and transport and information infrastructure, while those in areas such as competition policy, consumer protection and intellectual property rights are weaker and/or on a best endeavors basis. Kawai and Wignaraja (2011) stress the importance in the East Asian region for harmonizing the policies, rules and standards governing trade and investment. But harmonization is an agenda that even the EU has not achieved, having moved instead to the weaker and more decentralized principle of mutual recognition.

6.4.0.1 Comparing PTA Commitments with WTO Commitments

Roy et al. (2006) compare the commitments undertaken by 29 WTO members (counting the EC as one) for cross-border supply and commercial presence in services in 28 PTAs negotiated since 2000, and compare these with both the prevailing GATS commitments and the Doha Round offers at the time of those countries.

The authors find that PTAs appear to offer limited value added over GATS disciplines in the areas of rules governing safeguard mechanisms, subsidies, domestic regulation and the like. Their main contribution appears to be in their levels of commitments. A more detailed summary is given in Chap. 9 of this volume. Overall, the authors conclude (p. 33) that "PTAs generally have provided for significant improvements over GATS commitments, sometimes even leading to real liberalization of the market."

Fink and Jensen (2009) also examine the services commitments in PTAs negotiated in the 1990s and 2000s. They come to a similar conclusion to Roy et al. (2006)—in areas where there are no WTO disciplines, there tend not to be rules in PTAs either (safeguards, subsidies, procurement, domestic regulation). They also find that the tendency is for PTAs to have more commitments in sectors where countries have also made more extensive commitments in the GATS. Sensitive sectors such as health, transport and financial services as well as the movement of natural services suppliers tend to be subject to the fewest commitments.

But Adlung and Morrison (2010) have looked at evidence of where the services provisions in PTAs fall short of the same countries' GATS commitments. They find that instances of such "negative preferences" can be found in most recent agreements, including those involving some of the largest WTO members. Of the 56 PTAs whose contents (including sectoral classification) are compared with GATS commitments, 46 (or 80 %) contain some form of GATS-minus commitments in either their horizontal or sectoral sections. The authors also document some of the GATS-minus components in three particular agreements—the Economic Partnership Agreement between the EU and the CARIFORUM States, the AUSFTA agreement between Australia and the United States, and the PRC–ASEAN Agreement. They conjecture that such GATS-minus commitments are mutually conceded in "sensitive" sectors or tacitly accepted in view of "side-payments" in what they call non-WTO currency (including development finance).

Comparing PTA Commitments with Actual Practice

One recent comparison of PTA commitments with actual practice has capitalized on a pre-existing database of actual regulatory practice that was compiled for a different purpose. Barth et al. (2006) make use of a database on actual regulatory practice in banking as it stood around 2000, as reported in responses to a detailed World Bank survey. The database had been used previously to assess the impact of that regulation on banking performance (for example, Barth et al. 2004). In the more recent exercise, Barth et al. (2006) compare regulatory practice with actual WTO commitments in the financial sector for 123 WTO members.

The authors find significant differences between commitments and actual practice. A more detailed summary is given in Chap. 9 of this volume. In general, the authors find many instances where WTO commitments are significantly less liberal than actual practice. They also find instances where WTO commitments are more liberal than actual practice, particularly in developed countries.

As evidence about whether PTAs promote real liberalization, the findings are merely circumstantial. However, if WTO commitments lag actual practice by a significant margin, then even if PTAs improve significantly on WTO commitments, they may still themselves lag actual practice. Furthermore, if actual practice lags WTO commitments, as it appears to in a few cases, then there is clearly an enforcement problem that may also carry over to PTA commitments. One reason for the enforcement problem in a WTO context may be that trade partner countries are not equipped to check the compliance of all other WTO members. Such a monitoring problem may be less severe in a PTA context. But another reason for an enforcement problem may be that trade commitments are made by trade negotiators who are divorced from what is really going on in their own countries. This problem may well carry over to PTAs, especially in countries where problems of coordination among different government ministries are endemic.

Some recent, much more comprehensive evidence along similar lines is cited by Hoekman and Mattoo (2011). They report on research by Borchert et al. (2010) that has collected information on actual policies in the major services sectors of 102 countries—78 developing countries and 24 Organisation for Economic Co-operation and Development (OECD) countries. This information has been compared with GATS commitments for the 93 WTO members in the sample. The comparison shows that there is a very significant gap between applied and "bound" policies (the commitments) because most services liberalization around the world has been undertaken unilaterally. The Uruguay commitments are on average 2.3 times more restrictive than currently applied policies. Borchert et al. (2010) also look at the Doha Round offers made by 62 WTO members. They find that the best offers submitted so far improve on current GATS commitments by about 10 %, but remain on average twice as restrictive as actual policies.

According to Hoekman and Mattoo (2011), there are some PTAs that have induced significant market opening. They cite the example of the liberalization of telecommunications in several Central American countries as a result of the Central America Free Trade Agreement (CAFTA) agreement with the United States. But their general assessment is that although recent PTAs have wider sectoral coverage of services, they do not appear to have induced significant change in applied policies.

Roy et al. (2006) also attempt to assess whether PTA commitments lead to real liberalization. They do not make direct comparisons with regulatory practice, but look for instances where PTA commitments are phased in over time, using the phasing mechanism as an indication that real liberalization is taking place. They note that the group of countries making such phased commitments is fairly widespread, although it appears that financial services and telecommunications dominate. Most phase-out commitments have been contracted by countries as part of a PTA with the United States, although not exclusively.

Dee (2011) tracks actual policy changes in four services sectors in the ten ASEAN countries between 2008 and 2010, and gains some insight into how much has been driven by commitments under the ASEAN Framework Agreement on Services (AFAS). A brief summary of the policy changes affecting trade in medical, health, banking, and insurance services in ASEAN countries during 2008–2010 is shown in Tables 6.1 and 6.2. The table shows that there has been at least some progress in all four sectors.

Table 6.1 ASEAN's progress in liberalizing trade in healthcare services, 2008–2010

	Medical professionals	Health services
Brunei Darussalam	None	None
Cambodia	New mutual recognition agreement signed with ASEAN countries in 2009	None
Indonesia	Law no. 44/2009 covers medical professionals for hospitals. Hospitals can employ foreign medical professionals, but the employment must be intended for the purpose of knowledge and technology transfers. This rules out foreigners in unskilled positions. Permenkes no. 028 issued on 4 January 2011 says clinics cannot hire foreign healthcare workers. Foreign equity limits for medical and dental clinics (specialist only) have been raised from 65 to 67 %. Those for nursing have been raised from 49 to 51 % in Medan and Surabaya, and from 0 to 49 % in the rest of Indonesia	Law no. 36/2009 on health requires all foreign healthcare facilities to obtain operating license. Law no 44/2009 on hospitals regulates their establishment and management and introduces mandatory accreditation every 3 years. Foreign equity limits for hospitals and medical laboratories have been raised from 65 to 67 %. The minimum size of foreign hospitals has been lowered from 300 to 200 beds for ASEAN investors, though the hospitals still have to be specialist. Foreign medical professionals can be employed in hospitals and medical laboratories, but this must be intended for the purpose of knowledge and technology transfer. This now rules out foreigners in unskilled positions. Universal services obligations have been spelt out in law
Lao PDR	None	None
Malaysia	PROSPECTIVE: The Malaysian National Healthcare Financing Scheme (similar to Australia's Medicare system) may finally be implemented. The government is keen to push tele-medicine, and has also been promoting medical tourism. It has been promoting the recruitment of foreign doctors and specialists and establishing new medical colleges and twinning programs to raise the ratio of doctors per head of population	None
Myanmar	Same as for health services	Some easing of cross-border trade. Some joint venture hospitals have been established since 2008

Philippines	The process for issuing employment permits to foreign nationals has been extended from 1 to 3 working days. Otherwise, the lack of progress in liberalization stems from the constitutional provision that the practice of all professions in the Philippines shall be limited to Filipino citizens	A major policy change is the suspension for 1 year of the need to obtain a Certificate of Need, the only restriction on new entry of private hospitals. The DOH Administrative Order No. 2007-0027 created the improved quality assurance and monitoring program for clinical laboratories in the Philippines and rendered obsolete the DOH-BHFS Circular No. 3 Series of 2003, which suspends issuance of permit to new entry of laboratories. The process for issuing employment permits to foreign nationals has been extended from 1 to 3 working days. In 2009, the Health and Wellness Alliance of the Philippines was established to organize industry and government stake-holders involved with global healthcare and wellness services, tourism and retirement PROSPECTIVE: There are emerging demands for the amendment of the Republic Act 4226 or the Hospital Licensure Act to expand the coverage of the law to include health facilities other than hospitals
Singapore	None	None
Thailand	HORIZONTAL: One distinctive change is the replacement of the Working of Alien Act 1978 by the new act, Working of Alien Act 2008. Among other things, it extends the validity period of the work permit from not exceeding 1 year to not exceeding 2 years. However, non-immigrants visas are normally granted for 1 year	Same as for medical services
Viet Nam	None	The Health Insurance Law took effect on 1 July 2009, aiming to ease the load on provincial and central hospitals, and expand policyholder categories to include drug addicts and people with congenital defects who were previously excluded

ASEAN Association of Southeast Asian Nations, *BHFS* Bureau of Health Facilities and Services, *DOH* Department of Health, *Lao PDR* Lao People's Democratic Republic

Source: Dee (2011)

Table 6.2 ASEAN's progress in liberalizing trade in financial services, 2008–2010

	Banking	*Insurance*
Brunei Darussalam	Since the Ministry of Finance issued clarification on lending in 2009, foreign banks can only lend against local capital PROSPECTIVE: With effect from 1 January 2011, the Monetary Authority Brunei Darussalam will be establish as a Statutory Body to regulate the banking, finance and insurance sector, independent of the Ministry of Finance	None
Cambodia	An amendment was made in September 2009 to liberalize interest rate setting NOTE: Both the minimum capital requirement and the reserve requirement were changed in 2009 in response to the global financial crisis	None
Indonesia	None NOTE: Changes to banking industry regulation concerned a few prudential measures	None NOTE: The only change in insurance regulation during 2008–2010 concerned prudential measures New Law on Investment Promotion 2009 means that 100 % foreign ownership is allowed, the minimum foreign equity in joint ventures has been reduced from 30 to 10 %, and the term of licenses has been extended from 50 to 99 years. However, the government does not want to issue new licenses because of the small size of the market PROSPECTIVE: The Law on Insurance is expected to be amended to be more appropriate to the current situation of a more liberalized and open economy to the world and regional integration. In the coming years, the scope of the compulsory insurance-based social security system will be extended
Lao PDR	None	
Malaysia	In Nov 2010, the central bank announced several measures to curb property speculation as well as to address the rising household debt problem. Among these, the monetary regulator imposed a maximum loan-to-value ratio of 70 %, which will be applicable to the third house financing facility taken out by a borrower PROSPECTIVE: The Central Bank of Malaysia is currently preparing for a "new" Financial Sector Masterplan, which would further liberalize the banking and securities markets	None

Myanmar	None	Myanmar Insurance can supply insurance services including quasi-medical insurance for expatriates going abroad. In 2008 quasi-medical insurance did not exist
Philippines	None	None
Singapore	None	None
Thailand	The Bank of Thailand has permitted commercial banks to employ personnel of ASEAN nationality with unlimited numbers in any positions, but foreign institutions face consideration on a case-by-case basis. This policy change implements commitments under AFAS. A foreign bank with branches in Thailand is allowed to establish up to 2 additional branches by the approval of the Bank of Thailand. This implements commitments under the GATS	None
Viet Nam	In mid 2010, the Government removed the control over the lending interest rate (commercial banks could arrange the lending interest rate with customers), but the State Bank used some administrative procedures to impose the borrowing rate below 14 % (the rate that commercial banks in the Viet Nam banking association have committed). Circular 09 sets out stricter requirements for shareholders, especially founding shareholders, who wish to establish a joint stock commercial bank, and new longer timeframes of the application process for a license. Prior to 2010, foreign bank branches could lend against the parent capital but from 2010, branches have to lend against their own chartered capital, not their parent capital PROSPECTIVE: Under the Law on Credit Institutions that will take effect on 1 January 2011, the prime interest rate structure is abolished. The prime rate was eliminated as unreflective of the supply-demand relationship on the market and was viewed as interventionist by financial markets NOTE: Certain prudential requirements have been raised, including the minimum capital adequacy ratio	PROSPECTIVE: The draft amendment and supplement to the Law on Insurance Business would recognize the cross-border provision of insurance services by foreign insurance organizations and individuals. It would also recognize the right to set up branches of foreign non-life insurance enterprises in Viet Nam. It would also abolish ceding percentages. All are in accordance with Viet Nam's WTO commitments. It would expand the range of recognized insurance products and insurance enterprises

AFAS ASEAN Framework Agreement on Services, *ASEAN* Association of Southeast Asian Nations, *GATS* General Agreement on Trade in Services, *Lao PDR* Lao People's Democratic Republic, *WTO* World Trade Organization

Source: Dee (2011)

Not surprisingly, some of the recent policy changes in banking and insurance services involved a tightening of prudential regulation in response to the global financial crisis. Prudential regulation has a legitimate purpose of ensuring systemic stability. It is generally not regarded as a barrier to trade in financial services, and for this reason it is carved out of the GATS. Nevertheless, Viet Nam appears to have instituted stricter licensing requirements for banks to an extent that goes beyond purely prudential oversight. Within ASEAN, this is an isolated example of possible overreaction to the global financial crisis. In addition, both Brunei Darussalam and Viet Nam have required (or clarified) that foreign bank branches must lend against their local capital rather than their parent capital. This is a "grey area" measure—while it further constrains the activities of foreign bank branches, it also gives the local prudential authorities some control over the capital reserve requirements of foreign branches, rather than having to rely on the prudential oversight of the authorities in the branches' home countries.

The tables also show the extent to which countries in the region have instituted genuine trade reforms in response to commitments made under AFAS or the GATS. In banking, both Thailand and Viet Nam have instituted multilateral reforms in line with commitments under the GATS, while Thailand has also relaxed restrictions on hiring foreign personnel on a preferential basis under its AFAS commitments. In insurance, Viet Nam expects to implement a package of reforms in the near future in line with its WTO commitments. In health services, Indonesia has relaxed the minimum bed size for foreign-invested hospitals on a preferential basis. In medical professional services, Cambodia has implemented a mutual recognition agreement with its ASEAN neighbors. In all other respects, the reforms recorded in Tables 6.1 and 6.2 are unilateral and non-preferential, or if they have a regional dimension, it is because of geographical constraints rather than preferential commitments.

Some of the more notable unilateral reform efforts are the relaxations of interest rate controls in Cambodia and Viet Nam. Malaysia also awaits a new Financial Master Plan that will further liberalize the banking and securities markets in the near future. Lao PDR has implemented a package of reforms in the insurance sector, although at the same time, the government does not want to issue any new licenses. While this moratorium is explained because of the small market size, it also has the potential to offer protection to the existing government–foreign joint ventures. In Myanmar there has been a slight expansion in the range of insurance products on offer, although there has been no weakening of the monopoly position of Myanmar Insurance.

In the fields of medical and health services, there have been significant reforms in Indonesia and the Philippines, and a slight easing in Myanmar. In Indonesia, new legislation has been introduced to fill the significant gaps in the regulatory framework (Dee 2009). In a few cases, the introduction of explicit legislative guidelines has the potential to limit practices (such as the hiring of foreigners into relatively unskilled positions) that might have occurred otherwise. In most cases, however, the legislation will have somewhat reduced the scope for bureaucratic discretion. It also tightens the quality assurance framework in Indonesia by making the hospital accreditation process mandatory every 3 years. Finally, the Indonesian legislative reforms have also been accompanied by a slight easing of foreign equity limits. In the

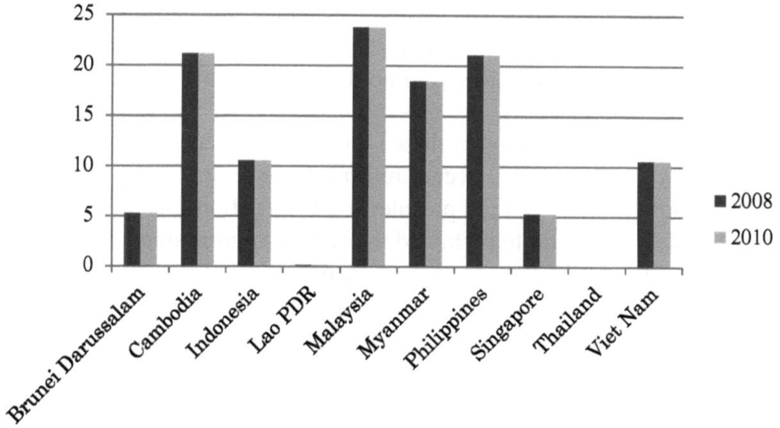

Fig. 6.1 Changes in ASEAN's restrictions on domestic medical services over time (prevalence in %). *Source*: Dee (2011)

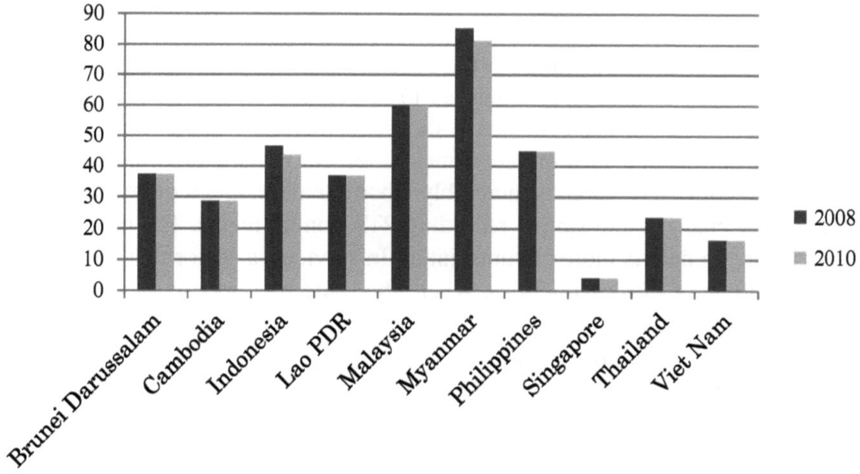

Fig. 6.2 Changes in ASEAN's restrictions on foreign medical services over time (prevalence in %). *Source*: Dee (2011)

Philippines, there has been a lifting of the regulatory restrictions on the entry of new hospitals and medical laboratories. In Myanmar there has been a growth in cross-border trade in medical and health services and some limited evidence of foreign investment occurring.

Thus there is evidence of worthwhile reform efforts in all four services. Some has been driven by AFAS or WTO commitments but in general, the more significant reforms have taken place unilaterally.

A further key question is whether the recent reforms have made a significant difference. This is indicated in Figs. 6.1 and 6.2, for domestic and foreign medical services providers respectively. These figures compare the overall prevalence of restrictions in 2008 and 2010. The differences reflect the reforms summarized in Table 6.1. The reforms have made only a slight difference to the overall prevalence of restrictions on foreign suppliers, and no difference to the prevalence of restrictions on domestic suppliers.

Comparable figures for the other three sectors are not reproduced here, but tell a similar story. In health services, recent reforms have removed the last restrictions facing domestic suppliers. But the prevalence of restrictions against foreign health services providers is still quite high, and the recent reforms since 2008 have made only slight inroads into those trade barriers. In banking also, the reforms have made only a slight difference to the overall prevalence of restrictions. In some countries, such as Viet Nam, banking reforms in some dimensions (as easing of interest rate controls) have been offset by a tightening in others (more stringent non-prudential licensing requirements). Thus there is evidence that ASEAN countries are still using unnecessary regulatory restrictions in place of better-targeted prudential requirements. Finally, there has been very little reform of regulatory restrictions on trade in insurance services between 2008 and 2010. In Lao PDR, legislative reforms have been essentially negated by the recent moratorium on granting new licenses. Insurance is a sector that is typically under pressure during WTO accession negotiations, so some ASEAN countries have already undergone market opening in this context. Other ASEAN countries will need to accelerate their reform efforts in this sector if the ASEAN Blueprint targets are to be met.

To summarize, empirical evidence to show conclusively whether formal regional institutional arrangements promote domestic reform is hard to come by. This is because the required research is incredibly labor intensive, and requires monitoring actual policy changes, not simply recording PTA commitments. The most compelling evidence to date is more circumstantial. In services, a sector that accounts for well over 50 % of most economies, where the trade barriers are overwhelmingly regulatory, even the best WTO Doha Round offers are on average twice as restrictive as actual practice. PTAs tend to improve on WTO commitments in services, at least in terms of sectoral coverage, if not in the depth of sectoral commitments or the disciplines on safeguards, subsidies, procurement and domestic regulation. But even if they improve on WTO commitments by a substantial margin, they are still likely to lag actual practice. It is on the basis of this and other evidence summarized above that Francois and Hoekman (2010) draw their conclusion—except in the EU, services trade reform has been primarily unilateral.

6.5 Why Has Reform Been Unilateral Outside the EU?

If PTAs have not succeeded in promoting regulatory reform in services outside of the EU, it is not because the reforms do not generate economic benefits. Francois and Hoekman (2010) survey recent econometric evidence showing that openness in a range of producer or intermediate services sectors is linked to productivity improvements and increased export performance in manufacturing. They also survey recent studies that have shown links between services sector liberalization and economic growth. Prospective studies have also highlighted the potential gains from future services trade reform. As noted by Francois and Hoekman (2010), these studies tend to show that services liberalization can generate much larger welfare gains that goods liberalization. One reason for this finding is that regulatory barriers in services can create deadweight costs, not just allocative inefficiencies of the sort generated by tariffs. Accordingly, services liberalization can generate larger welfare gains than tariff reform.

A recent example of such prospective studies is the study by the APEC Policy Support Unit (2011) into the impacts and benefits of structural reforms in the transport, energy and telecommunications sectors in APEC member economies. It found that $175 billion a year in additional real income (in 2004 dollars) could be generated from further reforms in the APEC region. APEC-wide, the projected gains from these structural reforms are almost twice as big as the gains from further liberalization of merchandise trade. Yet the sectors where the structural reforms occur are less than a quarter of the size of those engaged in merchandise trade. When structural reforms lead to lower real production costs, even by half as much as the report estimates, they create a return to reform effort that is much greater than that from border trade reforms.

So why have trade agreements (other than the EU) failed to deliver services reform (and by implication, other types of structural reform)? Hoekman et al. (2007) speculate on the reasons, some of which are relevant to domestic reform more broadly. They note that despite significant unilateral reform, barriers to trade and FDI still remain. One explanation is the standard political economy problems of resistance by vested interests. But the authors note that in the case of services (and other behind-the-border reforms more generally), the reciprocity mechanisms that have traditionally been used to counter the resistance by incumbent producers are much less effective. One of the key reasons is that in services, the balance is tilted in favor of incumbents because of regulatory concerns—it is hard to design trade commitments that distinguish or separate protectionist policies from those that have a legitimate domestic efficiency or social equity rationale. Hoekman and Mattoo (2011) also note that export interests may be weaker in services because services markets tend to be either very open or very closed, and in neither situation do exporters have a strong incentive to mobilize politically.

The desire to retain regulatory autonomy has clearly been a major consideration in services negotiations. The GATS explicitly recognizes the right to regulate. Francois and Hoekman (2010: 681) also observe

> The EU experience illustrates the difficulty for (unwillingness of) polities to converge on common norms and to allow for "regulatory arbitrage" even in situations where in principle all are agreed that common minimum standards exist.

This argument would also suggest a limited role for regional agreements to push domestic reforms more generally in those areas involving cross-border trade, when domestic regulatory regimes go head-to-head. They may have more success in promoting reforms in those areas involving FDI, where host country regulations unambiguously apply.

While these authors point out one of the key limits of reciprocity in dealing with the political economy resistance to reform, various authors have pointed out the limits of reciprocity in dealing with the economic externalities associated with reform. The arguments by Antràs and Staiger (2007) and Dee and Sidorenko (2006) have already been summarized above. In a similar vein, Hoekman and Mattoo (2011) note that when reforms reduce deadweight costs, the benefits of reform are fully internalized and the pressure for reform will be unilateral. Blanchard (2007) notes that when firms can deliver services via FDI, governments have less incentive to manipulate the terms of trade on cross-border trade, so once again, reciprocity is not needed.

Yet there is agreement that the EU alone has generated significant policy reforms. But it is *sui generis*—one of a kind. So what is it about the EU agreement that has contributed to its success? And what lessons if any can been drawn about the factors that can facilitate domestic reforms elsewhere?

6.6 What Is Special About the EU?

As noted above, the original EU Treaty contained broad commitments to the four freedoms—the free movement of goods, persons (both natural and legal), services, and capital. The real liberalization came in the enforcement of those broad commitments, a process that also led to increasingly broad definitions of what was meant by a violation.[7]

It is important to understand the process by which this came about. The legal literature points to two key decisions of the European Court of Justice. The first was the seminal decision in *Van Gend en Loos* (Case 26/62, Van Gend en Loos v. Nederlandse Administratie der Belastingen, 1963 E.C.R.) in which the European Court of Justice developed the doctrine of "direct effect". The other key decision was that in *Costa v. ENEL* (Case 6/64, Costa v. ENEL, 1969 E.C.R. 585) in which the Court developed the doctrine of "supremacy".

Under the doctrine of direct effect, certain provisions of the EU Treaty have direct legal effect such that individuals and enterprises can claim Treaty-based rights in member state courts, prevailing over contrary national rules. This doctrine meant that individuals and enterprises did not have to wait for the European Commission to challenge contrary state rules—they could take action themselves in their own national courts.

Under the doctrine of supremacy, Treaty law took primacy over national law. This doctrine leveraged off the doctrine of 'direct effect'. In *Van Gend en Loos,* the Court ruled that member states had 'limited their sovereign rights', and effected a permanent transfer of power to the 'new legal order' of the Community. The Court

[7] As noted above, the interpretation of violations became broader in the sense that it moved away from the notion of discrimination to one based on impediments to free movement. But in another respect, the interpretation of violations became narrower, because judicial interpretations of allowable derogations also became broader (Barnard 2010).

then relied on this point in establishing the doctrine of supremacy in *Costa v. ENEL*. As noted by Persaud and Goebel (1997), this was at the core of all other Court doctrines, because it achieved the binding nature of the Court's own judgments.

The Van Gend en Loos judgment laid down certain criteria for Treaty provisions to have direct effect (the provisions needed to be clear, precise and absolute in their terms, aimed at achieving individual rights, and did not necessarily require Community or member state legislation for their effective application). Over time, the Court has found that Treaty provisions having direct effect include those that define three of the four freedoms—Article 30 on the free movement of goods; Articles 48 on free movement of workers and 49 on the right of establishment; and Article 56 on the freedom to provide services. Other Treaty provisions have been found also to have *horizontal* direct effect, meaning that an individual or enterprise can appeal to EU law in a case against another individual or enterprise, not just against a member government. Treaty provisions in this category include Articles 101 and 102 on competition law and Article 157 on the right of equal pay for equal work between men and women.

The doctrine of direct effect has allowed individuals and enterprises to challenge a wide variety of national measures in their own courts or in the courts of other member states. As noted above, in trade matters these dispute settlement proceedings tended to be aimed initially at rules that discriminated on the basis of nationality. Over time, the Court's interpretations of what constituted a Treaty violation widened to include a range of rules that could not be objectively justified on grounds of compelling state interests (Persaud and Goebel 1997).[8]

The reason that we know so much about the power of this appeal mechanism is that national judges can send questions—preliminary references—to the European Court of Justice so as to obtain an interpretation of EU law when this is relevant to the resolution of a dispute in the national court.[9] The European Court of Justice responds with a preliminary ruling that the national judge is expected to apply to resolve the case. The vast majority of preliminary references involve an allegation on the part of an individual or enterprise that a specific national law or practice in the same country is incompatible with EU law (McNaughton 2011; Stone Sweet and Brunell 2011). So even if dispute settlement takes place in a decentralized manner in national courts, it leaves a shadow at the Community level in the form of preliminary references, and centralized data on these are available. The data show that the number of such cases has grown steadily, from 147 in the period 1961–1970 to 1,084 in the period 1991–1995 (Stone Sweet and Brunell 1998). The subject matter of these cases has also broadened, as was noted earlier. Furthermore, the preliminary ruling mechanism has been the key mechanisms through which the interpretation of what constitutes a Treaty violation has evolved over time.

In what way does this mechanism differ from the standard dispute settlement mechanisms embodied in trade agreements (either regional or through the WTO)?

---

[8] The doctrine of direct effect has also been extended beyond Treaty provisions, and also applies to certain Community directives.

[9] Lower national courts *can* refer such questions at their discretion; national courts of last resort are *required* to request the assistance of the European Court of Justice.

Stone Sweet, one of the pre-eminent legal scholars in the field, gives a legal perspective on this issue (Stone Sweet 2010; Stone Sweet and Brunell 2011).

He argues that the European Court of Justice and the WTO Appellate Body are in fact similar, in that both are more than mere agents of the contracting States in a principal–agent relationship. They are what he calls Trustee Courts of their respective treaty systems. He defines a Trustee Court according to three criteria:

- the court is the authoritative interpreter of the regime's law, and has the authority to review the legality of acts taken by the contracting States under the regime's law;
- the court's jurisdiction with regard to the contracting States is compulsory; and
- it is difficult, or impossible as a practical manner, for the contracting States, as principals, to reverse the court's important rulings on Treaty law.

He notes that unlike a simple agent, a Trustee Court has the authority to govern the principals themselves. It also has the power to expand or contract its own "zone of discretion". Classic examples of the use of these powers in the EU context are the doctrines of supremacy and direct effect. Also in an EU context, Stone Sweet argues that the member states conferred such authority on the European Court of Justice "in order to help them overcome acute commitment problems associated with market and political integration" (Stone Sweet and Brunell 2011: 4).

While Stone Sweet and Brunell (2011) claim that the WTO Appellate Body has similar powers, Pauwelyn (2005) argues that there are notable checks and balances on its behavior. The Dispute Settlement Understanding explicitly guards against judicial activism, by prohibiting panels and the Appellate Body from adding to or diminishing the rights and obligations of WTO members. Pauwelyn (2005): 49) also argues that the Dispute Settlement Body exercises political control over dispute settlement:

> *As the umbilical cord between the political and judicial branch, it is a crucial interface and forum of contestation or voice to which both panels and the Appellate Body are most receptive.*

Van den Broek (2009) also notes that current WTO dispute remedies are less than ideal. Compensation is often unrealistic because the defendant WTO member has to agree to it. Retaliation (raising levels of protection against imports from the defendant WTO member) involves shooting oneself in the foot. He argues that these aspects of WTO dispute settlement penalize the least developed WTO members in particular, a conjecture borne out by statistics on who uses the WTO dispute settlement process.[10]

Stone Sweet and Brunell (2011) consider how the European Court of Justice has dealt with the issue of legitimacy that its Trustee status creates. They argue that one strategy it uses to establish and maintain legitimacy is "majority activism"—the Court's rulings tend to line up with the actual practice found in the majority of member states. The Court also has a clear mandate—to construct and consolidate a

[10] Of the 356 complaints brought between 1995 and 2006, 227 were brought by high-income WTO members and only one was brought by a least developed country.

transnational, "European" identity, in part in opposition to nationalism. Its majority activism clearly serves that purpose. The authors argue that because the WTO has no comparable identity construction mandate, it has not developed a variant of majority activism as a way of securing its legitimacy, though they argue that perhaps it should.

The impression that one gets from reading this legal literature is that the differences between the European Court of Justice and the WTO Appellate Body are differences of degree rather than kind. To the extent that there are analytically identifiable differences, they tend to support the more popular notion that more has been possible in the EU because the ultimate goal has been not just the furthering of prosperity, but the prevention of world wars. Pauwelyn (2005) also notes differences in the degree of judicial activism. But here it is important to recall the distinction between a negative list agreement (such as the EU Treaty) and a positive list agreement (such as the GATS). There may have been more judicial activism in the EU because the nature of the agreement allowed more scope for it.

Nevertheless, there is a significant political economy difference between dispute settlement in the EU and the WTO that has received little attention in most of the legal literature. The doctrine of direct effect empowered a whole new set of domestic interests in favor of reform. As Burley and Mattli (1993) note, *importers* who objected to paying customs duties on their imports could invoke the Treaty of Rome to force their governments to remove them.

According to the standard political economy argument for regional rather than unilateral action, the interests of a country's exporters (in opening up foreign markets) need to be pitted against those of its import-competing industries (in keeping protection at home). The presumption is that the interests of consumers do not count politically because of the collective action problem of mobilizing large numbers of consumers with individually small stakes in the outcome.

At an economic level, this argument fails to recognize that exports are not per se "good" in an economic sense (the mercantilist fallacy)—it depends on the price at which they can be sold.[11] At a political level, this argument fails to recognize that there can be powerful domestic business interests that align with those of consumers—importers who sell directly to consumers, businesses that use imports as intermediate inputs and are equally hurt by import protection, or exporters who are hurt indirectly by the real currency appreciation that import protection tends to generate.

The doctrine of direct effect empowered at least some of those domestic pro-reform business interests. The significance can be illustrated in the context of the example developed by Krugman (1997: 118):

> When the United States recently imposed utterly indefensible restrictions on Mexican tomato exports, an Administration official remarked off the record that Florida has a lot of electoral votes while Mexico has none. The economically correct rebuttal to this sort of thing is to point out that the other 49 states contain a lot of pizza lovers: the politically effective answer is to subject U.S.–Mexican trade to a set of rules and arbitration procedures in which the Mexicans do too have a vote.

---

[11] Multilateral action can nevertheless help to overcome terms of trade externalities, as noted earlier.

What the doctrine of direct effect does is give the pizza lovers in the other 49 states a voice by proxy, by empowering tomato importers, who make money by selling to pizza shops, to complain about the actions of the Administration officials. So the politics of fighting protection is internalized, and no longer subject to concerns about loss of sovereignty.

Burley and Mattli (1993) note that this empowerment in turn contributed to the legitimacy of the European Court of Justice. The Court was seen as siding with the "little guy" against state bureaucracies, the "people" against the "power elites". And this was a powerful antidote to charges of antidemocratic activism.

Burley and Mattli (1993) also point out the more general benefits of depoliticizing a reform debate by framing it according to non-political criteria. In the case of the EU, with the forum being the European Court of Justice, the external frame of reference for debate was often the rule of law. In other forums (some of which will be discussed shortly), the external frame of reference may be economic growth and efficiency. Even when the politics of reform is entirely internal, it is useful to have a forum that can provide and safeguard such a non-political frame of reference. Burley and Mattli (1993: 72) describe the process as follows:

> Even an economic decision that has acquired political significance is not the same as a "purely" political decision and cannot be attacked as such. It retains an independent 'non-political' rationale, which must be met by a counterargument on its own terms. Within this domain, then, contending political interests must do battle by proxy. The chances of victory are affected by the strength of that proxy measured by independent non-political criteria.

The argument so far suggests that the unique feature of the EU that helped it to promote economic reform in sensitive, behind-the-border areas was that it overcame the problem of loss of sovereignty by internalizing the political battle to domestic interests, and yet still provided a non-political frame of reference for the debate.

Dee (2010) provides a number of case studies from around the East Asian region to demonstrate that this has been a common feature of institutional arrangements that have proved effective at promoting structural reform in that region. When it comes to structural reform, the vested interests with the strongest stakes in the outcomes are primarily domestic—very often the interests of incumbent producers against potential new entrants (domestic as well as foreign), consumers, and upstream and downstream industries. The key to promoting reform is to mobilize domestic pro-reform champions to act as a countervailing force against vested interests. One way to do this is to provide an independent, non-political forum and a frame of reference that stresses economy-wide benefits. A further characteristic stressed by Dee (2010) is that the forum should be transparent, in the sense of making public the arguments of the respective interests, and also making public any recommendations to government. In this way, the special pleading of vested interests can be revealed for what it is. Equally importantly, the pro-reform champions can also self-select on any particular issue.[12]

Examples of institutions that have promoted reforms in this way include the Productivity Commission and its predecessors in Australia (Banks and Wonder

[12] Note that under the processes of the European Court of Justice, even the issues self-select.

2010) and the Council on Economic and Fiscal Policy in Japan (Hosen 2010). McNaughton (2011) shows, for example, that the concerns that the EU Services Directive are intended to address are being dealt with domestically in Australia by the Council of Australian Governments and the research and recommendations of the Productivity Commission. Institutional examples from the Philippines (Llanto 2010) and Indonesia (Soesastro et al. 2010) illustrate how useful work to support structural reform could potentially take place within a medium-term economic planning framework. Old-fashioned economic planning is often seen as outmoded in an era of open markets and outward-oriented growth strategies, but a medium-term planning process can also provide a useful forum for detailed *ex ante* reviews of policy options, providing a lead in the policy development process. Such a medium-term focus can then bind successive governments and guard against excessive "short-termism" in policy development.

Many East Asian economies also have influential think-tanks that conduct impartial policy reviews and analysis, and therefore provide an open, independent forum in which the views of vested interests are subject to scrutiny using an economy-wide frame of reference. These organizations vary in the extent to which they sit inside or outside formal government structures, and the extent to which their contributions are used in the policy development process. But all have at least some of the characteristics of effective policy review institutions—independence, an economy-wide view, and transparent processes.

The problem of developing a mandate for structural reform is not confined to democratically elected governments. The PRC and Viet Nam also face the problem of managing vested interests. One strategy that Viet Nam has tried is a taskforce approach—putting together groups of experts from within and outside government to consider one particular area of reform (Vo and Nguyen 2010). According to He (2010), the PRC too is at the stage where reforms can potentially create losers as well as winners, and so it requires new strategies to deal with vested interests.

In none of these East Asian examples has an institution been given the powers of a Trustee Court to bind the actions of the government. This is the essence of the East Asian distaste for supranational institutions—no East Asian government would be willing to limit its sovereign rights in this fashion. But this does not mean that institutions with only advisory powers cannot influence policy outcomes. The country case studies in Dee (2010) demonstrate that they can, because ideas have influence by shaping debates, and transparent processes have influence by marshalling the winners as well as the losers from reform.

6.7 How to Shape Regional Institutions to Promote Domestic Reform?

The preponderance of evidence is that signing more PTAs will not promote domestic reform. The chapters may be written and the agreements signed, but the content will continue to be relatively empty so long as governments feel that such agreements impinge unduly on their sovereignty and their right to regulate. And one key reason that governments will continue to feel this way is that there is very little in PTAs to help governments deal with the domestic politics of reform.

Nor can great hope be placed in current WTO processes. Pauwelyn (2005) gives a careful examination of the likelihood of ongoing WTO success, particularly given its ever broader agenda. He concludes that (p. 58):

> The so-called bicycle club of trade must be disbanded. It takes exporters and producers as the core constituency of the system and assumes that, to keep their support, the world trade system requires ever more liberalization; otherwise, the bicycle will fall over. To survive as a legitimate organization, the WTO must extend its base to include consumers and citizens. It must, in other words, play out its strongest card: that genuine free trade benefits the masses, not the few. … The proxy of exporters/producers allegedly representing majority interests is no longer needed and can, in any event, no longer suffice.

It is instructive to look at recent proposals for how to restructure and revitalize the WTO. The immediate issues include whether to break away from a "single undertaking" (the decision-making rule that nothing is agreed until everything is agreed), the consensus rule, or to allow more plurilateral rather than multilateral agreements.[13] Examples of these kinds of proposals are found in the Sutherland Report (2004) and the Warwick Commission (2007).

The proposals also include the idea that WTO members should grant direct effect to WTO treaty obligations, so that individuals and enterprises can take action in national courts in the event of non-compliance by a WTO member. On the face of it, this looks like a promising move, since the doctrine of direct effect was instrumental in the EU's success in achieving domestic reform. To date, not even the EU has granted direct effect to WTO obligations, on the grounds that unless all other WTO members gave direct effect in the same way to the same provisions, the EU might put itself at a disadvantage *vis-à-vis* the other WTO members (for example, Van den Broek 2009). The move may well also create uncertainty for EU traders, because EU courts might have to give preference to WTO measures at the expense of *EU* measures. The general granting of direct effect by all members would overcome the EU's first objection.

But Trachtman (1999) disagrees with the proposition that WTO members should grant direct effect to WTO obligations. He argues that the currently weak enforcement mechanisms help the WTO to achieve democratic legitimacy—something that Stone Sweet and Brunell (2011) argue is currently lacking. Trachtman (1999: 678) argues that "direct effect without more direct democratic participation in formulation of the directly effective law raises as many issues as it resolves".

Pauwelyn (2005) makes a similar argument. He argues that the current WTO does not allow sufficient democratic participation (not just of the members states, but also of the various private interests within them) to ensure the loyalty required for members to put up with the more legalistic system that the WTO has become. This is in contrast to the EU, where progress was slow and incremental, but where loyalty was more or less maintained (see also the seminal analysis of the EU by

[13] The current WTO agreement on Government Procurement is plurilateral.

Weiler 1991).[14] Giving direct effect to WTO obligations would be a mistake, because it would achieve efficiency without loyalty.

Pauwelyn (2005) reviews the other major proposals that have been put forward to reform the WTO, not just in terms of the compliance it achieves, but more broadly. If a lack of democratic participation is the problem at the moment, then the solution is not to divorce trade negotiations even more from the "rough and tumble" of representative democracy (for example, Weiler 2001; Bhala 2001), nor is it to dispense with the current consensus rule (for example, Sutherland Report 2004). But nor does he think that the current dispute settlement process should be weakened (for example, Barfield 2001). As a legal scholar and former legal officer with the WTO Secretariat, the lesson he draws from the history of the WTO is that to be effective, it needed an independent and automatic enforcement mechanism—particularly once it started dealing with non-tariff barriers and behind-the-border measures.

As noted above, Pauwelyn (2005) argues that the problem of the WTO is that it remains focused primarily on non-discrimination instead of economic efficiency, and on the interests of producers instead of the interests of consumers. As such, it has been ripe for exploitation by special interests. Examples cited by Pauwelyn are the protectionist agreements on agriculture, antidumping and the former agreement on textiles, and win-lose agreements (which benefit some countries at the expense of others) such as trade-related intellectual property rights (TRIPS).

So Pauwelyn's solution is to propose more politics and participation in the WTO, not less. And he gives a number of concrete WTO-specific proposals to provide more capital city input into Geneva processes, and to give a broader range of actors a voice in WTO issues, if not a seat at the table. Van den Broek (2009) also urges a greater role for non-state actors in bringing pressure for WTO compliance via the "mobilization of shame". Pauwelyn also proposes a slight weakening of discipline (and more options for exit) by dispensing with the single undertaking and by not requiring a consensus of all WTO members that a new plurilateral agreement can be added to the WTO system.

If the current configuration of exporter and import-competing producer interests can no longer secure further trade liberalization in the WTO, as the current fate of the Doha Round suggests, then it is even less likely to secure deeper domestic reforms in either the WTO or in regional trade negotiating forums. These current forums are simply not equipped to help governments fight the necessary domestic political battles. The above proposals are worth considering if the WTO is to make progress on its current agenda. But in the context of a much broader agenda—domestic reform—a key question is whether it would be sufficient to give a greater

[14] When the doctrines of direct effect and supremacy were first developed, there were only six Member States of what is now the EU, and the legislative voting pattern in the Council of Ministers was by unanimity. Since then, there have been changes in the voting patterns in the Council, with the introduction and then modification of Qualified Majority Voting. In addition, a "co-decision" procedure has been introduced for legislation, under which both the EU Parliament and the Council of Ministers must consent to a measure for it to be adopted. These changes have contributed to the further/deeper integration of the EU legal system, and to further reforms at the domestic level in EU member states.

range of domestic interests a voice in a forum in which other governments also sit, or whether it would be even better to remove the other government(s) from the table.

The above economic arguments suggest that a reciprocity mechanism is weak or ineffective in achieving behind-the-border reform. So it does not help to have another government at the negotiating table, especially when this raises concerns about loss of sovereignty, to compound the problem of lack of democratic legitimacy. But this does not mean that regional institutions, or even the WTO for that matter, cannot assist domestic governments to push a domestic reform agenda.

This has been recognized recently by Hoekman and Mattoo (2011) in the context of services trade liberalization. They argue that a concerted, international effort to pursue regulatory cooperation could help to push the reform process along both unilaterally and in market access negotiations. They argue that two types of cooperation are needed. The first is international assistance with diagnosing prevailing policies (or the lack of them) and using this analysis to devise strategies for reform. This process could help to identify a menu of regulatory options for countries to consider. Aid for trade initiatives could also help with the implementation. A second type of cooperation is between regulators, explicitly focused on addressing regulatory externalities that impede trade. An example would be initiatives to improve the international mobility of workers, as international experience suggests that this requires the regulatory cooperation of both the home and host countries.

Dee and Findlay (2008) proposed a similar agenda, but also noted that further progress would be needed on domestic reform *before* further progress could be expected in market access negotiations. This would be the only way to overcome the quite legitimate concerns of developing countries that they were "not yet ready" for services trade liberalization.

Drysdale (2010) addresses more directly the kinds of regional institutions and mechanisms that could best support a domestic reform agenda. He stresses the importance of ownership of the reform agenda, something that is not helped if the reforms are seen to be dictated by outside organizations or by trading partner governments. He proposes regional support for those home-grown institutional mechanisms (such as those cited above) that help to generate successful domestic reforms. The key elements of regional support are capacity building and providing forums for experience-sharing. The domestic activities needing such support are *domestic* efforts to diagnose current policies and develop policy alternatives, in transparent *domestic* forums that allow the views of vested interests to be met and challenged by domestic pro-reform champions. The evidence above suggests that it was this aspect of the EU that accounts for its success in achieving domestic reform. So this aspect is worth the support of regional institutions.

Which members of the alpha-numerical soup of Asian regional institutions are best-placed to carry out this support? Drysdale (2010) and Soesastro (2010) point out that of all the current regional institutions, APEC has the track record of regional experience-sharing and mentoring. It has the sanction, through the Leaders' Agenda to Implement Structural Reform (signed in 2004). And it has started to develop the delivery mechanisms, for example through the establishment of the APEC Policy Support Unit. This is not to say that other regional institutions could not also start usefully working in this direction. What is critical is to recognize that the key to achieving domestic reform is to win the domestic political battle. This is what regional institutions need to support.

References

Adlung, R., & Morrison, P. (2010). Less than the GATS: 'Negative preferences' in regional services agreements. *Journal of International Economic Law, 13*(4), 1103–1143.

Antràs, P., & Staiger, R. (2007). Offshoring and the value of trade agreements. Centre for Economic Policy Research Discussion Paper 6966. London: Centre for Economic Policy Research.

APEC Policy Support Unit. (2011). *The impacts and benefits of structural reforms in transport, energy and telecommunications sectors. APEC#211-SE-01.1*. Singapore: APEC Policy Support Unit.

Bagwell, K., & Staiger, R. (1999). An economic theory of the GATT. *American Economic Review, 89*(1), 215–248.

Baldwin, R. (2006). Managing the noodle bowl: The fragility of East Asian regionalism. CEPR Discussion Paper No. 5561. London: Centre for Economic Policy Research.

Banks, G., & Wonder, B. (2010). The policy determinants of structural reform in Australia. In P. Dee (Ed.), *Institutions for economic reform in Asia* (pp. 63–87). London and New York: Routledge.

Barfield, C. (2001). *Free trade, sovereignty, democracy: The future of the World Trade Organization*. Washington, DC: The American Enterprise Institute.

Barichello, R. (2004). NAFTA and domestic agricultural policy reform: Observations from Canada. Working Paper No. 2004-08. Vancouver: Food and Resource Economics, University of British Columbia.

Barnard, C. (2010). *The substantive law of the EU: Four freedoms* (3rd ed.). Oxford: Oxford University Press.

Barth, J., Caprio, G., & Levine, R. (2004). Bank regulation and supervision: What works best? *Journal of Financial Intermediation, 13*(2), 205–248.

Barth, J., Marchetti, J., Nolle, D., & Sawangngoenyuang, W. (2006). Foreign banking: Do countries' WTO commitments match actual practices? Staff Working Paper ERSD-2006-11. Economic Research and Statistics Division. Geneva: World Trade Organization.

Bhala, R. (2001). The power of the past: Towards *De Jure Stare Decisis* in WTO adjudication (Part Three of a Trilogy). *George Washington International Law Review, 33*(3 & 4), 873–978.

Blanchard, E. (2007). Foreign direct investment, endogenous tariffs, and preferential trade agreements. *B.E. Journal of Economic Analysis and Policy: Advances in Economic Analysis and Policy, 7*(1), 1–50.

Borchert, I., Gootiiz, B., & Mattoo, A. (2010). *Restrictions on services trade and FDI in developing countries*. Mimeo. Washington, DC: World Bank.

Burley, A. M., & Mattli, W. (1993). Europe before the court: A political theory of legal integration. *International Organization, 47*(1), 41–76.

Carrubba, C., & Murrah, L. (2005). Legal integration and use of the preliminary ruling process in the European Union. *International Organization, 59*, 399–418.

Czaga, P. (2004). Regulatory reform and market openness: Understanding the links to enhance economic performance. OECD Trade Policy Working Papers No. 9. Paris: OECD Publishing.

Dee, P. (2005). The Australia-US free trade agreement: An assessment. Pacific Economic Papers No. 345. Canberra: Australia-Japan Research Centre, Australian National University.

Dee, P. (2008). Multinational corporations and Pacific regionalism. In J. Palacios (Ed.), *Multinational corporations and the emerging network economy in Asia and the Pacific* (pp. 232–266). London and New York: Routledge.

Dee, P. (2009). Services Liberalization toward the ASEAN economic community. In J. Corbett, & S. Umezaki (Eds.), *Deepening East Asian economic integration*. ERIA Research Project Report No. 1. Jakarta: Economic Research Institute for ASEAN and East Asia. pp. 58–96.

Dee, P. (Ed.). (2010). *Institutions for economic reform in Asia*. London and New York: Routledge.

Dee, P. (2011). Services Liberalization towards an ASEAN economic community. In S. Urata & M. Okabe (Eds.), *Towards a competitive ASEAN single market: Sectoral analysis*. ERIA Research Project Report 2010, No. 3, Jakarta: Economic Research Institute for ASEAN and East Asia. pp. 17–136.

Dee, P., & Findlay, C. (2008). Services: A 'Deal-maker' in the Doha round? In B. Blonigen (Ed.), *Monitoring international trade policy: A new agenda for reviving the Doha round*. London: Centre for Economic Policy Research and Kiel: Kiel Institute for the World Economy. pp. 49–63.

Dee, P., & Sidorenko, A. (2006). The rise of services trade: Regional initiatives and challenges for the WTO. In C. Findlay & H. Soesastro (Eds.), *Reshaping the Asia Pacific economic order* (pp. 200–226). London and New York: Routledge.

Drysdale, P. (2010). Introduction. In P. Dee (Ed.), *Institutions for economic reform in Asia* (pp. 1–6). London and New York: Routledge.

Ethier, W. (1998). Regionalism in a multilateral world. *Journal of Political Economy, 106*(6), 1214–1245.

Ethier, W. (1999). Multilateral roads to regionalism. In J. Piggott & A. Woodland (Eds.), *International trade policy and the Pacific Rim*. New York: St Martin's Press.

Ethier, W. (2001). The new regionalism in the Americas: A theoretical framework. *North American Journal of Economics and Finance, 12*(2), 159–172.

Fink, C., & Jensen, M. (2009). Services provisions in regional trade arrangements: Stumbling blocks or building blocks for multilateral liberalization? In R. Baldwin & P. Low (Eds.), *Multilateralizing regionalism: Challenges for the global trading system* (pp. 221–261). Cambridge and New York: Cambridge University Press.

Fink, C., & Molinuevo, M. (2007). *East Asian free trade agreements in services: Roaring tigers or timid pandas? Trade issues in East Asia*. Washington, DC: World Bank.

Francois, J. (1997). External bindings and the credibility of reform. In A. Galal & B. Hoekman (Eds.), *Regional partners in global markets*. London: Centre for Economic Policy Research.

Francois, J. (2005). Accession of Turkey to the European Union: Market access and regulatory issues. In B. Hoekman & S. Togan (Eds.), *Turkey: Economic reform and accession to the European Union* (pp. 123–146). Washington, DC: World Bank and Centre for Economic Policy Research.

Francois, J., & Hoekman, B. (2010). Services trade and policy. *Journal of Economic Literature, 48*(3), 642–692.

Gassebner, M., Gaston, N., & Lamla, M. (2008). The inverse domino effect: Are economic reforms contagious? KOF Working Paper No. 187. Zurich: KOF Swiss Economic Institute.

Graham, E., & Wada, E. (2000). Domestic reform, trade and investment liberalization, financial crisis, and foreign direct investment in Mexico. *The World Economy, 23*(6), 777–797.

Harms, P., Mattoo, A., & Schuknecht, L. (2003). Explaining liberalization commitments in financial services trade. Policy Research Working Paper No. 2999. Washington, DC: World Bank.

He, F. (2010). China's economic reform: Success, problems and challenges. In P. Dee (Ed.), *Institutions for economic reform in Asia* (pp. 195–211). London and New York: Routledge.

Hoekman, B. & Mattoo, A. (2011). Services trade liberalization and regulatory reform: Re-invigorating international cooperation. Policy Research Working Paper 5517. Washington, DC: World Bank.

Hoekman, B., Mattoo, A., & Sapir, A. (2007). The political economy of services trade liberalization: A case for international regulatory cooperation. *Oxford Review of Economic Policy, 23*(3), 367–391.

Hosen, M. (2010). Accelerating economic reform in Japan: The role of the Council on Economic and Fiscal Policy. In P. Dee (Ed.), *Institutions for economic reform in Asia* (pp. 53–62). London and New York: Routledge.

Kawai, M., & Wignaraja, G. (2011). Asian FTAs: Trends, prospects and challenges. *Journal of Asian Economics, 22*, 1–22.

Krugman, P. (1997). What should trade negotiators negotiate about? *Journal of Economic Literature, 35*, 113–120.

Kydland, F., & Prescott, E. (1977). Rules rather than discretion: The inconsistency of optimal plans. *Journal of Political Economy, 85*(3), 473–492.

Lewis, D. J. (2008). Integration of landlocked countries into the global economy and domestic economic reforms: The case of Lao People's Democratic Republic. Asia-Pacific Research and Training Network on Trade Working Paper Series No. 58. Bangkok: Asia-Pacific Research and Training Network on Trade.

Llanto, G. (2010). The policy development process and the Agenda for effective institutions in the Philippines. In P. Dee (Ed.), *Institutions for economic reform in Asia* (pp. 88–105). London and New York: Routledge.

Martin, W. (2001). Trade policy reform in the East Asian transition economies. Policy Research Working Paper No. 2535. Washington, DC: World Bank.

McNaughton, A. (2011). Integrating services markets: A comparison of European Union and Australian experiences. *Australian Journal of International Affairs, 65*(4), 454–468.

McNaughton, A., & Furlong, P. (2013). Services Trade Reform in the European Union—The EU Services Directive. In C. Findlay (Ed). *Priorities and Pathways in Services Reform, Volume 2: Political Economy Studies*. Singapore: World Scientific.

Ochiai, R., Dee, P., & Findlay, C. (2010). Services in free trade agreements. In C. Findlay & S. Urata (Eds.), *Free trade agreements in the Asia Pacific* (pp. 29–80). Singapore: World Scientific.

Park, I., & Park, S. (2008). Reform creating regional trade agreements and foreign direct investment: Applications for East Asia. *Pacific Economic Review, 13*(5), 550–566.

Pauwelyn, J. (2005). The transformation of world trade. *Michigan Law Review, 104*(1), 1–65.

Persaud, I., & Goebel, R. J. (1997). Achieving full effectiveness of community law: The court of justice's third stage of enforcement rules. *American Society of International Law Proceedings, 91*, 159–165.

Pitarakis, J. Y., & Tridimas, G. (2003). Joint dynamics of legal and economic integration in the European Union. *European Journal of Law and Economics, 16*, 357–368.

Plummer, M. G. (2007). 'Best practices' in regional trading agreements: An application to Asia. *The World Economy, 30*(12), 1771–1796.

Roy, M., Marchetti, J., & Lim, H. (2006). Services liberalization in the new generation of Preferential Trade Agreements (PTAs): How much further than the GATS? Staff Working Paper ERSD-2006-07. Economic Research and Statistics Division. Geneva: World Trade Organization.

Soesastro, H. (2010). A strategy for regional cooperation to promote structural reform. In P. Dee (Ed.), *Institutions for economic reform in Asia* (pp. 212–217). London and New York: Routledge.

Soesastro, H., Aswicahyono, H., & Narjoko, D. (2010). Economic reforms in Indonesia after the crisis. In P. Dee (Ed.), *Institutions for economic reform in Asia* (pp. 106–120). London and New York: Routledge.

Stone Sweet, A. (2010). The European court of justice and the judicialization of EU governance. *Living Reviews in European Governance, 5*(2), 1–50.

Stone Sweet, A., & Brunell, T. L. (1998). The European court and the national courts: A statistical analysis of preliminary references, 1961–1995. *Journal of European Public Policy, 5*, 66–97.

Stone Sweet, A., & Brunell, T. L. (2011). How the European legal system works: Override, non-compliance, and majority activism in international regimes. Mimeo. http://works.bepress.com/alec_stone_sweet/39 (accessed 1 April 2011).

Sutherland Report (2004). *The Future of the WTO: Addressing institutional challenges in the new millennium.* The Sutherland Report: A Report of the Consultative Board to the Director-General, Supachai Panitchpakdi. Geneva: World Trade Organization.

Tallberg, J. (2002). Delegation to supranational institutions: Why, how, and with what consequences? *West European Politics, 25*(1), 23–46.

Tornell, A., Westermann, F., & Martínez, L. (2004). NAFTA and Mexico's economic performance. CESifo Working Paper No. 1155. Munich: CESifo (University of Munich and Ifo Institute).
Trachtman, J. P. (1999). Bananas, direct effect and compliance. *European Journal of International Law, 10*(4), 655–678.
Van den Broek, N. (2009). Enforcing WTO compliance through public opinion and direct effect: Two proposals to enhance the compliance perspectives for least developed WTO members. *Frontiers of Economics and Globalization, 6*, 444–462.
Vo, T. T., & Nguyen, T. A. (2010). Institutional changes for private sector development in Vietnam. In P. Dee (Ed.), *Institutions for Economic Reform in Asia* (pp. 165–194). London and New York: Routledge.
Warwick Commission. (2007). *The multilateral trade regime: Which way forward? The report of the first Warwick Commission*. Coventry: University of Warwick.
Weiler, J. H. H. (1991). The transformation of Europe. *Yale Law Journal, 100*(8), 2403–2483.
Weiler, J. H. H. (2001). The rule of lawyers and the Ethos of Diplomats: Reflections on the internal and external legitimacy of WTO dispute settlement. *Journal of World Trade, 35*(2), 191–207.
World Bank. (2000). Trade blocs. World Bank Policy Research Report. Oxford: Oxford University Press.

Chapter 7
Institutions for Asian Integration: Innovation and Reform

Giovanni Capannelli and See Seng Tan

Abstract The formation of regional production networks in East Asia has occurred mainly through market forces, without much help from regional institutions in promoting the creation of a single Asian market. While this approach has served the region well in the past, the drastic changes experienced since the 2008–2009 financial crisis and the challenges Asian countries are facing—growing inequalities and competition, on the one hand, and enhanced threats to the environment and people's health on the other—have rendered more urgent the need for intergovernmental cooperation at global and regional levels. Asia's institutions for regionalism need strengthening through reform and innovation such as better governance and resourcing, greater and more effective participation and delegation of powers, overall streamlining of regional architecture, including the phasing out of outdated or irrelevant institutions and, where needed, the creation of new ones. Ultimately, given its rootedness in regional order, institutional efficacy is a function of the ability and willingness of its members, especially influential stakeholders, to collaborate.

Keywords Cooperation reform • Delegation • Efficacy • Governance

7.1 Introduction: Why Asia Needs Stronger Institutions for Regional Integration

The formation of regional production networks in East Asia has occurred mainly through market forces, without much help from regional institutions in promoting the creation of a single Asian market. Multilateral and unilateral policy actions—such as

G. Capannelli (✉)
Asian Development Bank Institute, Tokyo, Japan
e-mail: gcapannelli@adbi.org

S.S. Tan
Nanyang Technological University, Singapore
e-mail: issstan@ntu.edu.sg

G. Capannelli and M. Kawai (eds.), *The Political Economy of Asian Regionalism*,
DOI 10.1007/978-4-431-54568-2_7,

the Plaza Accord of 1985 and incentive packages to attract foreign direct investment—have played a major role in influencing the decisions of several multinational corporations to relocate their production facilities in Asian countries. So far, however, common regional institutions have not been very active in creating a common Asian market. The Association of Southeast Asian Nations (ASEAN) will establish the ASEAN Economic Community (AEC) by the year 2015, but the powers member countries delegate to the ASEAN Secretariat (ASEC) remain limited.

Such an approach to regionalism has served the region well. Since the 1970s developing Asian economies have grown much faster than those in any other region in the world due largely to the implementation of carefully planned national development strategies. Poverty in Asia has halved since the early 1990s and the overall welfare of Asian citizens has greatly improved. Why would Asia need stronger institutions to promote regionalism? Does Asia need eventually to follow a European approach to regional cooperation, with the creation of several major institutions such as a council of ministers, a regional commission, a parliament, and a court of justice, or is it better off with its current light institutionalization of regionalism?

What has worked well in the past may not work as well in the future. The global economic and political environments have changed drastically since the eruption of the global financial crisis in 2008–2009 and the challenges Asian countries are facing, both individually and collectively as a region, have become far more complex and with intricate global ramifications. On the one hand, increased Asian economic interdependence has come not without problems. Inequality has risen, increasing competition has negatively affected some economic groups, and the benefits of integration remain mostly limited within East Asia's production networks. South and Central Asian economies are still poorly integrated: the integration of labor, services, and financial markets is proceeding at a very slow pace. On the other hand, intergovernmental cooperation at global and regional levels is increasingly needed to manage major threats to the environment and people's health, to prevent the recurrence of financial and economic crises, and to ensure security and peace.

The institutional architecture for regional cooperation that has been taking shape in Asia—hitherto ad hoc and incoherent—may not be adequate to face these new challenges. Several reforms and innovations are needed to strengthen Asia's institutions for regionalism. The governance of existing institutions should be strengthened and made more effective and participatory, giving larger space to civil society and the private sector to contribute to defining their priorities and agenda, together with government agencies. Regional institutions should also be given more delegated powers to act on behalf of their member countries in order to improve regional commons, as well as more financial and human resources. Regional stakeholders should consider phasing out institutions which have already accomplished their mandate or which are no more effective, and creating new institutions whenever needed. At the same time, it bears reminding that regional institutions are rooted in regional order. Institutional efficacy as such is equally dependent on the ability and willingness of their members, especially great powers and influential stakeholders, to collaborate.

Based on a study completed in 2010 by the Asian Development Bank (ADB), this paper reviews some literature on the design and development of institutions for Asian regionalism and discusses the future needs for innovation and reforms of the regional institutional architecture having in mind the creation of a regional economic community of sorts. Although we refrain from defining the components and structure of such an economic community for Asia and from proposing a roadmap for its achievement, we follow the taxonomy of institutions for regionalism adopted by the ADB study and focus on key governance principles for such institutions. In doing so, we present cases studies of principles and institutions that worked and did not work well in the past, and suggest some needed policy action.

Section 7.2 of this chapter reviews the literature on Asia's institutions for regional integration and cooperation. Section 7.3 discusses the relevant governance principles for such institutions, including considerations on stakeholders and their agenda. Section 7.4 introduces a taxonomy of Asia's institutions for regionalism, while Sect. 7.5 compares ASEAN with the South Asian Association for Regional Cooperation (SAARC), which can be defined as the overarching subregional institutions in Southeast and South Asia. Section 7.6 analyzes three selected functional institutions that provide interesting examples of cooperation in different sectors and subregions. Section 7.7 concludes suggesting the need for reform and innovation to strengthen Asia's institutional architecture for regionalism.

7.2 Asia's Institutions for Regionalism: Overview of the Literature

The story of Asia's regional integration is distinct from that of Europe owing to different economic and political conditions. In Europe, an insecure regional environment following the Second World War, an equally unforgiving economic environment marked by high protectionism and widespread current account restrictions, an embedded liberalism that emphasized protection of labor relations and agriculture and, importantly, interventionist states that sought to satisfy such expectations, combined to render the region not particularly conducive to simple market-driven integration (Capannelli and Filippini 2010). Heightened societal expectations in the immediate postwar period coincided with the widespread feeling that traditional nation states had failed to provide their populations with economic security in the years between the first and second world wars and physical security after 1939.[1] Contrary to functionalist accounts that attribute European regionalism to non-state forces, others argue it was economic motives of emerging Western European welfare states that played a key part in driving regional integration in Europe (Moravcsik 1998; Moravcsik 2000; Puchala 1999).

[1] The crucial constituencies Western European governments sought to placate were the agricultural communities, workers, and dependents of the welfare state. Differences aside, the common solution was to raise wages and ensure full employment, enhance the living standards of the agriculture sector, and establish the modern welfare state (Milward 2000).

No such common cause and motivation impel Asia's economic integration. Today, Asian economic regionalism relies on an array of mostly uncoordinated processes, such as the People's Republic of China (PRC) unilateral opening during Deng Xiaoping's leadership, the concerted unilateralism of the Asia-Pacific Economic Cooperation (APEC) forum, the many bilateral and "plurilateral" free trade agreements (FTAs) that dot the region, global negotiations such as those under the World Trade Organization (WTO), and regional initiatives such as the ASEAN+3 (ASEAN plus the PRC, Japan, and the Republic of Korea) that emerged in reaction to the Asian financial crisis of 1997–1998 (Baum 1980; Dent 2008; Kawai and Wignaraja 2011; Ravenhill 2001). The combined impact of these initiatives has contributed to rapid economic growth marked by a considerable expansion of cross-border trade and financial flows, as well as an increasing integration within the region and with the rest of the world. As such, Asia has played host not only to swift-rising intra-regional investment and flows of managerial talent and other skilled labor, but also to the intensive development of regional supply chains and production networks. This has led some prominent economists to refer to the region as "Factory Asia" (Baldwin 2008).

In contrast to the scarcity of institutions for regional integration serving Asia in the immediate aftermath of the Cold War,[2] a dense web of overlapping regional and subregional institutions supports Asia's integration today. Figure 7.1 shows the main regional and transregional forums supporting Asian integration and emphasizes the fundamental role played by ASEAN in promoting Asia-wide integration, as it is around ASEAN that major groups such as ASEAN+3 and the East Asia Summit are revolving (ADB 2008).

Designed to foster cooperation on specific issues and solve policy problems, Asia's brand of functional regionalism is largely the consequence of ad hoc premises and rationales, where regional initiatives are formed in response to specific perceived needs (Tan 2010a; Woolcott 2009). This has led to a pan-regional architecture comprising a plethora of arrangements, each oriented toward a particular thematic purpose. For example, APEC focuses on promoting trade liberalization, whereas the ASEAN Regional Forum (ARF) promotes cooperative security and confidence building with a number of ASEAN dialogue partners (Kesavapany and Lim 2009; Ravenhill 2001; Katsumata 2009; Severino 2009a).

Despite these developments, there is growing concern among some regional stakeholders that while Asian institutions up to now have served the region well—primarily by not getting in the way of market forces—a fair amount of institutional retrofitting is required to ensure and enhance Asia's prosperity, stability, and security. Baldwin, for example, has argued that Asian regionalism is "fragile" since it relies

[2] In 1993, prominent international relations theorist Ruggie (1993: 4) wrote: "It was not possible to construct multilateral institutional frameworks [in Asia] in the immediate postwar period. Today [in 1993], the absence of such arrangements inhibits progressive adaptation to fundamental global shifts." For Ruggie, the absence of EU-like and/or NATO-like structures, or a Helsinki-like process in post-Cold War Asia essentially means "a reasonably stable balance is the best that one can hope to achieve" in Asia.

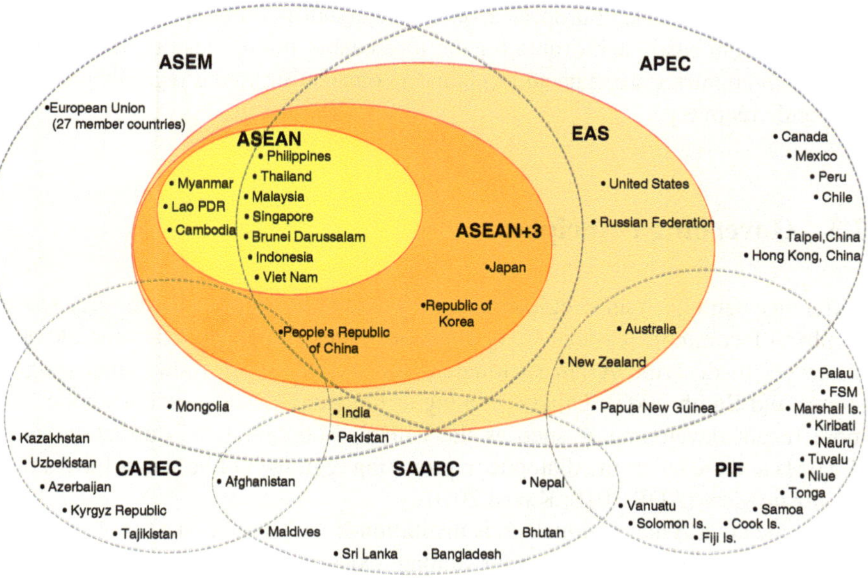

Fig. 7.1 Main regional and transregional forums for economic integration in Asia. *APEC* Asia–Pacific Economic Cooperation, *ASEAN* Association of Southeast Asian Nations, *ASEAN+3* ASEAN countries plus the People's Republic of China, Japan, and the Republic of Korea, *ASEM* Asia-Europe Meeting, *CAREC* Central Asia Regional Economic Cooperation, *EAS* East Asia Summit (includes ASEAN+3 countries, plus Australia, India, New Zealand, the Russian Federation, and the United States), *FSM* Federated States of Micronesia, *Lao PDR* Lao People's Democratic Republic, *PIF* Pacific Islands Forum, *PRC* People's Republic of China, *SAARC* South Asian Association for Regional Cooperation
Notes: (i) ASEM includes the European Union as a member; (ii) PRC's membership in CAREC is focused on the Xinjiang Uygur Autonomous Region
Source: Authors' update of Figure 7.1 in Asian Development Bank (ADB) (2008)

on three inherently unstable factors: (i) intraregional trade; (ii) unilateral liberalization and tariff reductions that are non-binding vis-à-vis WTO regulations; and (iii) the absence of "top-level management" to ensure bilateral trade tensions do not spill over into disputes or, worse, conflict (Baldwin 2008). Baldwin's third point—no overarching, leader-led framework—is a widely-shared concern, most recently highlighted in two former regional leaders' visions for a new regional architecture.[3]

More broadly, the Asian institutional architecture is perceived as fragile because, despite its growing web of regional intergovernmental organizations and groups created by civil society, Asia remains for the most part "institution-light" in the design, resources, delegated powers, extent of legalization, and efficacy of its existing institutions for integration (Evans 2005; Rathus 2010; Tan 2011). Considerably more diverse and widespread geographically than Europe, Asia also has no equivalent of the Franco–German cooperative arrangement—no local version of the Elysée

[3] Former Australian Prime Minister Kevin Rudd's vision of an "Asia-Pacific Community" and former Japanese Prime Minister Yukio Hatoyama's vision for an "East Asian Community."

Treaty, that is—on which European economic regionalism stands. Nor is a PRC–Japan rapprochement easily achievable for the foreseeable future, despite the significant roles both countries are expected to play in contributing to the region's post-crisis economic recovery.[4]

7.3 Governing Principles

Differences among Asia's regional and subregional institutions aside, they share a number of common features. It is these attributes that have led some skeptical observers to describe Asian regionalism as about process rather than progress (Jones and Smith 2007). Others, looking at the adoption of principles underlying more recent developments such as the Chiang Mai Initiative Multilateralization (CMIM) and the emerging dialogue in providing regional public goods have a more optimistic view (ADB 2010; Kawai 2010).

The idea that Asian regionalism is institution-light is based on a set of governing principles that are usually shared among existing organizations. First, Asia's regional arrangements tend to emphasize flexibility, informality, and consensus. Although decision-making rules are created to build consensus in a flexible way more than through strict unanimity, the process tends to limit decisiveness. Second, a general preference for non-binding and unilateral commitments means Asia's regional institutions operate under few explicit procedural rules, and delegate few tasks to standing secretariats. Put another way, their mandates and modalities are largely deliberative and/or advisory rather than distributive and/or regulatory.[5] Notable exceptions include APEC and arguably ASEAN that have introduced a set of targets and rules to govern actions of their members, although their agreements are still non-binding. As a result, the monitoring and enforcement powers of most regional institutions are slender. Third, regional organizations tend to specify only a few obligations for their members. Accession to regional institutions usually requires few policy changes or commitments. Asian regional institutions typically include all the economies in a given geographical area. This inclusivity is also expressed in terms of "open regionalism"—or regionalism with the least discriminatory

[4] Notably, Hatoyama's proposal for regional architecture had, as a foundation or pillar, PRC–Japan reconciliation and cooperation within (at least for early versions of the proposal) an EU-like organization for East Asia (Soeya 2010).

[5] Intergovernmental institutions are by and large consultative forums whose mandates are principally declaratory in orientation (that is, deliberative and/or advisory). While intergovernmentalism does not preclude institutions from legalizing (for example, the ASEAN Charter), they lack the power to regulate behavior among their members and to enforce rules, owing to the absence or weakness of compliance mechanisms and/or the strong norms of state sovereignty and nonintervention. On the other hand, supranational institutions (for example, the European Union) are empowered to regulate behavior among their members because of the availability of viable compliance mechanisms (that is, distributive and/or regulatory).

component for nonmembers—an idea formally affiliated with APEC's trade liberalization policy, but which also has a security connotation, as evidenced in Asia's security institutions—the ARF and, more recently, the ASEAN Defence Ministers' Meeting Plus Eight (ADMM+8)—designed for engaging the major powers (Garnaut 1996; Acharya 1997; Emmers and Tan 2011).[6] Fourth, as principally intergovernmental institutions, they tend to center on negotiations among governments rather than delegating authority to common regional or subregional bodies. Non-state actors, be they individuals or corporations, are not directly enfranchised. Here, the doctrines of national sovereignty, noninterference, and nonintervention are often invoked to justify decisions (or their lack of) undertaken that favor national interests over broader concerns. Fifth, they involve cooperation in specific fields by national governments that retain their sovereignty, rather than the creation and operation of a body or authority transcending those sovereign states. Economics and security are treated as compartmentalized or segmented issue areas. This implies that even though the proliferation of institutions in Asia can be described as web-like, they are not as interlocked as might be imagined.[7] Moreover, these institutions are rarely designed to incorporate links between the two domains. Sixth, existing institutions for Asian regionalism are thought of as confidence building exercises which aim to create an environment conducive to the cultivation of trust, and, on that basis, facilitate progressive though incremental integration.

The attributes described above have long been associated with the so-called "ASEAN Way". They have also been referred to as the "Asian Way" or "Asia-Pacific Way", given their import at the wider regional level (Acharya 1997; Haas 1989). It has also been noted how the ASEAN Way has indirectly influenced other institutions such as the Shanghai Cooperation Organization (Caballero-Anthony 2009). That said, it has been argued that the ASEAN Way is not unique to Asia since its features are common to the conventions that guide interstate relations in other parts of the world; in Severino's words, the ASEAN Way—for that matter, the governing principles of Asian regionalism—"is actually the way of the world" (Severino 2009b: 6)

While the so-called way of the world has hitherto served Asia well, there is growing acknowledgement among regional stakeholders that the existing regional architecture and its underlying conventions require revamping to address its fragility. But precisely what changes are needed, and how to achieve them, are crucial questions that will likely figure prominently in academic and policy debates on the future of Asia's regional architecture and its governing principles.

[6] As Singapore Prime Minister Lee Hsien Loong has opined, "the most robust and stable configuration for [Asian] regional cooperation is an open and inclusive one" (Lee 2006). The Plus Eight members are Australia, the PRC, India, Japan, the Republic of Korea, New Zealand, the Russian Federation, and the United States.

[7] Put another way, there is little or no clustering of existing institutions that would allow for tactical links among issues and the consequent reduction of transaction costs (Keohane 1984; Young 1999).

7.4 Taxonomy of Asia's Institutions for Regionalism

An ADB study (ADB 2010) conducted an inventory of Asia's intergovernmental organizations engaged in promoting regional integration. The list covers 40 institutions located in Asia's subregions (Table 7.1). This list includes institutions from four of Asia's subregions (Central, South, Southeast, and Northeast) and the Pacific. It also distinguishes between subregional, intraregional, pan-Asian,

Table 7.1 List of institutions for regionalism in Asia and the Pacific

Transregional (7)	
Overarching (4)	Asia-Europe Meeting (ASEM); Asia-Pacific Economic Cooperation (APEC); Eurasian Economic Community (EurAsEC); Forum for East Asia–Latin America Cooperation (FEALAC)
Functional (3)	ASEAN Regional Forum (ARF); Indian Ocean Rim Association for Regional Cooperation (IORARC); Shanghai Cooperation Organization (SCO)
Pan-Asian (2)	
Facilitating (2)	Asian Development Bank (ADB); UN Economic and Social Commission for Asia and the Pacific (ESCAP)
Intraregional (10)	
Overarching (2)	ASEAN plus the PRC, Japan, and Republic of Korea (ASEAN+3); East Asia Summit (EAS)
Functional (8)	ASEAN+3 Macroeconomic Research Office (AMRO); Bay of Bengal Initiative for Multi-Sectoral Technical and Economic Cooperation (BIMSTEC); Central Banks of Southeast Asia, New Zealand, and Australia (SEANZA); Coral Triangle Initiative (CTI); Credit Guarantee and Investment Facility (CGIF); Economic Cooperation Organization (ECO); Executives' Meeting of East Asia-Pacific Central Banks (EMEAP); Network of Asian River Basin Organizations (NARBO)
Subregional (21)	
Central Asia (3)	
Functional (3)	Central Asia Regional Economic Cooperation (CAREC); International Fund for Saving the Aral Sea (IFAS); UN Special Programme for the Economies of Central Asia (SPECA)
South Asia (4)	
Overarching (1)	South Asian Association for Regional Cooperation (SAARC)[a]
Functional (3)	Bay of Bengal Programme Inter-Governmental Organisation (BOBP–IGO); South Asia Co-operative Environment Programme (SACEP); South Asia Subregional Economic Cooperation (SASEC)
Southeast Asia (6)	
Overarching (1)	Association of Southeast Asian Nations (ASEAN)[b]
Functional (5)	Brunei Darussalam–Indonesia–Malaysia–Philippines East ASEAN Growth Area (BIMP–EAGA); Greater Mekong Subregion Economic Cooperation Program (GMS); Indonesia–Malaysia–Thailand Growth Triangle (IMT–GT); Mekong River Commission (MRC); South East Asian Water Utilities Network (SEAWUN)

(continued)

Table 7.1 (continued)

Northeast Asia (2)	
Overarching (1)	Trilateral Summit (TS)
Functional (1)	Greater Tumen Initiative (GTI)
Pacific (6)	
Overarching (1)	Pacific Islands Forum (PIF)
Functional (5)	Forum Fisheries Agency (FFA); Pacific Islands Applied Geoscience Commission (SOPAC); Secretariat of the Pacific Community (SPC); South Pacific Regional Environmental Programme (SPREP); South Pacific Tourism Organisation (SPTO)

[a]Since 2005, SAARC has launched many cooperation centers, programs, and initiatives. These include the SAARC Agricultural Information Centre, the SAARC Audio Visual Exchange Committee, the SAARC Coastal Zone Management Centre, the SAARC Development Fund, the SAARC Disaster Management Centre, the SAARC Documentation Centre, the SAARC Energy Centre, the SAARC Food Bank, the SAARC Forestry Centre, the SAARC Human Resource Development Centre, the SAARC Meteorological Research Centre, the SAARC Tuberculosis and HIV/AIDS Centre, the South Asian University, and the South Asian Growth Quadrangle

[b]A number of cooperation programs and initiatives operate under the ASEAN umbrella. These include the ASEAN Centre for Biodiversity, the ASEAN Centre for Energy, the ASEAN Centre for the Development of Agricultural Cooperatives, the ASEAN Coordinating Centre for Transboundary Haze Pollution, the ASEAN Council on Petroleum, the ASEAN Earthquake Information Centre, the ASEAN Foundation, the ASEAN Insurance Training and Research Institute, the ASEAN Intergovernmental Commission on Human Rights, the ASEAN Specialized Meteorological Centre, and the ASEAN University Network

Source: Asian Development Bank staff based on field interviews

and transregional institutions and it divides institutions into three categories (overarching, functional, facilitating) according to the role they play in promoting Asia's integration.[8]

Overarching institutions are "…umbrella arrangements with comprehensive purviews. They may be based on a vision of an integrated regional economy and creating a single regional market and regional community" (ADB 2010). They are typically set up to promote the idea of integration and regionalism in a number of areas and functions, and in the case of Asia their understanding of regionalism is usually inclusive. Most overarching institutions hold regular summits involving the heads of states or governments of their member countries and have established secretariats that coordinate their activities and link them with their constituting member agencies. The ADB study found, however, that in most cases these secretariats are not receiving enough delegated powers and human and financial resources from their members.

Usually these institutions have a body of normative frameworks that legitimize their existence, provide their governing principles, and specify the realm of their activities.

[8]Following ADB's classification, subregional institutions are those covering all or part of respective subregions; intraregional institutions cover at least two but not all subregions; pan-Asian institutions are those covering all Asia's subregions; and transregional institutions are those that link Asia to other regions of the world.

They also have various forms of feedback mechanisms to inform about their performance. At the subregional level, examples of overarching institutions include ASEAN in Southeast Asia and SAARC in South Asia; at the intraregional level, the ADB list includes ASEAN+3 and the East Asia Summit (EAS); while APEC and the Asia–Europe Meeting (ASEM) can be cited as two prominent examples of overarching institutions at the transregional level.

Functional institutions are arrangements focused on specific areas of cooperation and in some cases following a highly technical agenda. The spectrum of their activities is narrower than that of overarching institutions, while their aim is to internalize regional spillovers through collective action, to adopt common standards, and to share best practices.[9] Although functional institutions may lack a comprehensive vision for integrating their region beyond their specific sector, they represent an essential element of regionalism as they provide a unique ground for the region to come together on relevant technical areas underpinning wider integration projects.

Functional initiatives tend to focus on a limited geographical area, although some of them have been known to deemphasize geography and, in so doing, potentially impede any regionalizing imperative (Hurrell 1995). They deal exclusively with economic and/or development matters (such as trade, investment, finance, labor, infrastructure, and socioeconomic issues) that are to a large extent "depoliticized" (Tan 2009). Some of Asia's functional institutions enjoy a measure of delegation, particularly those in South Asia, whereas many of those in Southeast Asia are more properly considered "offshoots" under the hierarchy and purview of ASEAN. The ADB list includes functional institutions in Asia and the Pacific. At the subregional level, there are initiatives such as the Central Asia Regional Economic Cooperation (CAREC), the Greater Mekong Subregion (GMS) Economic Cooperation Program, the Greater Tumen Initiative (GTI), and the South Asia Subregional Economic Cooperation (SASEC). Examples of intraregional functional institutions include the ASEAN+3 Macroeconomic Research Office; the Bay of Bengal Initiative for Multi-Sectoral Technical and Economic Cooperation; the Coral Triangle Initiative; the Economic Cooperation Organization; the Executives' Meeting of East Asia–Pacific Central Banks; and the Network of Asian River Basin Organizations.

Asia's *facilitating* institutions for regionalism are the United Nations (UN) Economic and Social Commission for Asia and the Pacific (ESCAP) and ADB. These two organizations play a unique role as "service providers" to their member economies and their national and regional institutions to facilitate regional cooperation and integration. They can mobilize large funds from their internal programs and tap from sizable pools of resources from their partners and affiliates, due to the high level of reputation they command. Typically, they provide advisory, administrative, technical, and financial support. In subregions where overarching institutions are either weak or nonexistent, facilitating agencies play key roles in helping functional institutions contribute to regional cooperation and integration acting as catalysts

[9] An important qualification here is that most Asian institutions for integration are functional or issue-specific in orientation—true whether they are overarching, functional (as in this understanding), or facilitating arrangements.

and coordinators—or honest brokers— for regional initiatives, as capacity builders, and as providers of knowledge and information on regionalism, in addition to their role as funders of regional projects.[10]

The limited remit and scope of this study does not permit an investigation into all three categories of Asian institutions. What the following discussion seeks to do is to look at select illustrations of overarching and functional institutions focused on East and South Asia.

7.5 Overarching Subregional Institutions: Comparing ASEAN and SAARC

Two examples of overarching institutions are the subregional organizations operating in Southeast and South Asia: ASEAN and SAARC. These institutions have certain similarities as they both are intergovernmental arrangements operating in two large and dynamic subregions. Their decision-making structures are largely consensus-based, and their general approach is to adopt voluntary initiatives that are not legally binding. Their functions are typically related to advisory, non-deliberative roles, and they are (relatively) short on power delegation from their member countries. Nevertheless, these institutions display interesting differences.

ASEAN, established in 1967, is much further ahead than SAARC in terms of regional cooperation outcomes. In 1992, ASEAN leaders established the ASEAN Free Trade Area (AFTA); in 2003 they took the bold decision to create an ASEAN Economic Community (AEC) by 2015 (originally 2020).[11] In 2005, ASEAN leaders proposed the formulation of an ASEAN Charter, which was formally adopted in November 2007, establishing ASEAN as a rules-based institution with some binding legal obligations.

On the other hand, launched in 1985, SAARC, created as "an act of faith"[12] given the initial lack of any shared interest and/or aversion among its member countries, has shown fewer results than its Southeast Asian counterpart. From a 1993 agreement to gradually lower tariffs among member economies, leaders devised the South Asian Free Trade Agreement (SAFTA) in 2004, which entered into force 4 years later. However, SAFTA has been hampered by issues such as overall low intraregional trade ratios and an increasing income gap, Pakistan's refusal to extend most

[10] In is important to stress that neither ADB nor ESCAP make strategic decisions on regionalism, which are the purview of their member countries' governments and (to some extent) overarching institutions, striving instead to ensure that ownership of the programs and initiatives they finance and support rests with governments themselves.

[11] In addition to the AEC by 2015, ASEAN aspires to establish the ASEAN Political–Security Community (APSC, formerly known as the ASEAN Security Community or ASC) and ASEAN Socio–Cultural Community (ASCC). Taken together, the AEC, APSC, and ASCC will form the three pillars of the ASEAN Community.

[12] Indian Prime Minister Rajiv Gandhi's description of SAARC's creation at the first SAARC Summit in Dhaka in 1985 (Cherunilam 2008: 343).

favored nation (MFN) status to India, and subregional grievance against India's imposition of nontariff barriers to trade. Bilateral tensions and conflicts, with the Indo–Pakistani conflict being the most troublesome, have significantly impeded effective subregional cooperation.

Both institutions' secretariats, whose remits have principally been to furnish administrative support rather than been invested with powers of delegation, continue to be funded by very small budgets and did not aim to create regional bureaucracies promoting a more independent agenda for integration beyond the scope provided by intergovernmental cooperation structures. In the 1980s, ASEAN's iconic projects were managed by committees, but these were not given responsibility over the growing economic interactions and integration in the Southeast Asian region that was in effect driven largely by trade liberalization policies adopted by individual member countries. ASEAN has been able to enhance its secretariat, however, with the adoption of the charter and other initiatives to expand its institutional function. The charter was also an important step to improve ASEAN's compliance mechanisms, streamline its decision-making structure, and strengthen its dispute-settlement mechanism.

But several important factors continue to limit its role such as the principle of equal contribution to the secretariat's budget and the fact that it cannot take any major proposal or initiative without the full consent of member countries' government officials, be it in the form of its senior officials' meetings, senior economic officials' meetings, or high-level task force.[13] Delegation to the secretariat is limited to managing the dispute settlement mechanism and monitoring the implementation of the ASEAN Economic Community (AEC) Blueprint. This suggests that despite the progress made towards a rules-based regionalism, ASEAN remains robustly intergovernmental, with little delegation since it relies on "offshoots" rather than independent agencies to implement policy. An independent review recently conducted by the secretariat suggested that only about 30 % of the regional cooperation initiatives taken by ASEAN over the years have been actually implemented, raising a critical question over the effectiveness of the organization and providing an additional motivation for introducing further institutional reforms and innovation (Desker 2008).

As an intergovernmental institution, SAARC adopted an organizational structure similar to ASEAN's during its early years. A council of foreign ministers, assisted by a standing committee of senior officials, is entrusted with the formulation of policies, review of progress, and making decisions on new areas of cooperation, as well as the establishment of mechanisms that are deemed necessary. Much like ASEAN's committees, SAARC technical committees (or committees of experts) have been established to implement, coordinate, and monitor progress of its integration projects (Raghavan 1995). These committees focus their activities on infrastructure, science and technology, human development, and energy.

From a longstanding supporting role, SAARC secretariat's agenda has expanded to include coverage of issues such as regional connectivity and human development,

[13] On the limitations of the ASEAN Secretariat, pre- and post-charter, see Severino (2006).

as well as policy coordination in response to the 2008–2009 global financial crisis. But the implementation of SAARC's heralded iconic project, the South Asia Free Trade Area (SAFTA) is lagging behind. At the same time, however, a key innovation in SAARC is the creation of "regional centers"—13 currently exist—that focus on specific programs to facilitate regional cooperation at the ground level. Interestingly, the capital cost and administrative budget of each regional center are borne by the respective host country, while program budgets are shared by all member governments in proportion to their gross domestic product (GDP). The centers are overseen by the secretariat, which reports on their activities to the summit. The activities are approved by the program committee and the summit, whereas implementation responsibility rests with host country governments. This suggests that while concrete results in terms of closer regional integration may still take time to be seen, SAARC has made progress in its governance structure, as there is–on paper–a rather extensive delegation of responsibilities to separate institutions.

ASEAN clearly leads SAARC in overall economic integration. The introduction of the AEC Blueprint, accompanied by a system of score cards to monitor members' compliance with their commitments to move along the creation of a common ASEAN market have created a momentum. ASEAN's participation in the Group of Twenty (G20) meetings, albeit still as an observer, has further promoted the pivotal role it is playing to support wider Asian integration. However, SAARC has shown more innovation in delegation than ASEAN, whose structures and governing principles remain robustly intergovernmental.[14] That said, that there is an upside to ASEAN's centralism, not least in its ability as an institution led by leaders to push through bold initiatives such as AFTA.

7.6 Functional Institutions: Lessons from GMS, BIMSTEC, and AMRO

Functional economic initiatives in Asia have been most prominent in the areas of trade and investment, infrastructure and connectivity, as well as finance. We focus on three examples from East and South Asia: the Greater Mekong Subregion (GMS), the Bay of Bengal Initiative for Multi-Sectoral Technical and Economic Cooperation (BIMSTEC), and the ASEAN+3 Macroeconomic Research Office (AMRO). While the GMS is becoming an iconic example of successful subregional cooperation and can be used as a reference case for other institutions, BIMSTEC is relevant to show how functional cooperation can assist linking two of Asia's five main subregions: East and South. Finally, AMRO represents a unique example of

[14] An important exception to an otherwise delegation-challenged ASEAN is its various "growth area" initiatives. These include the Indonesia–Malaysia–Thailand Growth Triangle (IMT–GT) and the Brunei Darussalam–Indonesia–Malaysia–Philippines East ASEAN Growth Area (BIMP–EAGA) that were inspired by an earlier initiative among Indonesia, Malaysia, and Singapore (SIJORI) and have been endorsed by ASEAN officials.

institutional innovation in the area of financial cooperation that can be used as a blueprint for innovation and reform in other functional areas as well.

Launched by ADB in 1992, the GMS is a program aimed at facilitating economic development of the territories along the Mekong river basin, which extends from Yunnan Province and the Guangxi Zhuang Autonomous Region in the PRC, to Myanmar, Thailand, the Lao People's Democratic Republic, Cambodia, and Viet Nam. Two decades from its inauguration, the GMS today adopts a comprehensive approach to regional integration, covering activities from developing infrastructure, to promoting strategic industries, fostering the private sector, protecting the environment, and building capacity through specific training programs. Its institutional structure has also evolved and in addition to yearly ministerial conferences, since 2002 a GMS leaders' summit has been organized every 3 years. [15]

A feature of GMS has been a focus on following a bottom-up approach, driven by local authorities and communities more than by national governments, and establishing economic links among its members. Although ADB has continuously provided financial and technical support, the GMS institutional structure is directly organized by its member countries. Local constituencies have proposed and introduced new initiatives and funding has been sourced from member countries and international donors. As a result, the GMS has successfully narrowed the income gap and promoted a closer sense of community among its members. It is often cited as an example of successful subregional integration.

Created in 1997 from a Thai proposal to establish a link between Southeast and South Asia for promoting economic development through the implementation of technical cooperation projects among neighboring countries, BIMSTEC can be seen as the coming together of the "Look West" policy of Thailand and the "Look East" policy of India (Devi 2007). The group, comprising five SAARC countries (Bangladesh, Bhutan, India, Nepal, and Sri Lanka) plus Myanmar and Thailand, promotes technical cooperation in 14 priority sectors, each led by members on a voluntary basis.[16]

The development of cross-border infrastructure, especially for transport and logistics, is a key area of BIMSTEC cooperation. ADB, which became a BIMSTEC development partner in 2005, has assisted the group to promote and improve transportation infrastructure and logistics among its members. A trade negotiations committee was also established in 2004 to pave the way for an eventual free trade

[15] The first GMS leaders' summit was organized in 2002 in Phnom Penh, Cambodia, the second one in 2005 in Kunming, PRC, and the third one in 2008 in Vientiane, Lao People's Democratic Republic.

[16] Traditional priority sectors for BIMSTEC cooperation, agreed at its inception in 1997 are: (i) trade and investment, (ii) transport and communication, (iii) energy, (iv) tourism, (v) information technology, and (vi) fisheries. The following sectors were added at the ministerial meeting in 2005: (vii) agriculture, (viii) public health, (ix) poverty alleviation, (x) counter-terrorism and transnational crime, (xi) environmental protection and natural disaster management, (xii) cultural exchanges, (xiii) people-to-people contact; while (xiv) climate change was eventually added as the fourteenth priority sector at the ministerial meeting in 2009.

area although some observers do not foresee this development as likely to happen in the near future. BIMSTEC has no secretariat and its activities are coordinated by an office located in the Thai Foreign Ministry, but preparations are currently being made for the establishment of a permanent secretariat that could be in Bangladesh or Sri Lanka, as both have offered to serve as host countries.

In the area of regional financial cooperation, two of the main initiatives that emerged from the Economic Review and Policy Dialogue started by the ASEAN+3 countries after the Asian financial crisis of 1997–1998 are the Chiang Mai Initiative (CMI) and its multilateralization (CMIM), and the Asian Bond Markets Initiative (ABMI) (ADB 2008; Arner 2009; Gochoco-Bautista 2009; Capannelli 2011).[17] We discuss below the CMIM and the corollary decision to set up a regional surveillance agency under the AMRO, as it shows the ability of Asian governments to introduce an institutional innovation as an ASEAN+3 offshoot, with potential important implications for the future of regional economic cooperation.

The United States (US) veto to the creation of an Asian Monetary Fund (AMF), proposed by Japan in reaction to the 1997–1998 Asian financial crisis, led to the strengthening of Asia's financial cooperation. In particular, the first objective of Asian countries was to insure themselves against the recurrence of a similar, devastating crisis and taking from an existing ASEAN swap agreement introduced in 1978, they set up the CMI, or a system of bilateral currency swaps among regional monetary authorities to provide short-term liquidity to countries in immediate need. Launched in 2000, the CMI has expanded and the system of bilateral swap agreements was multilateralized in 2008, creating a common pool of regional funds—the CMIM—governed by a single contract and collectively managed by the ASEAN+3 countries (ADB 2010).

The ASEAN+3 finance ministers agreed at their 2009 meeting in Bali, Indonesia, on the main CMIM components, such as individual country contributions, borrowing accessibility, and the introduction of a regional surveillance mechanism to ensure that borrowers of CMIM funds would have enough capacity to repay their debt.[18] The size of its reserve pool was first increased from $80 billion to $120 billion, and in March 2012 it was doubled to $240 billion with ASEAN countries bearing 20 % of the fund's contributions and the other 80 % borne by the "Plus Three" countries. In particular, the intergovernmental resolution on the contribution shares of the PRC, Japan, and the Republic of Korea is grounded on an excellent outcome of financial diplomacy as Asia's two largest economies—the PRC and Japan—agreed to perceive themselves as equally sized, while allowing the Republic of Korea to position itself as holding a share equal to half of the two. The 80 % contribution share of the Plus Three countries was in fact equally divided between

[17] The ABMI, which was officially launched in 2003, aims to help recycling Asian savings into Asian investment by promoting the development of local currency-denominated bond markets, facilitating greater accessibility to the regional bond markets, and enhancing market infrastructure.

[18] The CMIM officially came into effect on 24 March 2010.

Table 7.2 CMIM financial contributions, borrowing arrangements, and voting power

Members	Financial contributions		Borrowing arrangements		Voting power			
	$ billion	% share	Multiplier	Quota ($ billion)	No. of basic votes	No. of votes based on contributions	Total no. of votes	% share
PRC (including HKG)	76.8	32.00					40.00	28.41
PRC	*68.4*	*28.50*	0.5	34.20	1.60	34.20	35.80	25.43
HKG	*8.4*	*3.50*	2.5	21.00	0.00	4.20	4.20	2.98
Japan	76.8	32.00	0.5	38.40	1.60	38.40	40.00	28.41
Republic of Korea	38.4	16.00	1.0	38.40	1.60	19.20	20.80	14.77
'Plus Three' Countries	192.0	80.00			4.80	96.00	100.80	71.59
Brunei Darussalam	0.1	0.03	5.0	0.30	1.60	0.03	1.63	1.16
Cambodia	0.2	0.10	5.0	1.20	1.60	0.12	1.72	1.22
Indonesia	9.1	3.79	2.5	22.75	1.60	4.55	6.15	4.37
Lao PDR	0.1	0.03	5.0	0.30	1.60	0.03	1.63	1.16
Malaysia	9.1	3.79	2.5	22.75	1.60	4.55	6.15	4.37
Myanmar	0.1	0.05	5.0	0.60	1.60	0.06	1.66	1.18
Philippines	9.1	3.79	2.5	22.75	1.60	4.55	6.15	4.37
Singapore	9.1	3.79	2.5	22.75	1.60	4.55	6.15	4.37
Thailand	9.1	3.79	2.5	22.75	1.60	4.55	6.15	4.37
Viet Nam	2.0	0.83	5.0	10.00	1.60	1.00	2.60	1.85
ASEAN	48.0	20.00			16.00	24.00	40.00	28.41
ASEAN+3	240.0	100.00			20.80	120.00	140.80	100.00

ASEAN Association of Southeast Asian Nations, *CMIM* Chiang Mai Initiative Multilateralization, *HKG* Hong Kong, China *Lao PDR* Lao People's Democratic Republic, *PRC* People's Republic of China

Source: ASEAN Secretariat and ASEAN+3 Macroeconomics Research Office

Japan and the PRC, which hold a 32 % share each in the CMIM, with the Republic of Korea contributing the remaining 16 % (Capannelli 2011).[19]

The small country bias in favor of the Republic of Korea is used as a more general principle in the governance of CMIM to not only allocate the 20 % contribution shares among the ASEAN countries, but also—and more importantly—to decide the multiplier used to determine the actual quota that each country can borrow, based on its financial contribution. As Table 7.2 shows, while the multiplier for large economies such as the PRC and Japan is only 50 % of their financial contributions, the smaller ASEAN economies can borrow from the CMIM five times as much their

[19] The PRC share is actually divided between a 28.5 % contribution from the PRC and a 3.5 % contribution from Hong Kong, China. Due to the nature of the CMI, based on the accumulation of foreign exchange reserves by Asian countries to be mobilized in case of short-term liquidity needs, representatives of the Hong Kong Monetary Authority have continuously shared a presence in CMI meetings with representatives from the People's Bank of China.

financial contributions. And in terms of voting power, the ASEAN countries collectively command a 28.41 % share of the total, which is relatively higher than their collective share of financial contributions (20 %).

Another important innovation introduced with the CMIM is a departure from a decision-making structure based uniquely on consensus to adopt a more flexible system allowing for a two-thirds qualified majority in the case of operational (lending) matters, while decisions on fundamental issues, such as agreements on the terms of lending, reviews of borrowing multipliers, membership, size, and IMF conditionality ratios, continue to be taken by consensus among the ASEAN+3 members. The CMIM voting shares also reflect a determination not to allow any of the Plus Three countries individually, nor all ASEAN countries together, to hold a veto power on decision making.

The decision to create the AMRO was officially made at the ASEAN+3 finance ministers meeting in May 2010. The mandate of this new institution, set up in Singapore in 2011, is to conduct regional macroeconomic and financial surveillance to ensure that borrowing countries can meet the repayment conditions of their debt. While some observers have noted that the combination of a regionally pooled fund of international reserves and a regional surveillance agency is similar to the de-facto creation of an AMF, more than a decade after the original Japanese proposal, others tend to stress the complementary relationship that the CMIM–AMRO combination will have with the IMF in its functions as both a financial crises-rescuing agency as well as a global and national macroeconomic surveillance institution (Kawai 2010; Capannelli 2011).[20]

The creation of the AMRO could indeed serve as a stepping-stone to the formation of an AMF. However, a fundamental issue concerns whether the AMRO will be able to build up its reputation as a technically solid and independent agency with strong macroeconomic surveillance capabilities. In particular, there is the need to develop an appropriate regulatory mechanism that could insulate the distinctive forms of state-led capitalism present in some of its members from the undesirable economic and political impacts of participation in the global political economy, while allowing them to take advantage of its benefits (Beeson 2003). The issue is basically whether the AMRO will be able to deliver as and when called upon for regulatory cooperation, standard harmonization, enhanced transparency, and multi-level governance, and more specifically to provide the surveillance and review process that a successful CMIM requires.

The success of the CMIM itself is yet to be tested as so far no country has applied for borrowing from the regional pool of reserves. For example, when both the Republic of Korea and Singapore needed liquidity support during the recent global financial crisis towards the end of 2008, they opted to request bilateral credit lines from the US Federal Reserve, the Bank of Japan, and the People's Bank of China

[20] The relationship between CMIM arrangements and the IMF is the subject of debate as under the current CMIM settings, any borrowed amount that exceeds 20 % of a country's quota is subject to IMF conditionality measures to avoid moral hazard. Several observers have argued in favour of an elimination of this IMF linkage.

instead of seeking to mobilize CMIM funds, which raises issues related to the appropriateness of the fund size. Other challenges facing the CMIM development concern the possible expansion of its membership, as countries such as India, for example, have repeatedly manifested a keen interested to be brought in, as well as a possible diversification of its activities, from emergency lending to the issuance of different financial assets which could eventually lead the CMIM and the AMRO to develop into a proper AMF, as a regional fund for monetary cooperation.

7.7 Strengthening Asia's Institutional Architecture Through Innovation and Reform

Referring to regionalism and the shaping of Asia's institutional architecture, a former top diplomat from the Republic of Korea, Han Sung-Joo, once mused, "Although it is underdeveloped, regionalism in Asia is complicated enough" (Evans 2005: 195).

The array of Asia's institutions for regionalism has emerged as a result of ad hoc decisions undertaken by policymakers in response to perceived, narrow functional expectations, be they economic or security in orientation. The shaping of these institutions did not follow a regional grand design like in the case of the European Union. While the existing regional architecture has served the region well so far, the pressing challenges wrought by globalization and transnationalism have made clear that its current structure is insufficient to guarantee the continued success of the regions' economies in a way that is sustainable, equitable, and compatible with global structures.

Indeed, the rapid proliferation of regional institutions in Asia since the financial crisis of 1997–1998 is the consequence of regional stakeholders' efforts to meet emerging challenges. Although more institutions for regional integration may be needed to perform functions which national agencies are not yet ready to delegate to regional organizations, there is a need to enhance existing institutions through an appropriate process of reform and innovation in order to make them more suitable to organize and sustain a regional agenda in the future. Of course, whenever existing institutions have fulfilled their mandate or become redundant, they should be phased out.

A prominent policy intellectual recently lamented: "…The Asia Pacific region has too many organizations, yet they still cannot do all the things we require of them. Instead of focusing on what we've got, we should look at what we need." (Gyngell 2007: 1).

But it is difficult to develop and agree on a set of objective criteria that can be used to assess the performance of regional institutions and suggest when it is time for them to be disbanded. According to US Secretary of State Hillary Clinton, Asia needs an institutional architecture that maximizes Asia's prospects for effective cooperation, builds trust among Asians, and reduces the friction of competition (Clinton 2010). But the what, how, and how much remain hotly debated considerations. Whether the future of Asia's institutional architecture for regional integration is to be found in the European model—with a region-wide council of ministers, a commission, a parliament, and a court of justice—is a proposition many know as misleading because Asia and Europe are two completely different entities, with distinct backgrounds, histories, endowments, socio-political structures, and economic systems. While the European Union remains an inspiration for many regionalists, it can hardly be used as a model for Asia (Capannelli and Filippini 2010). In addition, the problems that are currently affecting the eurozone economies, are casting a shadow in the eyes of many Asian analysts over the effectiveness of regional solutions.

Against this backdrop, it is important to look at three concerns that institutions for Asian integration need to address to effectively spread the benefits of regionalism beyond "Factory Asia": (i) bottom-up cooperation; (ii) institutions' lightness; and (iii) elite regionalism.[21] Ironically, these same factors have hitherto facilitated Asia's integration, but have now either become or are becoming hindrances to further progress.

Establish a Leaders-Led Regional Architecture

Asia is deemed fragile because its proclivity for unilateralism and non-regulation, as well as its lack of what Baldwin called "top-level management" (Baldwin 2008). It bears repeating that both the Rudd and Hatoyama proposals for a new regional architecture called for a single, overarching super-institution that would serve as a kind of "one-stop shop" for all things in Asia. In a similar vein, a taskforce on regional institutional architecture convened by the Pacific Economic Cooperation Council (PECC) called for the establishment of an "Asia-Pacific Summit" comprising the 21 APEC member economies and India for high-level discussions on key issues. The PECC report also urged the creation of a "Group of Ten" (G10), an informal caucus consisting of the Asia-Pacific members of the G20, which could ostensibly voice the collective concerns of all Asia-Pacific countries (Soesastro et al. 2009).

Despite ASEAN's wariness against stakeholders' recent promulgation of regional visions without prior consultation with ASEAN, the inclusion of the US and the Russian Federation in the East Asia Summit (EAS) has effectively turned the EAS into a de facto, top-tier institution. This could be the first step toward an overarching, leaders-led arrangement that would furnish the visionary guidance and "marching orders" for other proposed elements of the regional architecture. Key to this step would be the establishment of the Comprehensive Economic Partnership for East Asia (CEPEA), an ASEAN+6 plan that links the ASEAN+3 economies with those of India, Australia, and New Zealand. That said, others have argued that the EAS would benefit from the joint pursuit of the CEPEA as well as the East Asia Free Trade Area (EAFTA), which encompasses only the ASEAN+3 countries.[22]

[21] These considerations are discussed in Tan (2011).

[22] Singapore's Prime Minister Lee Hsien Loong made this observation (Tan 2010b).

Needless to say, a stable regional order will be crucial to such developments. The disagreements between the PRC and Japan in 2004–2005 over the inclusion of Australia, India, and New Zealand in the EAS serve as a somber reminder that no viable "top-level management" would be possible without the ability and willingness of the big powers—the PRC, Japan, India, the Russian Federation, and the US—to find common ground and agree to work together. On the other hand, whether ASEAN is prepared to countenance the prospect for such an institutional hierarchy over the extant variable geometry is a key consideration, particularly if ASEAN is not included within that management.[23]

Ultimately, what is needed is a structure for improving coordination of the initiatives of different subregional groups, reassuring other Asian countries about the intentions of those intent on pushing ahead with deeper integration, and providing a structure for fostering relations between integrating Asia and extra-regional powers. More likely, this need is best met through revamping existing institutions rather than creating new ones.

Streamline and Synergize by Forming Clusters and Linking Issues

Although Asia is no longer short on regional institutions, as the ADB study has well documented, the density, deepening, and intrusiveness of its architecture remains without a comprehensive region-wide vision. But even if Asia were to tread its own path for pan-regionalism, the concern is that more efficacy and effectiveness is needed of its institutions. Some experts believe Asia has too many institutions that do not get the job done. They call for practical reform of those arrangements in line with the concern for overall architectural coherence. Proposed reforms include, among other things, clarifying and streamlining institutional roles and responsibilities. On the other hand, other experts argue for reclaiming the APEC mandate as an economic forum focused primarily on trade liberalization and investment—and, by implication, preserving the compartmentalization—and strengthening those institutions as problem-solving or action-oriented mechanisms rather than just talk shops.

The persistent compartmentalization of issues in the existing regional architecture of Asia is counterintuitive in the light of the growing complexity and comprehensiveness of regional challenges posed by globalization and transnationalism. Issues like trade and finance, health and humanitarian concerns, and climate-related matters, can no longer be treated as separate from security concerns. The deliberate clustering of issues where tactical linkages can and should be made between and

[23] ASEAN members' dismay over the Rudd proposal, an early incarnation of which relied on a concert of powers without a key role for ASEAN, is a telling illustration. If anything, it could be argued that variable geometry and a fragmented and incoherent regional architecture benefits ASEAN since that renders difficult any attempt by any major power to control and define the regional process.

across institutions may be the way ahead in overcoming the silos that result from compartmentalization and segmentation. In this regard, the "whole-of-government" and "whole-of-society" strategies being adopted by some Asian countries in dealing with today's challenges suggests that concerted efforts are being undertaken. How these logics could serve as a guide for Asian regionalism is a key consideration.

Foster Closer Links with Global Institutions and Frameworks

Asia can take better advantage of global institutions and conventions. Asian economies are closely integrated with the rest of the world; Asia is the paradigmatic "open region." Fully exploiting the potential for regional economic integration therefore requires removing remaining barriers to cross-border competition in the region in ways that are compatible with Asia's economic links with other parts of the world. Building on existing global institutions and conventions is an obvious way of achieving this result.

Establish Binding Agreements

A limitation has to do with the default diplomatic and security model employed in Asian regionalism. A diplomatic convention that makes few to no demands on membership commitments, displays no precise and binding obligations, privileges consensus rather than decisiveness and favors noninterference, despite its usefulness in the early phases of Asian regionalism, is likely to be insufficient for overcoming emerging obstacles to deeper integration. Essentially, it preserves rather than revises the regional status quo. For sure, it is unrealistic to assume Asian institutions are prepared to make fundamental changes overnight. But the political commitment to introduce structural reforms by way of an evolutionary roadmap should be instituted—and, importantly, adhered to.

Improve Regional institutions' Governance and Endowments

These would include strengthening institutions' secretariats and creating efficient regional bureaucracies also by dedicating more human and financial resources, establishing clearer membership rules and adopt more majority voting, and delegating more responsibilities and powers from national agencies to common regional institutions.

Maintain Institutional Flexibility

A key part of streamlining existing regional institutions involves the dismantling of unproductive (or indeed counterproductive) organizations and various types of groups. Some overarching institutions have been described as little more than talk shops. That said, dialogue contributes to the building and sustaining of normative frameworks that play legitimating functions. Some functional institutions have also been consistently ineffective in meeting their economic targets. Policymakers will need to exercise judiciousness in deciding if any arrangement deserves to be discarded. At the same time, under-performing institutions could serve to meet the region's needs in other ways. In an era of economic uncertainty, strategic and tactical flexibility could prove to be a very important quality, and what seems a liability today could prove to be an asset tomorrow.

By the same token, countries should continue to develop institutions designed to exploit compelling functional opportunities. Subgroups of Asian countries stand to reap disproportionate benefits from functional initiatives that address their specific needs. Rather than waiting for the emergence of pan-Asian agreements, they can continue to push ahead on their own in groups of interested governments or at the subregional level, developing specialized institutional arrangements capable of exploiting these compelling opportunities. That said, even at the regional level, the creation of functional arrangements such as the CMIM and the AMRO is a good sign that the region is prepared to move things forward.

Encourage and Nurture Participatory Regionalism

Another limitation has to do with the elitism inherent in Asia's exclusively intergovernmental brand of regionalism. European regionalism is not free of elitist propensities either; indeed, whether one takes the "institutional" or "intergovernmental" side of the debate on European integration, the power of Europe's international secretariats as a key driver of regional integration is more or less assumed (Puchala 1999).[24]

By and large, Asia has precluded the inclusion of principles pivotal to European regionalism, such as subsidiarity, proportionality, pooled sovereignty, distribution of competences, delegation of powers, and enfranchisement of non-state actors. Certainly, Asia may not be fully ready for such practices. Nor are all these necessarily appropriate for Asia. Yet, ASEAN has indicated a willingness to incremental empowerment of ASEC, while SAARC has innovated a limited, yet creative delegation of functional powers by way of its "regional centers". The establishment of the

[24] As Eyal (2010: A2) has suggested, "the reality is that, for the EU, bureaucracy is not the means to an end; it is the very essence of activity. The EU always stood for the triumph of bureaucracy over history."

AMRO is another important development. To an extent, Asian governments have sought to accommodate the region's embryonic participatory regionalism, as demonstrated by the existence of parallel summits comprising civil society organizations, and the proliferation of semi-official dialogues and forums (for example, the Shangri-La Dialogue and other "second-track" activities). Arguably, these accommodations have rendered Asia–Pacific regionalism less exclusive than before. Be that as it may, "regionalism-elite" rather than "regionalism-*égalité*" remains its distinguishing feature. Eventually this implies more attention to involving civil society in the governance of regional institutions.

References

Acharya, A. (1997). Ideas, identity, and institution building: From the "ASEAN way" to the "Asia-Pacific way". *The Pacific Review, 10*(3), 319–346.

Arner, D. W. (2009). Developing Asia's financial norms and standards. Background Paper 3. ADB Study Finalization Workshop on institutions for regionalism in Asia and the Pacific. Shanghai. 2–3 December.

Asian Development Bank (ADB). (2008). *Emerging Asian regionalism. A partnership for shared prosperity*. Manila: ADB.

Asian Development Bank (ADB). (2010). *Institutions for regional integration. Toward an Asian economic community*. Manila: ADB.

Baldwin, R. (2008). Managing the noodle bowl: The fragility of East Asian regionalism. *Singapore Economic Review, 53*(3), 449–478.

Baum, R. (Ed.). (1980). *China's four modernizations: The new technological revolution*. Boulder, CO: Westview.

Beeson, M. (2003). ASEAN Plus Three and the rise of reactionary regionalism. *Contemporary Southeast Asia, 25*(2), 251–268.

Caballero-Anthony, M. (2009). Regional security institutions in Asia: Some insights on Asian regionalism. Background Paper 6. ADB Study Finalization Workshop on Institutions for Regionalism in Asia and the Pacific. Shanghai. 2–3 December.

Capannelli, G. (2011). Institutions for economic and financial integration in Asia: Trends and prospects. ADBI Working Paper 308. Tokyo: Asian Development Bank Institute. http://www.adbi.org/working-paper/2011/09/07/4689.economic.financial.integration.asia.trends.prospects/.

Capannelli, G., & Filippini, C. (2010). Economic integration in East Asia and Europe. Lessons from a comparative analysis. *Singapore Economic Review, 55*(1), 163–184.

Cherunilam, F. (2008). *International economics* (5th ed.). New Delhi: Tata McGraw-Hill.

Clinton, H. (2010). Clinton's remarks on regional architecture in Asia. Council on foreign relations. East West Center, Honolulu, HI. 12 January. http://www.cfr.org/publication/21218/clintons_remarks_on_regional_architecture_in_asia_january_2010.html.

Dent, C. M. (2008). *East Asian regionalism*. New York: Routledge.

Desker, B. (2008). Is the ASEAN charter necessary? RSIS Commentaries No.77/2008. Singapore: S. Rajaratnam School of International Studies. 17 July. http://www.rsis.edu.sg/publications/Perspective/RSIS0772008.pdf.

Devi, T. N. (Ed.). (2007). *India and Bay of Bengal community, the BIMSTEC experiment: Bangladesh–India–Myanmar–Sri Lanka–Thailand economic cooperation*. New Delhi: Gyan Publishers.

Emmers, R., & Tan, S. S. (2011). The ASEAN regional forum and preventive diplomacy: Built to fail? *Asian Security, 7*(1), 44–60.

Evans, P. (2005). Between regionalism and regionalization: Policy networks and the nascent East Asian institutional identity. In T. J. Pempel (Ed.), *Remapping East Asia: The construction of a region* (pp. 195–215). Ithaca, NY: Cornell University Press.

Eyal, J. (2010). EU foreign policy a mess. *The Straits Times*. 20 September: A2.

Garnaut, R. (1996). *Open regionalism and trade liberalization: An Asia-Pacific contribution to the World Trade System*. Singapore and Sydney: ISEAS/Allen and Unwin.

Gochoco-Bautista, M. S. (2009). Institutions for regional financial cooperation in Asia: Implications for regional economic cooperation. Background Paper 12. ADB Study Finalization Workshop on Institutions for Regionalism in Asia and the Pacific. Shanghai. 2–3 December.

Gyngell, A. (2007). *Design faults: The Asia Pacific's regional architecture*. Lowy Institute Policy Brief. Sydney: Lowy Institute for International Policy. 18 July.

Haas, M. (1989). *The Asian way to peace: A story of regional cooperation*. London: Praeger.

Hurrell, A. (1995). Regionalism in theoretical perspective. In L. Fawcett & A. Hurrell (Eds.), *Regionalism in world politics: Regional organization and regional order* (pp. 37–73). Oxford: Oxford University Press.

Jones, D. M., & Smith, M. L. R. (2007). Making process, not progress: ASEAN and the evolving East Asian regional order. *International Security, 32*(1), 148–184.

Katsumata, H. (2009). *ASEAN's cooperative security enterprise: Norms and interests in the ASEAN regional forum*. London: Palgrave MacMillan.

Kawai, M. (2010). Reform of the international financial architecture: An Asian perspective. *Singapore Economic Review, 55*(1), 207–242.

Kawai, M., & Wignaraja, G. (2011). Asian FTAs: Trends, prospects and challenges. *Journal of Asian Economics, 22*(1), 1–22.

Keohane, R. O. (1984). *After Hegemony: Cooperation and discord in the world political economy*. Princeton: Princeton University Press.

Kesavapany, K., & Lim, H. (Eds.). (2009). *APEC at 20: Recall, reflect, remake*. Singapore: Institute of Southeast Asian Studies.

Lee, H. L. (2006). Keynote address at the 5th International Institute for Strategic Studies' Asia Security Summit (Shangri-La Dialogue). Singapore. 2 June. http://www.iiss.org/conferences/the-shangri-la-dialogue/shangri-la-dialogue-archive/shangri-la-dialogue-2006/2006-plenary-session-speeches/keynote-remarks-he-lee-hsien-loong/.

Milward, A. S. (2000). *The European rescue of the nation-state* (2nd ed.). London: Routledge.

Moravcsik, A. (1998). *The choice for Europe: Social purpose & state power from Messina to Maastricht*. Ithaca, NY: Cornell University Press.

Moravcsik, A. (2000). De Gaulle between Grain and Grandeur: The political economy of French EC policy, 1958–1970. *Journal of Cold War Studies, 2*(2), 3–43. 2 (3): 4–68.

Puchala, D. J. (1999). Institutionalism, Intergovernmentalism and European integration: A review article. *Journal of Common Market Studies, 37*(2), 317–331.

Raghavan, S. N. (1995). *Regional economic cooperation among SAARC countries*. Bombay: Allied Publishers.

Rathus, J. (2010). Japan's early moves on the East Asian community. *East Asia Forum*. 21 March. http://www.eastasiaforum.org/2010/03/21/japans-early-moves-on-the-east-asian-community/.

Ravenhill, J. (2001). *APEC and the construction of Pacific Rim regionalism*. Cambridge: Cambridge University Press.

Ruggie, J. G. (1993). Multilateralism: The anatomy of an institution. In J. G. Ruggie (Ed.), *Multilateralism matters: The theory and praxis of an institutional form* (pp. 3–47). New York: Columbia University Press.

Severino, R. C. (2006). *Southeast Asia in search of an ASEAN community: Insights from the former ASEAN Secretary-General*. Singapore: Institute of Southeast Asian Studies.

Severino, R. C. (2009a). *The ASEAN regional forum*. Singapore: Institute of Southeast Asian Studies.

Severino, R. C. (2009b). Regional institutions in Southeast Asia: The first movers and their challengers. Background Paper 24. ADB Study Finalization Workshop on Institutions for Regionalism in Asia and the Pacific. Shanghai. 2–3 December.

Soesastro, H., Gyngell, A., Morrison, C. E., & Wanandi, J. (2009). *Report of regional task force on regional institutional architecture*. Prepared for the Pacific Economic Cooperation Council Standing Committee. June. Unpublished.

Soeya, Y. (2010). An East Asian community and Japan–China relations. *East Asia Forum*. 17 May. http://www.eastasiaforum.org/tag/eac/.

Tan, S. S. (Ed.). (2009). *Collaboration under anarchy: Functional regionalism and the security of East Asia. RSIS Monograph 15*. Singapore: S. Rajaratnam School of International Studies.

Tan, S. S. (2010a). ASEAN regional forum at 17: The Curse of "ad hoc-ism"? RSIS Commentaries 84/2010. 28 July.

Tan, S. S. (2010b). East Asia Summit 2010: Big step forward, or business-as-usual? RSIS Commentaries 141/2010. 4 November. http://www.rsis.edu.sg/publications/Perspective/RSIS1412010.pdf.

Tan, S. S. (2011). Is Asia Pacific regionalism outgrowing ASEAN? *RUSI Journal, 156*(1), 58–62.

Woolcott, R. (2009). Towards an Asia Pacific community. *The Asialink Essays, 9*(November), 1–4.

Young, O. R. (1999). *Governance in world affairs*. Ithaca, NY: Cornell University Press.

Chapter 8
Toward an Asian Economic Community?

Nagesh Kumar

Abstract The Asia and Pacific region has emerged as the growth pole of the world economy especially since 2000. However, in the aftermath of the 2008–2009 global financial crisis, sustaining the dynamism of Asian and Pacific economies would require a rebalancing in favor of greater domestic consumption and exploiting the potential of regional economic integration. This chapter argues that broader regional economic integration in Asia within the Comprehensive Economic Partnership of East Asia (CEPEA) framework, proposed for the Association of Southeast Asian Nations (ASEAN)+6 countries could be an engine of growth for not only the participating countries but also has the potential to enhance the welfare of the rest of the world by unleashing the synergies of Asian countries for trade creation besides making the region emerge as the third pole of the world economy alongside the North American Free Trade Agreement (NAFTA) and the European Union (EU). ASEAN members are Brunei Darussalam, Cambodia, Indonesia, Lao People's Democratic Republic, Malaysia, Myanmar, Philippines, Singapore, Thailand, and Viet Nam. The +6 countries are the People's Republic of China, Japan, Republic of Korea, Australia, New Zealand, and India. Furthermore, monetary and financial cooperation in the region has further possibilities of generating additional aggregate demand for sustaining their dynamism by efficiently intermediating between the region's excess savings and unmet investment needs. By forming credible schemes of regional economic integration, Asia will be able to seek its due place in global

Earlier versions of this chapter were presented as papers at the Conference on The Future of South-South Economic Relations held at The Frederick S. Pardee Centre for the Study of the Longer Range Future, Boston University, US on 24 September 2010.

N. Kumar (✉)
United Nations Economic and Social Commission
for Asia and the Pacific, New Delhi, India
e-mail: nkumar@un.org

G. Capannelli and M. Kawai (eds.), *The Political Economy of Asian Regionalism*,
DOI 10.1007/978-4-431-54568-2_8, © Asian Development Bank Institute 2014

economic governance and contribute to building a more democratic and multipolar world economy. Asian economic integration by increasing the interdependence of countries in the region will also ensure peace and stability.

Keywords Asian community • Connectivity • Governance • Market integration • Regional integration • Trade agreements

8.1 Introduction

Regional economic integration has been adopted as a strategy for development in different regions of the world since the 1990s following the formation of a single market by the European Union (EU) and of the North American Free Trade Agreement (NAFTA) by the North American countries. With the growing popularity of regional economic integration worldwide, more than half of world trade is now conducted between members of regional trading arrangements (that is, on a preferential basis) and not on a most favored nation basis. The Asia and Pacific region has been slow to respond to the global trend of regionalism and in exploiting the potential of regional economic integration. For historical and geopolitical reasons, the region has been better connected to the developed economies in the United States (US) and Europe than with itself.

Quite unexpectedly, financial crises acting as external shocks, help in promoting regional economic integration by highlighting regional interdependence and vulnerability. The Asian financial crisis of 1997–1998, for instance, led the Association of Southeast Asian Nations (ASEAN) to advancing the schedule of implementation of the ASEAN Free Trade Area (AFTA) and also to adopting the Chiang Mai Initiative (CMI) with three dialogue partners in monetary cooperation. The global financial crisis of 2008–2009 demonstrated the resilience of Asian economies such as the People's Republic of China (PRC) and India that continued growing robustly in the face of sharp contraction in the advanced economies around the world. It is now clear that the growth rate of demand for goods and services of the Asia and Pacific region in the US and Europe may not recover to precrisis trends as they try to restrain the debt fuelled consumption to unwind the global imbalances (ESCAP 2010). Therefore, Asian and Pacific countries will have to find new sources of aggregate demand to sustain their dynamism through expanding domestic consumption or regional demand. Hence, regional economic integration is likely to occupy a much more important place in the regional policy agenda in the coming years than before.

This chapter argues that the current phase of regional economic cooperation and integration is likely to be broader and more comprehensive in terms of coverage as countries in the region discover regional sources of demand and supply of resources. Deeper regional economic integration will enable the region to play its due role in global economic governance and will make it an anchor of peace and shared prosperity in the world economy.

8.2 Impetus for Regional Economic Cooperation in Asia

The Asian crisis of 1997–1998 highlighted the economic interdependence of the affected countries and thus underlined the importance of regional economic cooperation. The ASEAN countries expedited the implementation of the AFTA from 2008 to 2002 and moved to further deepen economic integration. The crisis also led to the CMI for monetary cooperation involving the ASEAN+3 countries.[1] A more important stimulus for regionalism seems to have come from the emergence of Asia as the center of final demand. With the emergence of large populous economies such as the PRC and India as powerful growth poles, Asia is quickly becoming the center of gravity of the world economy. For many products from mobile phones to motorcars to jet planes, the biggest markets are now in Asia rather than in the US and Europe. As a result more than 55 % of Asia's trade is now intraregional thus making regional economic integration an increasingly viable development strategy.

Global investment banks such as Goldman Sachs are projecting the PRC and India to emerge as the two largest economies in the world by 2050 (Wilson and Purushothaman 2003), a forecast that may be realized sooner in the postcrisis scenario with the uncertain and fragile recovery of advanced economies. The booming intraregional trade suggests the complementarities or synergies that have developed between economic structures of the Asian economies. Regional economic integration could help in their exploitation for mutual benefit. Although regional production networks have begun to be developed across Asia to exploit the synergies through vertical specialization, regional economic integration could help in expanding such opportunities and exploiting the potential of such rationalization or restructuring more fully. The slow progress of the Doha Round of multilateral trade negotiations and its inability to live up to the expectations of Asian countries has also contributed to the importance attached to regionalism.

Finally, as observed earlier, in the aftermath of the global financial crisis, Asian and Pacific countries may be forced to look inward and seek to exploit the potential of regional economic integration as a return to business-as-usual is rendered increasingly difficult by the compulsions of restraining debt fuelled consumption in the US and Europe as a part of unwinding global imbalances (ESCAP 2010; ESCAP 2011).

8.3 Emerging Patterns of Regional Economic Integration in Asia and the Case for Broader Arrangements

Asian developing countries made a number of attempts at regional economic cooperation in the 1970s promoted by the United Nations Economic and Social Commission for Asia and the Pacific (UNESCAP). These include the Bangkok

[1] ASEAN+3 members are 10 ASEAN countries plus the People's Republic of China, Japan, and the Republic of Korea.

Agreement established in 1975 that covered reciprocal tariff concessions between five member countries of Bangladesh, India, Lao People's Democratic Republic (Lao PDR), Republic of Korea, and Sri Lanka. In 2000, the PRC also joined the Bangkok Agreement. The Asian Clearing Union with seven members in the region (Bangladesh, India, Iran, Myanmar, Nepal, Pakistan, and Sri Lanka) came into being in 1974.

The expectations from these early initiatives have not been fully met for various reasons. For instance, the Bangkok Agreement (now known as Asia-Pacific Trade Agreement or APTA) suffered from its limited membership and product coverage given its positive list approach to liberalization, shallow preference margins, and lack of coverage of non-tariff barriers. The bulk of preferential trade under the Agreement comprises PRC–India trade that does not enjoy any other preferential arrangement.

Although set up in 1967, ASEAN members had limited cooperation in economic areas until AFTA was signed in 1992. Similarly, the South Asian Association for Regional Cooperation (SAARC) came into being in 1985 but did not adopt a program of economic cooperation until 1991 when the Committee on Economic Cooperation was formed. It created a SAARC Preferential Trading Agreement in 1995 and in 2004 eventually agreed to create a SAARC Free Trade Area to be implemented over 10 years from 2006. At the Summit held in Bhutan in 2010, it adopted a SAARC Agreement on Trade in Services and established the SAARC Development Fund.

Besides SAARC agreements, bilateral preferential trading arrangements between India and Nepal, India and Bhutan, and India and Sri Lanka have also contributed to economic integration in the South Asian subregion. Another notable initiative is the Bay of Bengal Initiative for Multisectoral Technical and Economic Cooperation (BIMSTEC) involving five South Asian (Bangladesh, Bhutan, India, Nepal, and Sri Lanka) and two Southeast Asian (Myanmar and Thailand) nations, bridging the two subregions. BIMSTEC adopted a Framework Agreement for a free trade agreement (FTA) to be implemented within 10 years at its first summit held in Bangkok in July 2004.

Initiatives in other subregions of the Asia and Pacific region include the Economic Cooperation Organization (ECO) initially formed with Turkey, Iran, and Pakistan as members in 1985 but later expanding its membership to cover Afghanistan and six Central Asian countries of Azerbaijan, Kazakhstan, Kyrgyz Republic, Turkmenistan, Uzbekistan, and Tajikistan. ECO established the ECO Trade Agreement in 2003. The Pacific Islands Forum (PIF) was set up as the South Pacific Forum in 1971 and has 16 member states including Australia and New Zealand and 14 independent Pacific island states. Twelve PIF members also signed the Pacific Island Countries' Trade Agreement in 2006 created within the framework of Pacific Agreement for Closer Economic Relations signed in 2001.

In the context of broader cooperation that brings countries from different subregions together, ASEAN's initiatives are exemplary. In the wake of the Asian crisis of 1997–1998, ASEAN countries expedited the implementation of AFTA from 2008 to 2002 and moved on to deepen economic integration further to an ASEAN

Economic Community by 2020, a goal that was later expedited to 2015. The crisis also led to the launch of several regional initiatives such as the CMI in the area of monetary cooperation that involves ASEAN together with the PRC, Japan, and the Republic of Korea—the ASEAN+3 countries.

In addition, ASEAN's policy of engaging key Asian countries as dialogue partners has provided much needed cohesion in the Asian region as is clear from the numerous schemes for regional and bilateral free trade arrangements that are at different levels of implementation. The PRC, India, Japan, the Republic of Korea, Australia, and New Zealand have all negotiated FTAs (the so-called "+1 FTAs") with ASEAN and are also engaging each other. Dialogue partnership is also leading to more inclusive broader groupings. An important initiative was the launch of the East Asia Summit (EAS) in December 2005 in Kuala Lumpur as an annual forum participated by ASEAN and all its dialogue partners. Bringing together 16 of the largest and fastest growing economies in an annual summit level dialogue, EAS was widely expected to pave the way for broader regional arrangement in Asia that could be the third pole of the world economy.

To sum up, major initiatives towards regional economic integration led by ASEAN include:

- Subregional attempts to form FTAs and further deepen economic integration to form an ASEAN Community;
- FTAs or comprehensive partnership arrangements between ASEAN and its dialogue partners (the PRC, India, Japan, and the Republic of Korea) and also between ASEAN and CER (Australia–New Zealand)—or the +1 FTAs;
- FTAs or comprehensive arrangements between individual ASEAN countries and ASEAN dialogue partners, for example Japan–Singapore, India–Singapore, and India–Thailand; and
- FTAs or comprehensive arrangements between the dialogue partners themselves, such as India–Japan, India–the Republic of Korea (already signed) and Japan–PRC–the Republic of Korea, and India–PRC (under study).

From this complex web of free trade arrangements linking ASEAN and its dialogue partner countries, a virtual Asian or East Asian economic community is emerging (Fig. 8.1). It has been argued however that the subregional or bilateral attempts at regional cooperation such as these while desirable are unlikely to exploit the full potential of regional economic integration in Asia and hence are suboptimal (for details see Kumar 2005). This is because the extent of complementarities are limited at the subregional levels because of similar factor endowments and economic structures within an immediate neighborhood as is clear from low proportions of intra-subregional trade such as within ASEAN or SAARC. At the broader Asian level, on the other hand, the diversity in the levels of economic development and capabilities are quite wide thus providing for more extensive and mutually beneficial links.

Recent quantitative analysis at ESCAP shows that complementarities between subregions are greater than within the subregions (ESCAP 2011). Furthermore, bilateral arrangements do not provide a seamless market because of different scopes and coverage and rules applicable to different FTAs producing an Asian noodle

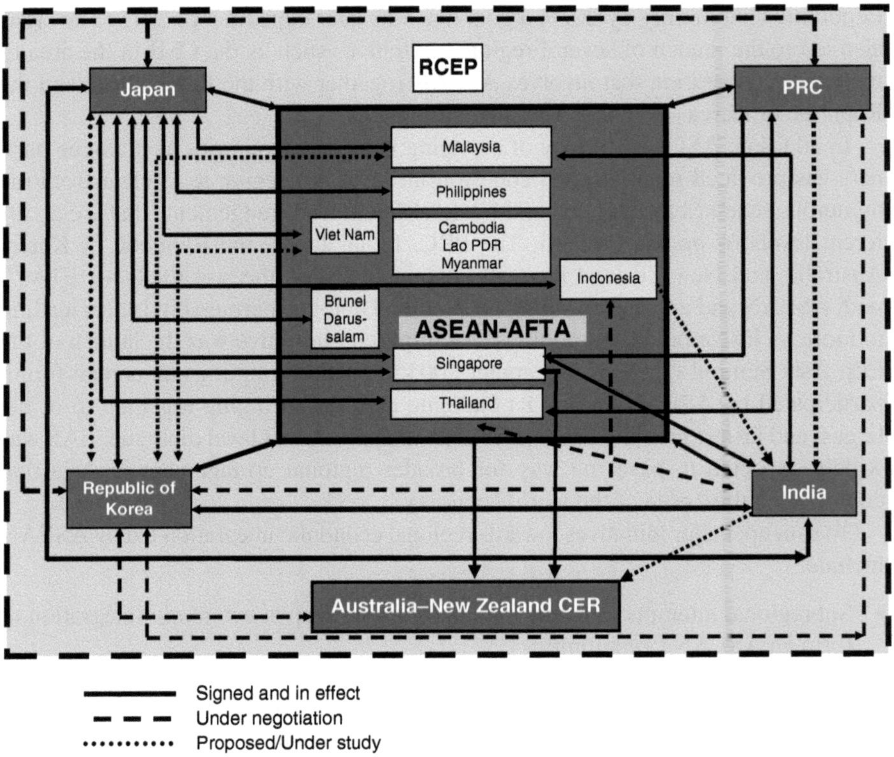

Fig. 8.1 An emerging virtual Asian community. *AFTA* ASEAN Free Trade Area, *ASEAN* Association of Southeast Asian Nations, Lao PDR Lao People's Democratic Republic, *CER* Closer Economic Relations, *PRC* People's Republic of China, *RCEP* Regional Comprehensive Economic Partnership
Source: The author based on information available from the Asia Regional Integration Center of the Asian Development Bank. www.aric.adb.org

bowl syndrome and increasing transaction costs for businesses. As one observer pointed out, without some form of overall regional framework within which to work, capital, human, and natural resources may all be deployed at less than their optimal values (Rowley 2004). Hence, a case has been made for a broader regional arrangement coalescing various bilateral FTAs between Japan, ASEAN, the PRC, India, and the Republic of Korea (JACIK) countries that will facilitate the optimal utilization of Asia's resources and synergies for the benefit of all countries (Kumar 2004; Kumar et al. 2008).

The Prime Minister of India, Manmohan Singh made a case for an Asian Economic Community (AEC) combining, to begin with, ASEAN countries, the PRC, India, Japan, and the Republic of Korea as an "arc of advantage" across which there would be a large-scale movement of people, capital, ideas, and creativity, thereby creating a community that would release enormous creative energies (Singh 2004). Recognizing the need for deepening regional economic integration in the aftermath of the global financial crisis, other leaders of the region also articulated their own visions of broader pan-Asian economic communities at the Fourth East Asia Summit held in Hua Hin, Viet Nam in October 2009. The Philippines made a case for "Asian economic cooperation including through the possible establishment of an economic community of Asia." Japan made a case "to reinvigorate the discussion toward building, in the long run, an East Asian community based on the principle of openness, transparency, and inclusiveness and functional cooperation," and Australia proposed to build an "Asia Pacific community in which ASEAN will be at its core" (East Asia Summit 2009). The leaders' perceptions about the relevance of broader integration are widely shared as a survey conducted by the World Economic Forum and Taylor Nelson Sofres revealed that over 37 % of new Asian leaders view an extended Asia, comprising ASEAN, the PRC, India, Japan, and the Republic of Korea, as the most desirable model of economic integration, with only 26.8 % preferring ASEAN+3 (WEF 2003).[2]

As EAS brings together all the JACIK countries as well as Australia and New Zealand, a start can be made on broader regional integration in the EAS forum. The Second EAS held in Cebu, Philippines, on 15 January 2007 endorsed the preparation of the track-II feasibility study of a Comprehensive Economic Partnership of East Asia (CEPEA) involving ASEAN+6 countries. The Fourth East Asia Summit in 2009 adopted the final report of the CEPEA study group set up as a follow up to the Cebu meeting in 2007. The group found a fruitful case for deeper regional integration in the EAS region involving three pillars of liberalization, facilitation, and cooperation implemented in parallel (CEPEA Study Group 2009). The leaders agreed to a consideration by the senior officials—the CEPEA proposal along with an East Asia FTA (EAFTA) combining ASEAN+3 countries in parallel.

Combining 16 of the largest and fastest growing economies of Asia and the Pacific with significant complementarities, the CEPEA grouping is a potential third pole of the world economy. The grouping has a population of 3.2 billion people or half of the world's population (Table 8.1). In terms of purchasing power parity, the CEPEA will have a combined gross national income exceeding $20 trillion accounting for nearly 30 % of the global income is much larger than either NAFTA or the EU. EAS exports will equal $3.3 trillion compared with $1.6 trillion from NAFTA. The combined official reserves of the CEPEA economies, at $4 trillion in 2008 (and over $5 trillion now), are much larger than those of the United States and the EU combined. Clearly, the region would have sufficiently large market and financial resources to support and sustain expedited development. With both the PRC and India together in one grouping, CEPEA would be ahead of its western counterparts in terms of dynamism and would quickly emerge as a growth pole of the world economy.

Therefore, CEPEA has the potential to create a regional grouping that could be comparable in size with NAFTA and the EU but much more important in terms of its dynamism and hence constituting a third pole of the world economy. Besides

[2] The survey took place at the World Economic Forum's New Asian Leaders Retreat in Seoul in June 2003, covering all participants and invitees and other Asian-based global leaders for tomorrow.

Table 8.1 Proposed East Asian community in relation to the EU and NAFTA in 2008 ($ billions)

Indicator	EU(27)	NAFTA	CEPEA(16)
Gross national income (PPP)	15155	17041	20699
(% of world total)	(21.88)	(24.60)	(29.89)
GDP	18328	16683	13943
(% of world total)	(30.27)	(27.55)	(23.02)
Exports	4584	1603	3324
(% of world total)	(37.05)	(12.95)	(26.86)
International reserves	494	205	3934
(% of world total)	(7.17)	(2.98)	(56.98)
Population (millions)	496	444	3240
(% of world total)	(7.42)	(6.63)	(48.39)

CEPEA Comprehensive Economic Partnership in East Asia, *EU* European Union, *GDP* gross domestic product, *NAFTA* North American Free Trade Agreement, *PPP* purchasing power parity

Note: CEPEA (16) refers to Association of Southeast Asian Nations (10), Japan, People's Republic of China, India, the Republic of Korea, Australia, and New Zealand

Sources: Author based on World Bank. *World Development Indicators Online* (accessed 20 September 2010); International Monetary Fund (IMF). *Direction of Trade Statistics 2010* (CD-ROM)

the potential welfare gains accruing from economic integration exploiting the synergies, such a grouping would help Asia play its due role in global economic governance commensurate with its increasing economic weight (Kumar et al. 2008). CEPEA could be a good stepping stone for building a broader and more inclusive Asian economic community in due course.

8.4 Gains from Broader Economic Integration

A number of recent studies have found considerable evidence of complementarities between Asian countries in their production and trade structure (Kumar 2004; Kumar et al. 2008). Using the Global Trade Analysis Project database (GTAP 6) with the World Bank's LINKAGE model, an ADB study (Brooks et al. 2005) generated projections of income and trade to 2025 under different scenarios to examine the relative impact of regional integration vis-à-vis global trade liberalization. The findings suggest that regional trade and integration could offer Asia great potential for rapid and sustained growth. The ADB study also finds that much of Asia's gains from global trade liberalization could be realized by a regional initiative alone. Significantly, it finds that the combined gains from removing tariff and structural barriers to Asian trade far outweigh those from global tariff abolition. Hence, regionalism should be a very high priority for Asia. Furthermore, the ADB study suggests that regional integration would promote Asian economic convergence, raising average growth rates, and benefiting poorer countries. In particular, greater regional integration would propagate commercial linkages and transfer the stimulus of Asia's rapid growth economies, particularly the PRC and India, to their lower income neighbors. A recent ADBI study has also reported substantial potential welfare gains of up to $284 billion from regional economic integration in the EAS or ASEAN+6 framework which are in tune with previous studies and larger than any alternatives (Kawai and Wignaraja 2008; CEPEA Study Group 2008.)

8.5 Strengths, Weaknesses, Opportunities, and Threats of a Broader Asian Economic Community

A Strengths–Weaknesses–Opportunities–Threats (SWOT) analysis of the proposed Asian economic community as outlined above suggests a number of strengths and opportunities but also some weaknesses and threats. The *strengths* arise from a range of profound complementarities among the EAS members as some economies are endowed with natural resource bases (for example, Australia) while others are large importers of them; some are dominated by manufacturing (such as the PRC, Japan, and the Republic of Korea), and others are dominated by services (such as India and the Philippines). The group has some of the fastest growing economies of the world such as the PRC and India and some of the largest economies such as Japan, the PRC, and India. There are net exporters such as the PRC, Japan, and the Republic of Korea, and most of the ASEAN countries, but also net importers like India. Collectively, they are endowed with large human and financial resources besides natural resources.

As observed earlier, a number of simulation studies have confirmed that substantial welfare gains for the participating countries resulting from CEPEA are to be much larger than alternatives. Furthermore all the six dialogue partners have concluded their FTAs with ASEAN and some of the dialogue partners have also concluded bilateral FTAs between themselves (such as India–the Republic of Korea and India–Japan). These FTAs, together with AFTA provide a valuable foundation for a broader regional grouping in Asia and the Pacific with EAS members as the core. Many Asian and Pacific countries share centuries old civilizations and cultural links and enjoyed vibrant intraregional trade in pre-colonial times (Sen 2007; Shankar 2004; Frost 2008).

The *opportunities* arise from the fact that Asian and Pacific countries will need to rebalance their economies in favour of greater domestic and regional consumption as the of aggregate demand in the US and Europe decline in an effort to unwind the global imbalances in the aftermath of the global financial crisis. Another opportunity arises from public opinion in support of regionalism as evident from the statements of different leaders as well as perception surveys as observed earlier. The slow progress in the Doha Round of multilateral trade negotiations spares trade negotiators to work on the regional arrangements. Furthermore, a broader arrangement between CEPEA members would reduce the transaction costs for the businesses of the region caused by the noodle bowl syndrome and would facilitate efficiency-seeking industrial restructuring. Regional economic integration bringing developed and developing countries into a single arrangement could help in narrowing development gaps by facilitating the building of productive capacity through industrial restructuring in poorer economies.

The *weaknesses* and *threats* arise from the perceived lack of a strong political will and leadership for driving the agenda of a broader grouping. ASEAN has been the driving force behind the process, but its first priority is to complete the ASEAN community building process. A broader integration agenda can also get slowed down by the lack of coherence between the members as some prefer a less inclusive EAFTA that is vehemently opposed by others. This is despite the fact that a more inclusive arrangement has a greater viability given the range of synergies and beneficial welfare effects. Some bilateral political sensitivities between a few countries also tend to slow down the progress. However, one may argue that a broader grouping would help to diffuse the bilateral tensions and sensitivities. The lack of regional institutions, deeper financial markets, and well developed transport connectivity are other weaknesses.

On the balance, in the Asian economic community agenda, the favorable factors tend to overwhelm the negatives. In any case the political differences between Asian countries may not be as strong as they were between European countries before they moved towards the agenda of European economic integration. The European leaders were able to see the value that integration brought to all the members and agreed to put aside the differences and moved ahead. Hopefully the Asian leaders will also see the compulsion of deepening and broadening their economic integration especially in the post-crisis period and will begin to push the agenda.

8.6 Priority Areas for Cooperation Under an Asian Economic Community

The discussion above has shown that CEPEA would significantly enhance welfare not only for participating countries but also for the rest of the world with possibilities of trade creation. There are a number of other areas where regional cooperation could be fruitful such as in strengthening connectivity, financial architecture, energy security, and science and technology, among others. A few key priorities are summarized, as follows.

Framework for Balanced and Equitable Integration: CEPEA—An RTA with a Difference?

The track-II CEPEA study has envisaged CEPEA to have the three pillars of liberalization, facilitation, and economic cooperation as a part of a single undertaking to make it a balanced framework. CEPEA should target liberalizing regional trade and investment regimes in a phased manner by 2020 with provisions for safeguards for sensitive products, and differential treatment for countries at different levels of development and dispute resolution. Care must be taken in designing the regional economic integration programs in such a manner that they keep equity, employment generation, social transformation, and social safety nets for the vulnerable sections of society and balanced regional development at their heart so that they represent regionalism with an "Asian face." Therefore, economic cooperation with the objective of narrowing the development gaps between countries and regions has to be an integral part of the scheme of regional economic integration.

Economic cooperation could cover the creation of structural funds based on contributions by the member countries on the basis of capacity to pay. These funds should provide economic assistance to lagging regions within the member countries for capacity building, infrastructure development, and assisting underprivileged sections of the population in trade liberalization adjustment, connectivity improvement, and enterprise-level technological capability development. By balancing efficiency and equity, the Asian arrangement could emerge as a role model for trade liberalization in multilateral as well as regional contexts.

Strengthened Physical Connectivity, Transport, and Energy Networks

Market integration would not be effective unless accompanied by strengthened physical connectivity and other networks such as energy grids, information and communication technology (ICT) connectivity, and transit facilitation. Thus far, for historical, political, and topographical reasons, the region has been better connected with Europe and North America than it has been with itself. Over time the region has improved its highway and railway networks, but it cannot use the infrastructure effectively without the legal and regulatory framework for vehicles, goods, and people to move across borders and transit in countries.

Currently, many international movements are hindered by slow and costly processes, formalities, and procedures. The cost of red tape is considerable and often wipes out the benefits of tariff reductions enacted since the 1990s. In future the region will need an integrated, multimodal transport system. For this purpose, it can, for example, build intermodal transfer points, also known as dry ports, where goods, containers, or vehicles can be transshipped using the most efficient mode of transport—along with facilities for product grading, packaging, inspections, and trade documentation processing. The areas surrounding dry ports can then emerge as growth poles, bringing new investment and employment opportunities to impoverished hinterlands while reducing the pressure on coastal areas.

UNESCAP's work has resulted in the signing of intergovernmental agreements on the Asian Highway and the Trans-Asian Railway. These networks when completed along with a regional network of dry ports, which is in progress, would assist in substantially strengthening the physical connectivity of the region. Similarly, among other initiatives, the region needs to strengthen the network of pipelines to transport hydrocarbons from major production centers to major consumption centers, to boost energy security (Tuli 2008).

A More Developed Regional Financial Architecture

The combined foreign exchange reserves of CEPEA countries now add up to over $5 trillion and comprise the bulk of such reserves in the world. It has been argued that because of a lack of a regional framework for their deployment in Asia, these funds have been invested in low yielding US treasury bonds and should be able to contribute to Asian development more meaningfully. This is matched by a substantial deficit for investments in the infrastructure development needs of underdeveloped parts of Asia running into $800 billion per year for the next decade (ADB and ADBI 2009). India alone requires $1000 billion for infrastructure development over the 5 years, as part of its 12th Five Year Plan (2012–2017).

The objective of financial cooperation in Asia should be to leverage the combined strength of foreign exchange reserves of the region's countries for their mutual benefit. There is a growing consensus that Asia needs a regional institution for mobilizing its foreign exchange resources for its own development as well as for achieving stability of real effective exchange rates and for an orderly response to external shocks. Even conservative commentators like Martin Wolf now acknowledge the importance of Asia to have its own regional monetary and financial institutions (Wolf 2004). Studies have shown that there is growing macroeconomic interdependence between Japan, the Republic of Korea, and ASEAN. Such interdependence is likely to include the PRC and India, besides Australia and New Zealand, with ongoing reforms, liberalization, and growing intraregional trade and investments (Kawai and Motonoshi 2005).

A number of important initiatives have been taken in the area of monetary and financial cooperation in Asia over the past decade including the CMI and the development of Asian bond markets. However, these initiatives need to be deepened and broadened to cover all systemically important countries in the region to be effective (ESCAP 2011).

There is also a growing consensus that a more ambitious attempt needs to be made toward regional financial cooperation to provide institutional intermediation between the region's growing foreign exchange reserves and its unmet infrastructure financing needs. Abdullah Ahmad Badawi, former Prime Minister of Malaysia, suggested that Asian countries could use "a fraction" of their massive foreign exchange reserves as capital for a fund that would invest in basic economic infrastructure including super highways and super railways linking and binding the East Asian community. Asia has the resources to set up a regional mechanism with a large capital base that would enable it to undertake funding of infrastructure development without putting pressure on government budgets in the member countries

(ESCAP 2011; Agarwala and De 2008). Asia also needs relative stability of exchange rates to facilitate its growing intraregional trade that has approached nearly 55 % of Asia's trade.

One area of cooperation is the creation of a regional unit of account such as an Asian currency unit (ACU) that could bring about relative stability of intraregional exchange rates. Integration of capital markets to enable companies to list themselves and raise capital across borders in other countries in the region is another key priority.

Global Governance

Regional economic integration is likely to strengthen Asia's role in global economic governance. Although Asian countries hold two thirds of the world's foreign exchange reserves, decision-making in Bretton Woods institutions, for instance, is dominated by the US and Europe. By forming credible schemes of regional economic integration, Asia will be able to seek its due place in global economic governance and contribute to building a more democratic and multipolar world economy. Asian economic integration, by increasing the interdependence of countries in the region, could also ensure peace and stability as Prime Minister Manmohan Singh of India argued.

8.7 Roadmap for Progressive Deepening of Regional Economic Integration Toward an Asian Economic Community

An economic community represents a stage of deeper economic integration. The vision of forming an economic community should be achieved in a progressive manner over the next 15–20 year period with successive deepening of the integration. The stages involve completion of a free trade agreement as included in CEPEA over 5–8 years from inception, and to move further to build a customs union within 10 years. The next stage is to build a common market allowing free movement of factors of production, say by 2025 and finally to the economic community which involves macroeconomic policy coordination by 2030.

Usually the most critical stage is an FTA as it involves detailed negotiations and has to encounter various sensitivities and vested interests. Once an FTA has been agreed to and implemented, movement to other stages becomes smoother partly because business restructuring across the region to take advantage of the FTA provisions begins to create an integrated market. Hence, expediting the CEPEA implementation is the key to forming an economic community along with supportive infrastructure development and trade and transport facilitation. In that context, one way of jump-starting the formation of a broader regional trade arrangement would be for all six dialogue partners to multilateralize their ASEAN+1 FTAs, subject to some safeguards as may be considered important by countries. Once these FTAs have been multilateralized, it will be easier to harmonize rules and regulations including agreeing to new cumulative rules of origin, and adopt a single broader agreement that could even be opened for accession by other countries in the Asia and Pacific region.

8.8 Concluding Remarks

Broader regional economic integration in Asia within the CEPEA framework could be an engine of growth for not only the participating countries but also has the potential to enhance the welfare of the rest of the world by unleashing the synergies of Asian countries for trade creation especially in the context of the 2008–2009 global financial crisis. The participating countries need to deepen their ongoing cooperation further in shaping CEPEA toward the creation of an integrated or seamless Asian market as a stepping stone of an even broader Asian economic community that could emerge as the third pole of the world economy alongside NAFTA and the EU. The integration of markets needs to be complemented by strengthened physical connectivity and transport facilitation across the region.

Development of the regional financial architecture to leverage the region's substantial foreign exchange reserves for mutual benefit presents further opportunities of generating additional aggregate demand by efficiently intermediating between the region's excess savings and unmet infrastructure investment needs. By forming credible schemes of regional economic integration, Asia will be able to seek its place in global economic governance and contribute to building a more democratic and multipolar world economy. Asian economic integration and the increasing the interdependence of countries in the region will also ensure peace and stability.

The prospects of broader regional economic integration in Asia and the Pacific region have improved since November 2012 when a decision was taken at the ASEAN Summit in Phnom Penh to launch negotiations on the Regional Comprehensive Economic Partnership (RCEP) involving the ASEAN+6 countries. Through this initiative, ASEAN is de facto assuming a leadership role in moving forward the CEPEA framework in the form of the RCEP. Another development of interest is the ESCAP's 68th Commission Session in Bangkok in May 2012 that focused on regional economic integration and adopted a resolution asking ESCAP to convene a ministerial conference on regional economic integration in 2013 to consider recommendations of the study *Growing Together: Economic Integration for An Inclusive and Sustainable Asia-Pacific Century* (ESCAP 2012). The study recommends a four-pronged scheme with a long-term vision of building an economic community of Asia and the Pacific:

- Coalescing the numerous bilateral and subregional trading arrangements of the region into a broader regional trading and economic cooperation arrangement with built-in safeguards and flexibilities for poorer countries.

- Creating seamless physical connectivity across the region to spread the benefits of economic integration to lagging regions through transport, energy, and ICT links, and the adoption of best practices in trade and transport facilitation.
- Strengthening financial cooperation for closing development gaps and to ensure the optimal use of the region's resources for mutual benefit.
- Promoting economic cooperation for addressing shared vulnerabilities and risks such as energy and food insecurity, natural disasters, pressures on natural resources, social exclusion, and rising inequalities.

The study supports the RCEP as a nucleus of an incipient broader region-wide regional trade arrangement to which other countries in the region can join in due course. The ESCAP ministerial conference to be convened in late 2013 will hopefully move the agenda of regional economic integration forward.

References

Agarwala, R., & De, P. (2008). Reducing global imbalances and accelerating growth: Role of regional financial cooperation in Asia. In N. Kumar et al. (Eds.), *Asia's new regionalism and global role: Agenda for the East Asia Summit* (pp. 203–220). New Delhi and Singapore: RIS and Institute of Southeast Asian Studies.

Asian Development Bank (ADB), & ADB Institute (ADBI). (2009). *Infrastructure for a seamless Asia*. Tokyo: Asian Development Bank Institute.

Brooks, D., Roland-Holst, D., & Zhai, F. (2005). *Growth, trade, and integration: Long-term scenarios of developing Asia*. Manila: Asian Development Bank.

CEPEA Study Group. (2008). Report of the track two study group on comprehensive economic partnership in East Asia (CEPEA). Tokyo. 20 June. http://www.thaifta.com/thaifta/Portals/0/cepea_report.pdf.

CEPEA Study Group. (2009). Phase II Report of the track two study group on comprehensive economic partnership in East Asia (CEPEA). Tokyo. 3 July. http://www.dfat.gov.au/asean/eas/cepea-phase-2-report.pdf.

East Asia Summit. (2009). Chairman's statement of the 4th East Asia Summit. Hua Hin. 25 October. http://www.15thaseansummit-th.org/PDF/25-08_EAS%20Statement.pdf.

ESCAP. (2010). *Economic and social survey of Asia and the Pacific 2010*. Bangkok: United Nations Economic and Social Commission for Asia and the Pacific. http://www.unescap.org/pdd/publications/survey2010/download/Survey2010.pdf.

ESCAP. (2011). *Economic and social survey of Asia and the Pacific 2011*. Bangkok: United Nations Economic and Social Commission for Asia and the Pacific. http://www.unescap.org/survey2011.

ESCAP. (2012). *Growing together: Economic integration for an inclusive and sustainable Asia-Pacific Century*. Bangkok: United Nations Economic and Social Commission for Asia and the Pacific. http://www.unescap.org/pdd/publications/themestudy2012/index.asp.

Frost, E. L. (2008). *Asia's new regionalism*. Boulder, CO: Lynne Rienner.

Kawai, M., & Motonoshi, T. (2005). Macroeconomic interdependence in East Asia: Empirical evidence and issues. In Asian Development Bank (Ed.), *Asian economic cooperation and integration: Progress, prospects, challenges* (pp. 213–268). Manila: Asian Development Bank.

Kawai, M., & Wignaraja, G. (2008). EAFTA or CEPEA. Which way forward? *ASEAN Economic Bulletin, 25*(2), 113–139.

Kumar, N. (Ed.). (2004). *Towards and Asian economic community: Vision of a new Asia*. New Delhi and Singapore: RIS and Institute for Southeast Asian Studies.

Kumar, N. (2005). A broader Asian community and a possible roadmap. *Economic and Political Weekly, 40*(36), 3926–3931.

Kumar, N., Kesavapany, K., & Yao, C. (Eds.). (2008). *Asia's new regionalism and global role: Agenda for the East Asia Summit*. New Delhi and Singapore: RIS and Institute for Southeast Asian Studies.

Rowley, A. (2004). Asian integration needs and overarching framework. *New Asia Monitor, 1*(1), 6.

Sen, A. (2007). *Asian immensities*. Keynote Address in Commemoration of the 60th Anniversary of UNESCAP. Bangkok. 28 March.

Shankar, V. (2004). Towards an Asian economic community: Exploring the past. In N. Kumar (Ed.), *Towards an Asian economic community: Vision of a new Asia* (pp. 3–40). New Delhi and Singapore: RIS and ISEAS.

Singh, M. (2004). Speech at the ASEAN–India business Summit, New Delhi. October.

Tuli, V. (2008). Regional cooperation for Asian energy security. In N. Kumar, K. Kesavapany, & C. Yao (Eds.), *Asia's new regionalism and global role: Agenda for the East Asia Summit* (pp. 247–260). New Delhi and Singapore: RIS and Institute of Southeast Asian Studies.

Wilson, D., & Purushothaman, R. (2003). Dreaming with BRICs: The Path to 2050. Goldman Sachs. Global Economic Papers No.99. http://www2.goldmansachs.com/ideas/brics/book/99-dreaming.pdf.

Wolf, M. (2004). Asia needs the freedom of its monetary fund. *Financial Times*. 19 May.

World Economic Forum (WEF) (2003). Press Release. 18 June.

Index

G. Capannelli and M. Kawai (eds.), *The Political Economy of Asian Regionalism*,
DOI 10.1007/978-4-431-54568-2,

S

MIX
Papier aus verantwortungsvollen Quellen
Paper from responsible sources
FSC® C105338

FSC
www.fsc.org

If you have any concerns about our products,
you can contact us on
ProductSafety@springernature.com

In case Publisher is established outside the EU,
the EU authorized representative is:
Springer Nature Customer Service Center GmbH
Europaplatz 3, 69115 Heidelberg, Germany

Printed by Libri Plureos GmbH
in Hamburg, Germany